Colleen Stan:
The Simple Gifts of Life

iUniverse, Inc.
New York   Bloomington

The Simple Gifts of Life
Dubbed by the Media "The Girl in the Box" and "The Sex Slave"

iUniverse books may be ordered through booksellers or by contacting:

iUniverse
1663 Liberty Drive
Bloomington, IN 47403
www.iuniverse.com
1-800-Authors (1-800-288-4677)

Because of the dynamic nature of the Internet, any Web addresses or links contained in this book may have changed since publication and may no longer be valid. The views expressed in this work are solely those of the author and do not necessarily reflect the views of the publisher, and the publisher hereby disclaims any responsibility for them.

ISBN: 978-1-4401-1837-1 (pbk)
ISBN: 978-1-4401-1838-8 (ebk)

Library of Congress Control Number: 2009922573

Printed in the United States of America

iUniverse rev. date: 02/24/2009

Colleen Stan: The Simple Gifts of Life

Dubbed by the Media "The Girl in the Box" and "The Sex Slave"

Jim B. Green

In Memory of Marie Elizabeth Spannhake, and Dedicated to my Daughter Danielle -- Colleen Stan

Contents

List of Illustrations

Preface

The memoir of Colleen Stan is a great story. It takes the reader into a world of modern slavery few of us have witnessed. How many of us have had our character truly tested? How many of us have come face-to-face with evil? How many of us have not only survived, but put our lives back together again?

What man has not dreamed of having a sex slave and what woman has not dreaded being abducted by such a man. Thankfully, such situations are rare, not to mention against the 13th Amendment to the U.S. Constitution. For Colleen Stan, the dread of being kidnapped became real. In her story, she shares the emotions, pain, and her eventual triumph over evil. She tells of her early life, faith, and desire to live a normal life once freed from slavery.

We use the word hero or heroine freely in our society, perhaps too freely. The word "super hero" has been created to compensate for its overuse, but what is a hero? A hero is not just a survivor, but a person who has gone on to live life to the fullest. Survival sometimes depends on luck, but getting one's life back to normal requires hard work. As an amateur historian, I have always admired the Holocaust survivor who went on to lead a full and complete life or the pioneer who lost a husband or wife, yet still milked the cows before sunset. That's a true hero and that's what is great about the human spirit, the ability to rebound. Colleen Stan is one such heroine.

If you met Colleen today, you would be surprised to learn of her previous life as a slave. You would be shocked to learn of the torture and despair she endured. You would be even more surprised at how well she has adjusted and returned her life to normal. Today, Colleen is a happy woman who enjoys life to the fullest. However, she will never completely free herself from the ghosts of her past. While interviewing Colleen for this book, I noted an increased tension in her voice when she got to the part about the knife being pressed against her throat. The ghosts remain near and occasionally visit her late at night.

Colleen is not a perfect woman. She has made many mistakes in her life, including hitchhiking alone which was a major factor in her abduction. One book agent wanted to market her story to the Christian audience because of Colleen's deep faith in God. How many people can say their faith has been truly tested? How many people can say they have been crucified? Who can say they can relate to the suffering of Jesus Christ and still maintain their faith? The book agent backed away when he read about her illegal drug use, child out of wedlock, and multiple marriages. No, Colleen is not a perfect Christian, but she is a person who prays daily and keeps her faith in God more so than most people, including myself. People of religion will appreciate and benefit from her story.

After her ordeal, Colleen claimed to be a "harder person" who was slow to trust people. My experiences with Colleen proved the opposite. I found her to be a kind, gentle, trusting soul. Colleen is the same nice person today, as the young woman who climbed into the backseat of her abductor's car in 1977. Her spirit and love of life has not been crushed.

A most sincere thanks to Colleen Stan for trusting me with her life story and to Debbie King and Marilyn Barrett, long time friends of Colleen. Many others who have helped Colleen will be acknowledged by Colleen in the text of her story.

During the interview process, Colleen talked freely about all aspects of her life. In writing this book, I interviewed only Colleen. I wanted this book to be her story and her story alone. I decided not to interview other people, instead I asked Colleen to describe the other people in her own words. However, I did conduct an extensive search for written material concerning her life, much of it found to be inaccurate or incomplete. I have tried to maintain historical accuracy throughout the book and exclude my own opinions. As the writer, my job was to capture Colleen's words on paper and give her the final edit authority as to the content of this book. This book is Colleen's life, in her words, using her feelings, and her points of view. As the reader, you must place yourself in Colleen's shoes and ask yourself, "What would I have done in her place."

Colleen Stan and Jim Green, Hawaii, 2003

This is the true story of Colleen Jean Stan.

Jim B. Green
February 23, 2008
Fort George G. Meade, Maryland

Chapter 1 - My Story

"We know through painful experience that freedom is never voluntarily given by the oppressor; it must be demanded by the oppressed." - Dr. Martin Luther King, Jr.

On a warm May afternoon in 1977, deep in the pine-covered mountains of Northern California, my life suddenly and dramatically changed. A large, sharp butcher knife was pressed against my throat.

"Put your hands above your head!" he demanded.

Being overtaken with shock and fear, I found myself paralyzed and unable to respond. He pressed the tip of the knife harder against my throat.

"Put your hands above your head!" he demanded once again, in a menacing voice.

Shock and fear were replaced with panic as I realized the man was going to kill me if I didn't obey. Still unable to speak, I slowly raised my hands above my head. I was being abducted.

I didn't know it at the time, but life as I had known it for 20 years had come to an end. The cultural norms I had been taught as a young woman no longer applied. Social skills such as conversational ability, a sharp mind, and intellect were no longer of value to me. A new set of social skills would have to be learned fast if I expected to stay alive.

I soon found myself sealed in a box the size of a coffin in which light, fresh air, and sound were excluded. Food, water, and information were strictly rationed. Punishments came frequently and randomly with no explanations. Questions were rarely permitted, and correct answers were never given.

All was taken away from me including my personality, self-esteem, and sense of security. Even my name, Colleen, was replaced with the single letter "K." Most painful was the lack of human contact. No gentle hand touched me and no kind words comforted me. My cloistered world was filled with silence, isolation, and fear.

I was soon to learn new rules applied in this dark world. I had to learn fast to stay alive. I hardened myself for what lay ahead with

1

my personality becoming stoic and void of emotion. I soon became submissive and compliant. I cried often, but only in private. Eventually, I stopped crying altogether.

Why had I been kidnapped? Why was I being punished so cruelly? Who were these evil people? What were they going to do with me? Why me?

I learned in time, I had not been abducted for money since my family was of average means. Nor had I initially been abducted for sex, although rape did occur later. I had been kidnapped for a more sinister purpose. I was a surrogate to take the pain and humiliation for another woman. The other woman, my abductor's wife, reserved the love and kindness for herself. My qualifications for this position were my youth, beauty, and gender.

With everything taken from me, I turned to the Lord for help. I had always believed in God, but as a young person I had relegated religion to the back of my mind. Now I needed Jesus more than ever. I prayed hard and sought His help in understanding my situation and staying alive. My faith was the only light I had to see through the darkness.

After eight months, I was presented with a contract and forced to sign myself into slavery for life. I surrendered everything except my soul, which I told my abductors belonged to God. Physical restraints were replaced with even more effective mental barriers that were reinforced with cold, raw fear. "The Company," an international slave organization, would be responsible for my security. Any attempt to escape would result in unspeakable torture for me and danger to my family.

At first, escape was never far from my mind. However, like a ship sailing out to sea, the chances of swimming back to shore became less probable as time passed. I eventually accepted my status as a slave for life. To avoid painful punishments, I worked hard at being a good slave. In time, I was granted increased privileges and pseudo-freedoms. I was allowed to care for my captor's children and was presented to the outside world as their babysitter. No one suspected I was a slave or knew about the evil that went on in a single-wide mobile home parked at the end of a quiet street.

In 1981, I was rewarded with a short visit to my parents during which fear kept my lips sealed. My limited freedom ended when I was told to crawl into a 15 inch high, tomb-like box under my abductors waterbed. The door to the box was bolted shut, and I was confined in the box 23 hours a day for the next three years. My isolation was so complete even my abductor's two young daughters thought I had gone home.

Once released from the box in 1984, I was reintroduced to the neighbors and allowed to seek employment as a maid at a local motel. One hot August morning, the fear that I had lived with for so long was suddenly removed. Two days later, I found myself on a public bus traveling back to my family. It was hard to contain my emotions as fellow passengers on the bus assumed I was just another traveler like themselves. I was finally free after seven years, two months, 20 days, and 17 hours.

After I arrived home, I realized that the rules of life had changed once again. Now, I was expected to assert myself and make decisions. I slowly integrated back into the world finding both a job and boyfriend. Like all released hostages, I had learned to appreciate the simple gifts of life. A beautiful sunset followed by a starlit sky and a simple drink of water in the middle of the night were deeply appreciated.

However, not all the effects of slavery had been removed. I still had trouble trusting people, especially men. My body and soul had scars that I will carry with me for the rest of my life. I was no longer the carefree person I had been prior to my abduction. I was plagued with fear, guilt, and anger.

With the police investigating my abductor, I was finally able to get answers to questions that had been plaguing me from the beginning. Why was I kidnapped and tortured so much by these people? Why were they so evil? What had I done to deserve such punishment? Why me?

To my horror, I learned I was not their first victim. A young woman before me had suffered a painful death on her first night of captivity. She now lies in an unmarked grave somewhere in the mountains near where I was kidnapped.

During the trial of my abductor, I was accused of being a willing participant. I found myself defending my actions while in bondage. The news media dubbed me "The Girl in the Box" and "The Sex Slave" in their coverage. When I testified in court, the man who had brought me such pain sat 10 feet in front of me with a smirk on his face. After the verdict, the man's smirk disappeared.

As the years passed, I enjoyed my freedom and became a functional member of society. My status as a victim changed to that of a survivor. I traded fear for anger towards the man who had taken so much from me. I still live with physical pain and periodic nightmares, but these are a small price to pay to be out of bondage and alive.

After returning home, the road of life still had its share of bumps and potholes. I sought love in marriage, only to be disappointed by men who lied about their criminal past and abused alcohol along with me. Most rewarding was the birth of my daughter after a difficult pregnancy. She made the struggles of life well worth the effort.

Throughout my life, I have maintained my faith in the Lord. It's people, not God, who bring evil into the world. God gives people free choice, and some people choose evil over good. I have never blamed God for my hardships. Instead, I have thanked God for giving me the strength to endure. Without my relationship with the Lord, I never would have survived.

Each year, I wanted to write about my experiences and the lessons I had learned. However, when I started to write a cold feeling came over me. I couldn't continue. It's still painful and difficult to talk about, much less write about, all the pain.

How does one describe a fear so strong it paralyzes your soul? How can anyone convey pain so awful you shut your emotions down to survive? What words do I use to illustrate the darkness in the box that confined me for so many years? How does one write about isolation so complete that you pine for human contact? How do you place words on paper to describe endless silence?

Except for a handful of television appearances and fewer newspaper interviews, I have never told my story. This will be my first book. Previous publications about my story were based on police reports and trial records. Such bureaucratic documents omit my personal faith, perspectives, and emotions. Television shows and newspaper articles, by their nature, tend to be short on substance and details. My story will reveal personal information about my life before, during, and after my years of captivity. I wanted the story to be truthful and complete.

I wanted my story told for four reasons:

1. During the trial, an expert witness reported that my abduction was unparalleled in FBI history. No other person had been kidnapped for such a long period of time and subjected to such isolated confinement and torture. In fact, when the case was taken to trial, many of the things done to me were not against California law. Stretching me on a rack, electric shocks, and confining me to a coffin-size box for years was not contemplated by California legislatures when the laws were drafted. This omission of laws has today been corrected. My story must be told so that such crimes don't pass from the collective consciousness of the public and lawmakers. Evil should never be allowed to hide in forgotten memory.

2. Over the years, I have realized most people don't understand what it's like to be a hostage. Like Patty Hearst before me, they keep asking, "Why didn't you fight or try to escape? How could you believe what your abductors told you? Why did you write love letters and tell your tormentor you loved him? When you got home, why didn't you go straight to the police? Weren't you angry when you got home? After what you have been through, how can you be normal? How could you keep your faith in God?"

These are the questions I want to answer. These are the same questions you see today in newspapers and on television when a hostage is released. Survivors are asked the same questions because the media and public don't understand what it's like being held in captivity. It doesn't matter if you're a victim of crime, prisoner of war, or a slave, the emotions of the survivor are the same. The press and general public need to understand these emotions because someday they may serve on a jury dealing with a kidnapping, have a family member abducted, or be a victim themselves.

3. Most crimes occur in minutes or days at the most. Rarely is a person illegally taken from society for long-term confinement. Mostly women, but also some men, boys and girls, have been kidnapped with the intension of holding the victim for long periods of time for torture or sexual purposes. Recently, a number of such crimes have come to light when the hostages escaped or were rescued.

In 2008, Elisabeth Fritzl was released, after 24 years and seven children, from a windowless cellar in Austria. In 2007, 13 year old Ben Ownsby and 15 year old Shawn Hornbeck were rescued from a man's apartment in Missouri. Natascha Kampusch emerged in 2006 after eight years of captivity in an underground vault in Austria. Elizabeth Shoaf escaped after 10 days from an underground dungeon in South Carolina by stealing her captor's cell phone and text-messaging her mother. Tanya Kach was confined by a man in Pennsylvania for 10 years until 2006. Lena Simakhina and Datya Martynova were held by a Russian factory worker as sex slaves in an underground cellar for over three years until 2004. San Fusako, a Japanese woman, was held captive for nine years until 2000. A shake-up of the Belgium government occurred in 1996 after four girls died and two survived an ordeal in the basement of a man's house. Sabine Dardenne, one of the survivors, wrote about her ordeal, *I Choose to Live,* published in 2006. In 1993, Katie Beers was freed from an underground vault in New York after 17 days. A man abducted a seven year old boy named Steven Stayner in California and raised him as his son for seven years until 1980. The list goes on and on. Sadly, even now someone is probably being criminally held against their will.

Many of these stories end with people who survived. Once back home, they must jump-start their lives, readjust to a normal life, and deal with questions from the media and friends. They must transition from fear to anger and being a victim to being a survivor. The process isn't easy, and it's different for each individual, but some generalizations can be made.

By telling my story, I hope, in a small way, to help survivors and their families understand the impact of being a hostage. I lack a Ph.D. in psychology, but I do have real-life experiences that give me insights into areas in which most people have never known. Perhaps my story will help someone, or their family members, during the recovery phase. I hope my story will help the general public, and especially the media, in understanding why hostages do what they do and say what they say while in captivity.

4. Anyone plunged into a dark abyss must quickly formulate a survival strategy to stay alive. Letting go or committing suicide was

never an option for me because I wanted to live. Some people will rely on the discipline gained during police, military, or sports training. I turned to my faith in God. It was my faith, along with day dreams of happier times, which sustained me through the dark years of confinement. The general public doesn't know and the news media fails to report on the role of faith in surviving a hostage situation.

This is my story as I experienced it. It's not the story of the man or woman who abducted me. They must tell their own stories. I can only tell you what they did to me, along with what I saw with my eyes, and heard with my ears. I will present my personal opinions on religion, the Stockholm syndrome, and the people who abducted me, but I leave it to the reader to make judgments and to evaluate my opinions.

Many of the dates and measurements in my story were obtained after my release. At no time was I keeping a private diary or taking measurements of my surroundings. Most quotations have been reconstructed from my best memory. I have tried to maintain the emotions of the moment in my quotations. I have also tried to remain faithful to truth and accuracy throughout my story.

The names of the two young daughters of my abductors have been changed to protect their innocence and privacy. For the same reason, I have used only the first name or changed the name of some individuals.

I must apologize to the reader for the graphic and painful details in my story. I didn't want simply to say the man hurt me, because that would fail to convey the true horror of those seven years. Who would describe the Holocaust or the events of September 11, 2001, in euphemistic language? I want my story to convey the pain and despair of the situation. However, time tends to fade the memory, and many of the events remain painful for me to retrieve even to this day.

I must thank the handful of people who were kind to me during my captivity even though they had no idea I was a slave. To them, I was just a sad, unhappy young woman who went by the name of Kay. I also want to thank the many people who knew me as Colleen and helped in my recovery with love and understanding. I will try to include all of your names, but please forgive me if I overlook anyone. Most important, I want to give thanks to the Lord on whose words I survived.

I will start with my last chance to escape before the knife was placed against my throat. A strange voice coming from deep within me tried to warn me, but I chose to ignore the voice, to my everlasting regret.

My name is Colleen Stan, and this is my story.

Chapter 2 - Warnings

As I stared out the window, I wondered, "Why am I having these feelings?" The voice persisted, "Jump out the window, run, and never look back." The voice was coming from somewhere inside me and was compelling all the way to my soul.

I could see the beautiful oak trees and wild grasses of Northern California through the window. It was Thursday afternoon, May 19, 1977, and I was traveling to nearby Westwood to see my good friend Linda Smith. I wanted to surprise her and wish her a happy birthday. The weather was warm and beautiful as I stood in the restroom of a combination gas station, café, and bar in Paynes Creek, trying to cool off and clean up. This all-in-one establishment was about all Paynes Creek had in the way of businesses.

"Climb out the window and get away. It's your last chance. Get out and run," the voice persisted. I was apprehensive and didn't understand the warnings.

"Why? Why do I want to climb out of the window and run?"

As I washed up at the sink, the voice continued for about a minute. It was forthright and sincere, but most of all, it was persistent. As I looked in the mirror, I could see the open window behind me. I continued to question my feelings and the warnings.

"What am I running from?"

I couldn't identify the voice so I ignored it. I decided it was all crazy, shrugged it off, and failed to heed the warnings. I didn't know it at the time, but that moment in a public restroom was my last chance to escape.

I returned to the car that was giving me a ride to Westwood. The driver had a smirk on his face, but the woman had an inviting smile that greeted me as I emerged from the restroom. The baby in the woman's arms appeared happy, and I felt secure. I climbed into the back seat of their car and continued my journey to Linda Smith's house. I didn't have another thought about the incident in the restroom, not until much later.

Things seemed to be on schedule, and I was glad I would be arriving in Westwood before dark. It was such a relief, because my day had not gone well up to that point.

I left Eugene, Oregon, early in the morning. I had spent the night before with my boyfriend Mark. When I awoke to the sound of the neighbor's barking dog, I knew I had to go to Westwood. In addition to visiting Smith, as I called her, I could also see my sister-in-law Sandra and another close friend, Sara.

Being young with a free spirit, I was very impulsive. I did what I wanted to do and when I wanted to do it. I was 20 years old and unsure what I wanted from life, but I knew the world was mine to conquer. It was a beautiful morning, and the sun was shining brightly through the window shades. All the birds were singing, and the air was fresh and clean. I knew I had to go to Westwood to surprise Smith. In my mind, the decision was made.

As I lay in bed, I stared up at a tapestry Mark had hung from the ceiling. Suddenly, as if by magic, I saw an evil, awful-looking face of a person in the middle of the tapestry. Mark was in the bathroom washing his face and getting ready for work. He said something to me, but I was only half listening. The frightening face in the tapestry had mesmerized me.

I suddenly realized Mark was talking about his ex-girlfriend. I continued to stare at the tapestry as I responded, "Was she an evil woman?"

"Yeah, how did you know?"

"I didn't know," I said. "I was just looking at an evil face in your tapestry." Later, I wondered if the face in the tapestry was a warning of things to come. It didn't matter because I was going to Westwood anyway.

As Mark drove me back to my apartment, I told him it was Linda Smith's birthday and I wanted to travel to Westwood and surprise her.

"I don't think that's a good idea, Colleen. It's too far away," Mark said, with concern in his voice.

I knew Mark was right, but my mind was set on going. Being headstrong and impulsive were my strong characteristics. Everyone knew once I set my mind on doing something, I would do it. Neither Mark nor anyone else was going to stop me from going.

"I'm throwing a party on Sunday and would like for you to attend. My father and brother will be there, and I want you to meet them," Mark said.

"Don't worry, I'll be back by Sunday in time to meet your family."

"It's not safe for you to travel that far," Mark pleaded.

"I'll be fine. If I can't find a way home, I know Smith will give me a ride back. Don't worry, I won't miss your party."

I kissed Mark good-bye as he dropped me off at my apartment. He was late for work and sped off down the street. I didn't know it, but it would be years before I would speak to him again.

I wanted to drive my old Saab automobile to Westwood, but knew the car's better days had long passed. My father had given me the car after he purchased it from my husband, Tim Stan. The motor was a two-cycle engine requiring the oil and gasoline to be properly mixed in the correct ratio to achieve a smooth-running car, something you would never find in a vehicle today. I never mastered the mixing process, which resulted in a car that wouldn't run. I believe I pushed that car more than I drove it.

Bus fare and a rental car were out of the question, for financial reasons. "Oh well," I thought. "I'll just hitchhike to Westwood."

Hitchhiking wasn't new to me. My roommate Alice and I had hitchhiked all around Eugene with a sense of complete safety. It was while hitchhiking that I met Mark. Hitchhiking to Westwood wasn't a big deal, but I had to admit I had never hitchhiked that far before by myself. Smith was at least eight hours away.

When I opened the door to the apartment, I announced to my roommates that I was going to Westwood. "It's Smith's birthday, and I want to surprise her. Would you guys give me a ride to Interstate 5? My car won't start, so I'm going to hitchhike."

"Colleen, that's not safe," Alice said. Bobby, her boyfriend, agreed. "You shouldn't be hitchhiking that far by yourself."

"Guys, my mind is made up. Thanks for your concerns, but I'm going. Seeing Smith on her birthday is important to me. Would you give me a ride to the interstate?"

Alice and Bobby finally agreed to give me a ride to Interstate 5, so I started packing a few clothes and personal things inside my sleeping bag. I tied my Pendleton jacket around my waist in case it got cold in the mountains. My driver's license, Social Security card, a hair brush, lotions, makeup, and birth control pills were in my blue purse. I didn't have a lot of money, so $20 had to see me through. I didn't have much breakfast that morning, because I wanted to get on the road early. Above all else, I wanted to arrive in Westwood before dark.

Around 7:00 in the morning, we all climbed in Bobby's old pickup truck and headed toward Interstate 5, the main north-south highway between Oregon and California.

"Colleen, please don't go," my roommates pleaded with me one more time.

"Don't worry, I'll be safe. I plan on being back for a party Mark is throwing on Sunday."

We hugged and said our good-byes on the shoulder of the highway. After Alice and Bobby pulled away, I set my sleeping bag down and put my thumb up in the air to hitch a ride.

Colleen Stan Hitchhiking

I had over 400 miles to travel, so I was glad for the early start. I would go south from Eugene, Oregon, on Interstate 5, until I got to Red Bluff, California. From Red Bluff, I would head east on Highway 36 into the mountains until I arrived in Westwood. Situated high in the Southern Cascade Range, Westwood is surrounded by tall pines and fast-moving mountain streams. The air is cool, clean, and healthy.

The surprise would be complete since Smith didn't have a telephone. The only telephone I had was a pay phone down the street from my apartment. I was excited and looking forward to seeing Smith and all of my friends.

After five minutes, a little red Porsche pulled off the interstate and stopped directly in front of me. The driver, a handsome young man, looked out the passenger side window and asked me where I was going.

"South to California," I said.

"I'm from Salem," he replied, "and I'm only going as far as Cottage Grove."

Salem was 60 miles north of Eugene, and Cottage Grove was only 17 miles south of where I was standing. "Great," I replied, figuring it was at least a start, and I needed to get started to make my destination before dark.

I hopped in the sleek-looking sports car and thanked him for the ride. As we talked, he told me he was a college student on his way home. Twenty minutes later, we arrived at the Cottage Grove exit. He pulled over on the shoulder so I could catch another ride. "Thanks a lot," I said as the little red sports car sped away.

Once again, I had to wait only a short time before a big semi-truck whizzed past and put on its brakes. The rig stopped a short distance down the interstate, and the driver got out and walked around as if inspecting his truck. As I ran over to him, I wasn't sure if he had stopped to check his load or give me a ride.

As I approached the truck, the man turned around and asked, "Where you going, young lady?"

"I'm going to Red Bluff and then east on Highway 36. "

"My partner and I can give you a ride to Red Bluff. We're heading to Southern California," the truck driver shouted over the noise of the passing traffic.

"Great," I said. Luck must have been with me because I was having no trouble getting rides.

The truck driver took my sleeping bag and put it in a storage compartment below the truck cab. He opened the door, and I climbed up the high steps into the cab. "Thanks a lot," I said, sensing everything was going my way.

As we pulled onto the highway, the other driver, a much younger man in his 20's, emerged from the sleeping compartment behind the cab. He appeared to be surprised to find a woman in the cab.

"What's going on?" he asked. There were probably strict rules concerning picking up hitchhikers, but the old man, in his 40's, was the senior driver and the young man did whatever he was told.

We traveled 120 miles south on Interstate 5 to Grants Pass, Oregon, where some of their freight had to be dropped off. The truck was hauling boxes of grape juice in one quart plastic containers. After they made their delivery, it was time for lunch. All three of us went to a buffet-style restaurant that the truckers had previously visited. The two men insisted on paying for my lunch, I accepted their offer, and thanked them for their kindness.

After lunch, we continued on our journey with the younger man driving and the older man in the sleeper taking a nap. The young driver, who seemed friendlier then the older driver, told me he was new to truck driving. We talked, and I felt relaxed as we traveled down the highway, making good time. We passed some of the most beautiful scenery in America, including snow-covered Mount Shasta, which stands 14,162 feet in elevation.

Just before we got to the California truck inspection station at Dunsmuir, approximately 120 miles south of Grants Pass, the old driver woke up and crawled out of the sleeper.

"You need to hide in the sleeper, or we'll get in trouble," the old man said as the truck entered the off ramp.

"Okay," I said in a naïve way as I got in the sleeper.

We went though the inspection station without any problems, but as we pulled back onto the interstate, the old man hopped into the sleeper with me. Immediately, he started trying to kiss and fondle me. His hands were all over my body. The young man was driving, but I'm sure he heard what was going on behind him.

"No, leave me alone," I shouted as I broke free of his grip and jumped out of the sleeper back into the cab. The young man, looking sheepish, didn't say a word. After the old man had fallen asleep, the young man apologized for the old man's behavior.

"It's not your fault that your partner is a nasty old man," I said, with anger in my voice.

When we got to Red Bluff, the driver pulled over at the Highway 36 exit to let me out. The young man got out of the truck and retrieved my sleeping bag from the compartment below the cab.

"I'm sorry for my partner's behavior," he said again in an apologetic manner.

Before I departed, the young man went to the back of the truck, opened the trailer door, and pulled out a quart container of grape juice.

"Good luck on your trip," he said as he handed me the container of grape juice.

"Thanks for the ride and grape juice," were my last words to him as I walked up the off ramp to Highway 36. It was 4:00 in the afternoon, and I had traveled 325 of my 400 mile journey. I was still hoping to make Westwood before dark.

The Highway 36 overpass crosses above Interstate 5 in Red Bluff. Once I had walked to the top of the overpass, I set my sleeping bag on the pavement and stuck out my thumb. It wasn't long before a car stopped.

The car was full of young guys who said they would be glad to give me a ride. I surveyed the situation and decided it wasn't safe. Five of them to one of me were poor odds from my point of view, especially after confronting the dirty old man in the truck.

"Thanks for the offer, but not today," I said. The guys sped off east on Highway 36.

As I stood waiting for the next car, I surveyed the small town of Red Bluff from the overpass. Red Bluff was a town of around 9,000 people at an elevation of 342 feet. Most of the cars and trucks speeding up and down Interstate 5 never notice Red Bluff unless they need food or gas. Being far from Los Angeles and San Francisco, both in miles and culture, the town had more of a rural or country feel. Some people would call Red Buff a redneck town. The downtown portion was west of the overpass, while to the east lay a string of gas stations and fast-food restaurants. Red Bluff was just a transfer point for me, or so I thought at the time.

Five minutes later, another car with a young couple stopped to offer me a ride. They looked safe, but they were only going a short distance down Highway 36. Once again, I thanked them and sent them on their way.

The day had grown warm, and the hot sun felt good on my face as I stood next to the highway. A high-pressure system was over the Oregon-California state line, bringing mostly clear skies. The temperature for Red Bluff that day was forecast to range from a high of 65 degrees to a low of 50 degrees. It felt warmer standing next to the black asphalt highway.

It must have been hard for anyone driving down Highway 36 to miss seeing me standing on the side of the road. I was 20 years old with long auburn hair that hung down to the middle of my back. My white complexion matched my blue eyes and freckles. People tell me I had a sweet smile and a look of innocence. I was 5 feet, 6 inches tall and weighed around 135 pounds.

Unknown to me at the time, my Capricorn astrological forecast for the day read in part, "Be analytical--don't rush to judgment. You do best by observing, waiting, planting seeds for future." I never took astrological signs seriously, but maybe I should have on that particular day.

I was wearing a white wrap top, which was a type of shirt that wrapped around my body. One side of the wrap top tied on my right side, and the other tied on my left side. The garment had a "V" neckline and short sleeves that covered only the top portion of my arms. The wrap top left my midsection exposed. However, my Pendleton jacket was tied around my waist, reducing the amount of skin showing.

The wrap top was popular among young people as were my bell-bottom jeans. I had on some jewelry and a pair of Earth Shoes on my feet. The Earth Shoes, which were also popular at the time, were tan with little shoe laces. The soles were thick with the heel lower than the toe. "Like walking in sand on the beach" was how they were advertised. Overall, I was within the normal fashion trends of the day for a young woman in her early 20's.

This was the image the driver of the next car saw through his front windshield. A cobalt-blue, two-door, 1971 Dodge Colt with front bucket seats pulled over and stopped in front of me. A man and woman were in the car, and the woman held a small baby in her arms.

Through the open passenger window, the woman asked, "Where're you going?"

"I'm going to Westwood," I told them hoping they were going farther than the previous couple.

Colleen Stan Prior to Abduction

"We're heading that way," the man said. "Climb in."

"Thanks for stopping," I said, as the woman opened her door and pulled the bucket seat forward so I could get in the backseat. She cradled the baby in her left arm. I tossed my sleeping bag in the backseat and then awkwardly climbed in wishing their car had four doors. I felt my luck had changed, and now I would make it to Smith's place before dark.

The man and woman shared many things in common with me. They didn't appear to be well off financially. The man, approximately age 23, looked like a mechanic who had just gotten off work. His clothes and blond hair were dirty and greasy. He was wearing a blue work shirt, jeans, and work boots. His wife, about age 19, had long, wavy black hair and was dressed in shorts and a t-shirt. They both wore glasses. The baby was blond, like her dad, and looked to be around eight months old. I assumed they were married and the child was theirs. I felt secure with the couple, because the presence of the baby reassured me I was safe.

I sat on the right side of the car directly behind the woman. My sleeping bag was in the unoccupied seat to my left. As we waited for the traffic to clear before pulling back on the highway, I opened the container of grape juice the truck driver had given me. The heat of the day, along with the fact I had not drank anything since lunch at Grants Pass, made me very thirsty. As I put the open container to my lips, the man hit the gas, and the car bolted forward. Grape juice ran down my chin and on to my white wrap top.

"You creep," I wanted to say, but didn't because I was grateful for the ride. I took the jacket from around my waist and wiped the juice off my front. When I looked up, I noticed the man was staring straight at me through the rearview mirror. I continued to wipe the juice off, knowing it would soon dry and become sticky. I couldn't help thinking that the man purposely accelerated the car onto the highway when he saw me put the juice bottle to my mouth. This made me feel uneasy, but I chose to ignore it.

After a short distance, we made a left turn where Highway 36 splits with Highway 99. As we began our gradual climb into the mountains signs of human habitation, such as houses and automobile traffic, decreased. We continued through dry ranch country with tall grass and sparse trees. An occasional outcropping of lava would come into view just off the road. Lassen Peak, a nearby volcano with an elevation of 10,457 feet, had last erupted in 1914. Prior to the Mount St. Helens eruption in 1980, Lassen was the last volcanic eruption in the continental United States. Scientists used the Lassen area to learn how the vegetation and animal life of Mount St. Helens would recover.

"Why are you going to Westwood?"

"It's my friend's birthday, and I want to surprise her," I replied.

"She doesn't know you are coming?"

"No, it will be a complete surprise."

"Where are you coming from?"

"I started in Eugene, Oregon, and have been hitchhiking all day."

I was growing tired of the questions and just wanted to look out the car window and watch the scenery. I assumed they were just curious about the person they had picked up.

"How old are you?"

"I'm 20."

"Do you hitchhike often? "

"I do for short trips, but this is my first big trip."

"Are you married?"

"Yes, but I'm no longer living with my husband."

It occurred to me the couple were almost too curious about my life. The questions kept coming, and I kept responding. Later, I would realize they had a lot of information about me, and I had no information about them. I was tired and didn't really care about them. I continued to answer their questions politely because they had stopped to give me a ride. I was grateful, but I wanted only to relax and stare out the window.

"I'm going to pull over up here for some gas," the man said after we had traveled about 25 miles.

Paynes Creek was little more than a gas station and a few houses on the side of the road. The gas station, known as Hogawaller Flats, contained a small café, a bar, and a couple of pool tables. It served the few ranchers and farmers in the area.

I took advantage of the stop to pull a fresh t-shirt from my sleeping bag and rush to the restroom to clean up. It felt good to wash the sticky grape juice off my skin. The water was refreshing, but the voice from within was disturbing.

"Jump out the window, run, and never look back," the voice said.

Since the instructions from the voice didn't make sense, I ignored it. I removed the juice-stained wrap top and replaced it with a dry t-shirt. Then I folded the wrap top and walked out of the restroom. The man and woman were waiting for me at the front door. The man had a smirk on his face, but the smiling face of the woman made me completely forget the strange message I had received in the restroom.

Gas Station at Paynes Creek, 1989

I had chosen to ignore all of the warnings I had received, including the evil face in the tapestry, the lascivious old man, the grape juice spill, the man staring at me through the rearview mirror, the unending questions from the couple, and the powerful voice in the bathroom. I had an uneasy feeling, but all I could think about was getting to Westwood before dark.

In addition to the gas, the woman had purchased some candy in the café. As I hopped back in the car, the woman offered me a single chocolate peanut butter cup. The candy made me thirsty, but I knew better than to take a drink of the grape juice I was carrying. As we pulled out of the gas station and headed east up the mountain, I didn't realize my last chance to escape had passed.

Chapter 3 - Abduction and First Night

As the car headed east out of Paynes Creek, the first thing I noticed was a weird wooden box on the seat next to me. It had not been there before. It was in the shape of a cube, measuring about a foot on each side. Leather hinges were visible, along with leather reinforcement strips on the edges. I didn't know the purpose of the box, so I disregarded it. Later, the strange box would play a significant role in my life.

As we ascended the mountain along an isolated stretch of highway, we approached Lassen Volcanic National Park which is surrounded by a dense forest of tall pine trees. I loved the mountains with their snow fed streams and towering peaks. Unlike Riverside, California, where I was from, the air in the mountains was pure and clean. I was happy knowing I would soon be in Westwood, about 40 miles away, before dark. Fatigue was the only thing dampening my excitement.

"Do you mind if we make a short stop to check out some ice caves? We've heard they're just off the road," the woman said.

"Will we make it to Westwood before dark? "

"Yes, it won't take long," she answered.

I didn't want to infringe on their kindness and generosity. After all, they had stopped and given me a ride. How could I, sitting in the backseat, say no to a short visit?

After some searching, the man made a left turn off the highway onto a dirt forest access road. I didn't see any signs on the highway for ice caves, but I figured they knew the way and didn't question them.

We had probably driven a quarter of a mile down the road when the man stopped the car and turned off the engine. The pine trees around the car were very tall, and I could hear the sounds of running water. A small creek was a few yards away from where we had stopped. There were no cars, homes, or people for miles around. The air was quiet and still. It was around 5:00 in the afternoon.

The man and woman, with the baby, got out of the car and walked down to the creek to get some cool mountain water. I chose to wait in the backseat of the car with the door open. I was in a hurry and didn't want to hold things up by getting out of the car with them.

I glanced out the window and could see the woman and baby at the creek, but the man wasn't in sight. For just a second, I had lost track of him.

Suddenly, the bucket seat in front of me was thrown forward and the man jumped into the backseat with me. A large, sharp butcher knife was in his hand and pressed against my throat.

"Put your hands above your head," he ordered.

I froze in fear. All I could think was, "Oh, my God, I can't believe this is happening to me." I was petrified and couldn't move. My mind was in shock as adrenalin started pumping through my arteries.

"Put your hands above your head," he said again as he pushed the knife harder against my throat.

I did as I was told, subconsciously noting both of us were shaking. I was shaking out of fear, while he was probably shaking from nervousness. A pair of handcuffs came out of his back pocket and passed before my eyes. Quickly, one wrist and then the other were cuffed behind my back. Now I was his captive with no way to escape. I feared this was the beginning of the end for me. I was going to die!

The man picked up the knife and placed it against my throat again. "Are you going to do as I tell you?"

I was petrified and couldn't speak, but was able to node my head, "Yes."

Then he secured a cloth blindfold over my eyes. He pulled something down over my head and face that fit like a harness. A wide leather strap covered my mouth and encircled my head; another strap went under my jaw. Two additional straps went up the sides of my nose and joined together at my forehead. From my forehead, the strap continued over the top of my head and was secured to the wide strap at the back of my head. Now my jaw was locked securely in place, rendering me unable to open my mouth to scream. Any attempt to talk with this gag in place would be difficult. Lastly, he tied my ankles together with a rope.

The speed and precision of his movements indicated the man was well rehearsed. This wasn't an ad hoc abduction. Instead, the man had positioned the restraints in his car beforehand. Later, I thought back on the situation and realized the couple had been out hunting female quarry. I was their catch.

My mind was still in a state of shock. I couldn't believe what was happening to me. "Oh, my God, he's going to kill me," was my deepest fear.

Unbeknownst to me, the worst was still to come. Now the purpose of the strange box in the backseat next to me became evident. The 20 pound box worked like a clam shell with a round hole designed to fit around my neck. With the box in the open position, half of a semicircle was in the lid while the other half was in the base of the box. When closed, the two halves clamped down tightly on my neck, locking my head in the box. Two latches secured the head box, as it was called, preventing light, sound, and fresh air from entering.

Now it was my turn to experience the device as the man positioned my head in the box and slammed it shut. The neck hole, which I had not seen in the car, clamped down tightly on my neck. The inside of the box was insulated with foam rubber and carpet that was contoured to fit my head. Breathing immediately became difficult.

The human head contains four of the five senses. Within the head box, vision, hearing, taste, and smell were suppressed or eliminated. My vision was of darkness, sound was muffled, taste was of a leather gag, and smell was of foam and carpet. My sense of touch was not impaired by the head box. I could feel the suffocating device on my head, the handcuffs on my wrist, and the rope on my ankles.

My sleeping bag was unfurled and placed on top of my prostrate body in the backseat of the car. All control had passed from me to the man with the sharp knife.

With the head box on me and sleeping bag over me, I began to overheat. I felt as if I were about to have a heatstroke. Fear ran through my veins causing my body to shake out of control. Sweat began rolling down my body as my mind entered a state of shock and disbelief. Fear overtook me as my mind tried to decide if fight or flight was my best option. Neither option was open to me as I lay fully restrained. I was trapped and helpless.

"Oh God, please help me," I prayed.

Even with the head box on, I could still hear muffled noises such as the car door closing after the woman and baby returned. Since the woman didn't say anything, I concluded she knew beforehand of the plot to abduct me. For some unknown reason, she placed the baby on top of the sleeping bag covering me. When the baby started to cry, she took the baby back.

The man got in and started the engine. I could feel the car moving over the dirt road and making a right turn onto the highway. We headed west back down the mountain toward Red Bluff. Since I couldn't hear the man or woman speak, I assumed they drove in silence. Even if they had spoken, I'm not sure I could have understood what they were saying.

"What kind of people were they? Were they going to kill me? If so, why didn't they kill me in the woods? What had I done to deserve this? I knew this wasn't God's fault. He or His angels had tried to warn me, but I wouldn't listen. What is going to happen next?"

Soon, I could hear traffic noise, which indicated we were back in Red Bluff. I considered sitting up, hoping someone might see me. A woman with her head in a box would surely draw attention and surely bring help. I also thought about screaming, but realized no one would hear me with my mouth gagged and locked in the head box. I abandoned the ideas as stupid, knowing the man would probably kill me on the spot. My options were few in number. I was trapped.

The car stopped briefly as the woman got out and walked away. After a few minutes, the car stopped again and, I assumed, the woman got back in the car. I wondered, "What was going on, and where was I being taken?" Fear, like I had never known before, gripped me.

As we drove, it appeared we were departing Red Bluff since the traffic noise faded away. A short time later, the car came to a stop, and the engine was turned off. The man removed the sleeping bag and unlocked the head box. I was allowed to sit up, but all other restraints, which included the handcuffs, gag, blindfold, and ankle ties, remained in place. The cool air felt good against my sweaty skin, and I could breathe a little freer. My body continued to shake out of control with hysteria not far behind.

I could smell food. What kind of sick people are these two? I was restrained and gagged while they are having a family picnic. I began to pray, "Oh God, please help me. Please Lord, protect me from these evil people."

I was thankful for the few moments of relief, but it didn't last long. Back in the head box I went with the sleeping bag again draped over my body. The car started, and we began driving around. I had a feeling the couple were waiting until it was dark. "Oh God, please don't let them kill me," I prayed.

We continued to drive until the car made a series of sharp turns and suddenly stopped. The engine was turned off. The man got out this time, and the woman and baby stayed with me in the car. After a minute or two, the man returned, and it sounded as if the woman, with the baby I assume, got out and walked away. Now I was alone with the man. He got in the backseat with me and unlatched the head box.

"Sit up," he ordered. In a stern voice, he said, "Are you going to do what I tell you?"

"Yes," I answered with clenched teeth behind the gag. My ankles were untied, but the gag, blindfold, and handcuffs remained.

"Get out of the car," he commanded. Once out of the car, he gripped my shoulders from behind and guided me forward. I walked 16 steps down a narrow concrete walkway until I came to a set of porch

steps. I struggled up three steps, through a screen door, and into a screened in back porch that served as a laundry room. With the head box off, I discovered I could see a little if I looked down between the blindfold and the bridge of my nose. I could see what I thought was the base of a washtub in the laundry room.

I passed through the backdoor into the house and was guided to the right. I could tell I was in a kitchen because a stove came into my limited field of view. Five steps later, I felt the man turning me to the left as he tightened his grip on my shoulders. I

Back of Oak Street House, 2006

25

walked down 14 steep steps into a basement, which unbeknownst to me, was my descent into hell. It would be months before I would be allowed back up those 14 steps. "Oh God, please help me," I prayed, "What are these people going to do to me?"

Stairway to Basement, 2006

Basement, 2006

My body was shaking so uncontrollably I could hardly walk. The basement was musty and smelled of mold and dust, but was cooler than the outdoors. When I got to the bottom of the stairs, the man turned me to the left, and walked me to the center of the basement.

"Step up," his harsh voice commanded.

From under the bottom of the blindfold, I could see a green-and-white Coleman ice chest. I stepped up and could feel the man unlocking my left wrist from the handcuffs. He took my handcuffed right wrist and quickly locked it to a pipe above my head. Now I was standing on the ice chest with my right hand cuffed to a pipe in the ceiling. On the left side of my body, he started removing my shoes and clothes. "Oh no, he's going to rape me," I thought.

Next, he attached a three-inch-wide, thick brown leather cuff to my left wrist, which in turn was attached to a hook in a wooden beam of the ceiling. Now I was undressed on the left side of my body with my left wrist attached to the beam. At no time were both my hands free. Then he repeated the procedure on the right side of my body. As he worked, I could smell the sweat and grease on his body. He was shaking, as was I, except his shaking was from excitement, whereas mine was out of fear. I could sense darkness and evil flowing from this man.

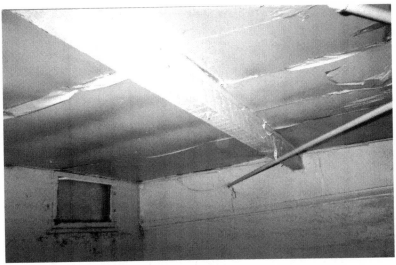

Wooden Beam in Basement, 2006

Fear ran through my body like I had never known before. I was so horrified I couldn't stop trembling and shaking. My legs were so weak I had trouble standing on the ice chest. Finally, I was completely naked except for my socks. My socks came off later, but I can't remember exactly when. My wrists were in leather cuffs attached to the beam in the ceiling with body formed the shape of the letter "Y." My hands were three feet, eight inches apart.

"What are you going to do to me?" I asked behind the gag.

"Shut up," he said callously as he ran his hands up and down my body. The feeling of his hands running over my body made me want to throw up. This was all foreign and frightening to me as I had no control. "What have I gotten myself into?" I thought.

Without any warning, he kicked the ice chest out from under my feet. All of my weight suddenly transferred to my wrists. The pain shot down my arms to my shoulders and ribs. My hands went numb as my feet dangled in the air. The pain was excruciating, unlike anything I had experienced before. There was no way to ease the pain as breathing became increasingly difficult. Later, I would refer to this as being hung up, but others would call it a form of crucifixion.

In pain, I tilted my head back and surveyed the basement through the bottom of the blindfold. I could see I was in a cinder block basement with two small windows high on the opposite wall. The windows were covered with black plastic. I could also see the wooden beam I was attached to and a pipe running diagonally across the ceiling. Some items were hanging on the wall, but I couldn't identify them.

Suddenly, to my horror and disbelief, I saw a magazine on a table in front of me opened to a picture of a naked woman suspended by her wrists from the ceiling. I broke down at that point. "Oh God, who are these people, and what have I gotten myself into?" I sobbed uncontrollably.

There was more to come. The man went upstairs and brought down the woman. They took off their clothes and started to have sex on a table in front of me. "Oh God," I cried as full impact of the situation sunk in on me.

"Keep your head down," the man snapped at me.

I quickly lowered my head, but it was too late. He jumped up from the table and grabbed something off the wall. I heard the crack of a whip and felt the sting of pain as a whip struck my back. I realized the items on the wall, I previously couldn't identify, were whips.

Again and again, the whip came down on my back. The whip wrapped around my body leaving long, red welts. The pain from the suspension, and the whipping became unbearable. The pain was deeper than just my body. It was an assault on my whole being, right down to my soul. Sweat ran down my body as I lifted my legs and flailed them about. The pain was more than I could bear.

"Shut up and relax," the man ordered. "It'll be over sooner."

The whip struck my flesh again and again. I was confused and didn't understand what was happening to me. Finally, I was able to stop kicking my legs and hung there quietly crying between sobs.

Thoughts flooded my mind such as, "Who are these people? Why are they doing this to me? What is their plan, and how did I become a part of it? What did I do to deserve such painful punishment? What was I being punished for? Was I being whipped because I was crying? Who wouldn't cry under these circumstances?"

After 15 minutes, the man put a smaller box under my feet. I couldn't stand flat-footed, but had to stand on my toes. This brought some relief to my wrists and arms, but only for a short time. Soon, I was transferring my weight back and forth between my wrists and my toes. "God, please help me," I prayed.

I searched my mind for answers and remembered a friend who, years before, had mentioned people who were into something called sadism. "Is sadism what these people are about? What is sadism anyway?" I had no experience and wasn't sure of the exact meaning of sadism. In time, I would learn sadism is sexual gratification gained through causing pain or degradation to others. I was in the hands of a sadist!

The man and woman went back to having sex as I stood on my tiptoes. My body was wracked with pain, and my mind was panicking. I asked myself, "How did I ever let myself get into this situation? How could I have been so stupid?"

When they had finished, the woman got dressed and went back upstairs. I was alone with the man. He came over to me and ran his hands over my body again as if to admire his prize. There was nothing I could do except stand on my toes and cry softly. I tried to keep my sobs quiet because I didn't want to make the man angry. He would whip me again. In fact, he seemed to enjoy beating me with the whip.

This man was no stranger to evil. His basement was fully equipped to fulfill every fantasy in his twisted mind. He had deprived me of my freedom and subjected me to humiliation and pain like I had never known before. My spirit was crushed by his sadistic acts.

Suddenly, the small box was kicked out from under me. The pain came back with a vengeance. Flashes of light indicated a souvenir photo was being taken. Later, I learned the man developed his own film in private.

Thankfully, I was not suspended as long the second time. The ice chest came back under my feet, and he released my wrists from the ceiling. My hands were still numb as he replaced the leather restraints with small chains. The chains were secured with small padlocks.

"Step down," he commanded. With his hands grasping my shoulders, he guided me to an area under the stairs. My legs were so wobbly I could hardly walk. "Sit down," he ordered. I quickly obeyed.

He scooted me into a box that was shaped like a crate and open at one end. The box was not tall enough for me to sit up straight, but I could stretch my legs out flat. My bare back faced the open end of the box. The chains on my wrists were attached to the upper inside corners of the box, and my ankles were secured to the bottom inside corners.

The head box was then clamped on my head, with claustrophobic effect. The head box was then secured to the top, middle of the open end of the box. The neck hole in the head box was smaller than my 13¼ inch neck, creating a feeling of strangulation. With the gag and blindfold still in place, I was having trouble breathing. Soon my arms, chained above my head, began to ache.

As I sat in total darkness, I cried and prayed to God for His help. The minutes slowly turned into hours as a claustrophobic, choking feeling overtook me. I began to hyperventilate as each breath felt like my last. I knew I wouldn't last the night. My only escape would be death. The pain became intolerable as my wrists became bruised by the chains. In desperation, I kicked my feet against the sides of the box, and I tried to scream as best I could.

Suddenly, a pair of hands touched my back. I screamed out in fear as my body became tense. After opening the head box, the man asked in an angry voice, "What's wrong?"

"I can't breathe. Please let my hands down," I pleaded through the gag.

"Shut up," he said, with no compassion in his voice. "If you don't shut up, I'll cut your vocal cords. I've done it before, and I'll do it again." The head box was clamped shut again, pinching my neck.

A few seconds later, I could feel a cord or belt being wrapped around my chest and upper waist. He tightened it until it became even more difficult to breathe. Then I felt something sharp being inserted between my thighs. It felt like a prickly hair roller. He kept trying to get something to work, but finally gave up leaving the cord or belt wrapped tightly around my ribs. Years later, I would learn he was trying to electrically shock me, but couldn't get the phallic-shaped device or corset-like constriction to function.

Breathing was now even more difficult, but I suffered in silence rather than risk drawing his wrath. I was quickly learning that a sadistic person enjoys inflicting pain on a helpless person. "Oh God, please help me. What should I do? How could I have been so stupid? How could I have let this happen?"

I never knew when I was alone or when the man was behind me silently admiring the red welts on my naked back. Periodically during the night, I would suddenly feel the touch of his hands. My body would flinch, confirming to him I was still alive. It seemed as though I could feel his eyes on my back. Years later, the man confirmed my feelings when he told me he stayed in the basement all night watching me suffer.

I fought all night in spite of the pain in my wrists and the burning in my lungs. The restraints prevented me from changing positions to prevent my arms and legs from falling asleep. My body hurt as the hours ticked by. I felt certain I would see death before I would see another sunrise.

My mind began to wander back to my childhood. In the fifth grade, I had a teacher who was very strict and stern. She tolerated nothing but obedience from her students. If anyone violated her rules, the offender would be subjected to humiliation and physical punishment in front of the class.

Jacob was a boy who had liked me since the first grade, and I liked him. During class, he would do things to get my attention. I would try to ignore him and not make a scene, because I knew the teacher would punish him by striking a ruler across his fingers. The whole class was scared to death of this teacher. She was the first truly cruel person I had known as a child.

One day, 20 minutes before the bell, I had to go to the restroom. I raised my hand to ask permission.

"Wait until the bell," the teacher said.

I looked at the clock and prayed I would make it. Five minutes later, I once again asked to be excused only to receive the same answer. By the third time I asked, it was too late. I jumped from my seat and ran for the girl's restroom. Inside a stall, I cried and tried to clean up my dress.

My friend Marcy came into the restroom and asked, "Colleen, are you okay?"

"No, I'm not. I can't go back to that classroom."

The teacher had given Marcy a permission slip for me to go to the office and call my mom. When Mom arrived, I told her I was sick. She took me home, where I spent the rest of the day in bed. I knew I would have to return to school the next day. How could I ever face that classroom again? My shame and humiliation were more than I could bear.

The following morning, no one said a word about my accident. The teacher probably put the fear of God in the class. She never apologized, but she did treat me better for the remainder of the year.

Also in the fifth grade, my class was shown a graphic film about the Holocaust during World War II. I didn't really understand the film at the time, but the images terrorized me. Dead bodies were being thrown into pits by soldiers wearing gauze medical mask on their faces.

When I got home, my mom and step-father were going out for the evening. I didn't tell Mom about the film or my trauma. When the babysitter told me it was time to go to bed, I became hysterical. The Holocaust film was more than I could comprehend, and it terrorized my soul.

Back in the basement, I wondered if something like the sadistic teacher or the Holocaust film had terrorized the man who kidnapped me. Had he been so humiliated he hated all women? Was I the subject of his revenge? How could one human being treat another human being so badly? Why did his wife, assuming she was his wife, allow such violence against another woman? I was searching for answers and found none.

My wrists were bruised, and my lungs were burning from hours of gasping for air. Even though I was in severe pain, my faith calmed me. I knew God was with me. His angels helped me bear the pain and protected me from this evil man. God's calming hand was upon me, and I knew I had to be patient. In time, an opportunity would come for me to escape.

As morning approached, I could feel the temperature in the basement cooling. By now, I was totally exhausted with no fight remaining. As I relaxed, I discovered that breathing was easier. Slow breaths reduced the panic, but did little to ease the claustrophobic conditions or pain. Never in my life had I been through such an exhausting ordeal.

Suddenly, I felt my wrists being released. The small chains remained locked on my wrists, but it was good to have my arms lowered. The latches on the head box were opened, and the head box was removed. The musty basement air smelled fresh to me after being in the head box all night. The cord or belt wrapped around my chest and the prickly hair roller device between my legs were also removed. The blindfold and gag continued to encircle my head. The man reached in the box and disconnected my ankles, freeing me from his evil torture box.

"Stand up," came the command.

I staggered to my feet too tired to fight anymore. He gripped my shoulders from behind and walked me across the hard, cold concrete floor.

"Climb up," he said, after placing my back against a long, high table.

As I was getting on the table, I pleaded through my gag, "When will you let me go?"

"Soon," he answered, as he positioned me on the table face up. I was being introduced to yet another of his evil creations. In time, I would come to know the long table as "the rack".

The rack was a hard, wooden table three feet high, eight feet long, and three feet wide. The height of the table was designed to give the man easy access to me without bending over. The base of the rack was strong and well supported. This was the same table used by the couple to have sex when I was suspended from the ceiling.

The small chains dangling from my wrists were hooked to the upper corners of the rack. Ropes were used to secure my ankles to the lower corners. I was now naked, blindfolded, gagged, and spread-eagled, as I lay on my back. The only concession to my comfort was my sleeping bag was under me. The man was finished except for one last item. The head box was once again clamped over my head, plunging me back into silence and darkness.

Once I was securely attached to the rack, silence filled the basement. I assumed the man had gone upstairs. I was alone and exhausted. In a short time, I would drift off to sleep. It had been a long night, and the sleep would prepare me for what was to come later.

Chapter 4 - Rules

When I awoke, I didn't know the time of day. I didn't even know if it was daytime or nighttime. My head was surrounded by carpet, foam rubber, and wood. There was no vision, only black emptiness. Musty carpet was the smell in my nose, and leather from the gag was the taste in my mouth. My body remained on the rack with my movements severely restricted. I could shift my weight from side to side, arch my back, and wiggle my fingers and toes. I needed to blow my nose, but couldn't because I was as helpless as a baby.

In this bleak world my mind began to drift. I thought of my friends back in Eugene, Oregon. "If I had listened to their advice, I wouldn't be in this situation. Hitchhiking was a stupid thing to do. I wish I had never been so headstrong and free spirited."

I met my friends, Bobby and Alice, at my mom's boarding house in Riverside, California, in January, 1977. They were from Oklahoma City, and I loved the little twang in Alice's voice. Bobby worked as a part-time carpenter, and Alice cared for her two year old son, Tomac. Their plan was to stay at the boarding house until they had enough money to travel to Oregon. They were young and out to discover the world, and I, with my youthful spirit, wanted to join them.

When the time came in early March, I packed my belongings in my old Saab automobile and told my family I was leaving with Bobby and Alice. My family thought I was a little hasty running off to Oregon with no real destination in mind, but they knew I was determined to go. They wished me luck and asked me to stay in touch, which I did.

My boyfriend at the time, Eric, wasn't happy to see me go either. Our parting was inevitable since he was moving to the beach for the summer. Before I left, I told him I loved him and gave him a kiss.

Bobby and Alice packed their belongings in his forest-green, 1949 Ford pickup. With me following in my Saab, we drove north on the coastal highway to the Redwood National Park in Northern California. We camped out under the stars and cooked on an open fire among the gigantic redwoods. It was like being with God. I was having the time of my life without a care in the world.

If you had wondered over to our campfire after sunset, you would have evaluated me as a relaxed, fun-loving girl, who tended to trust people. My easy going personality, free spirit, and desire for adventure would have been evident. You would have noted I was wearing jeans with a red or purple top, my favorite colors, and sandals. I didn't care much for television, but I loved classic rock music with performers such as The Stones, Janis Joplin, and Jimi Hendrix. If you asked, I would have told you about my poster of Jim Morrison on my bedroom wall back home. My favorite breakfast food was fresh yogurt made with blueberries or raspberries and granola. You would have discerned a lack of direction in my life, but realizing I had recently turned 20, you would have understood that I was out to explore the world. I think you would have liked me and envied my free life style.

Colleen's 20th Birthday

Our trip ended abruptly outside Eugene, Oregon, when my old Saab suddenly died on the side of the road. We were low on money so Eugene, out of necessity, became our new home. We checked into a seedy motel in the downtown area which was good, since I lacked both money and transportation.

I telephoned my family and told them to send me money from my last job along with my tax refund. With the cash Bobby and Alice had, we were able to get a small apartment across the street from the motel. My roommates slept in the bedroom while I slept on a twin-mattress in the living room. Slowly, we collected furniture and other items to fill the apartment. Bobby worked as a carpenter, Alice stayed with Tomac, and I started looking for work.

"Are you a college student?"

"No, I'm not," I answered honestly during job interviews. I should have answered "yes" since Eugene is a college town. Employers wanted college students, not someone whose car had broken down on the side of the road.

Lacking a job, I had plenty of time to explore Eugene. Alice and I would hitchhike around town when Bobby took the pickup truck to work. We were careful and never had any problems hitchhiking on the streets of Eugene.

One spring day I was hitchhiking by myself along the McKenzie River, near Eugene, when two guys in an old Chevy pickup stopped to offer me a ride. They both had long hair which was the norm in the late 70s. I instantly trusted them and jumped in between them in the front seat. Their names were Mark and Marty, and they shared an apartment in Eugene. Mark set up mobile homes while Marty worked as a tree planter. In time, Mark would become my boyfriend. As we talked, I told them I was looking for a job to earn some extra money.

"I have some friends who pick moss for extra money," Mark said.

As he described the work, it sounded like something I could do and enjoy. Moss that grows on trees was in demand by florists who used it in flower arrangements. Working in the serenity and peacefulness of the woods sounded heavenly to me. I thanked God for my new friends as we drove back to Eugene.

My roommates and I were soon exploring the woods around Eugene for moss-laden trees. East of the city the moss was too wet and stuck to the trees, but to the west we found an ample supply of quality moss. We would load Bobby's pickup with moss and deliver it to a man who would pay us $40 to $60 per load. The man would resell the moss to florists in Southern California. The moss money, as I called it, went for groceries, utilities, and rent. It helped us survive in Oregon.

As a youth, I occasionally used illegal drugs recreationally. Mark and I smoked marijuana twice, and once someone came over to his apartment with cocaine which we snorted. It was my lack of money that curtailed any serious use of pot or coke. My roommates and I were too poor to support an illegal drug habit. All of our money went towards rent and groceries.

My boyfriend Mark was a native Hawaiian from Honolulu. He had come to the mainland to get away from, as he called it, the commercialization of Hawaii. Too many cars, highways, and tourist had destroyed the island way of life for him.

"I'll never return to Hawaii," he said, with conviction in his voice.

"How about your mother?" I asked, thinking about her back in Honolulu.

"If she wants to see me, she can visit me in Oregon," Mark replied.

"Mark, that's not a nice thing to say about your mother."

Mark was always nice to me, and I loved his dark, suntanned skin which was the opposite of my white complexion. Over a two month period, we had grown close to each other. I remembered spending my last night of freedom with him in his apartment. Mark told me …he ….

Suddenly, I was snapped back into reality. Fear shot through my body as I realized I wasn't alone. Someone was unlatching the head box. My wrists and ankle restraints were unhooked from the rack.

"Sit up," the man ordered.

I had not eaten, drank, or been to the restroom in over 24 hours. A bedpan was the first order of business. With my blindfold and wrist chains remaining in place, I was guided to a chair with a plastic bedpan, the type one receives during a hospital stay. This was a first for me, using a bedpan and doing so in front of a stranger. This left me too nervous and embarrassed to go to the restroom. I surely needed to go, but nothing happened.

"I can't go with you watching," I told him through the gag.

"All right," he said, walking a few steps away.

Being blindfolded, I never knew if he had his back turned towards me or was still staring at me. Later, he would walk to the top of the stairs, but I'm sure he never left the basement.

"When will I get to go home?" I asked.

"Soon," he replied.

I asked the same question over and over. Each time I would receive the same answer time and time again. After a couple of months, I would give up asking because I knew the answer. However, I never gave up hoping and praying for freedom.

Now, I was to have my first meal. The gag was removed from my mouth and, while still blindfolded, I was handed a plate filled with potatoes au gratin along with a 24 ounce glass of water. For me, eating while blindfolded with chains dangling from my wrists was also a new experience.

After I had finished, the chains were removed and replaced with the dreaded leather cuffs. I knew what was next. The cuffs were attached to hooks in the ceiling and the support under my feet was kicked out. The pain radiated from my wrists down my arms to my shoulders and ribs. My toes searched in vain for something to support my weight. This time I knew it was futile to scream. After 15 long, painful minutes the ice chest was slipped under my feet. I was taken down and the leather cuffs were replaced with the small chains and locks.

"Lie down," he ordered, after walking me over to the rack.

He fastened my arms and legs to the table as before, and then clamped the head box back on returning me to a world of darkness. In my silent isolation, I never knew if the man had departed or was glaring at my exposed body. After a few minutes without feeling the touch of his hands, I concluded he had departed the basement and I was at last alone. Years later, I would learn a panel in his bedroom closet could be removed giving him a view of the basement from upstairs. Even when in his bedroom, he could monitor my activities without my knowledge. I was to stay chained to the rack for another 23 hours.

On the second day, I was trashing around on the rack pulling at my restrains, crying, and moaning. Suddenly, I heard the latches on the head box being unsnapped. The head box was slowly opened, but the blindfold and gag remained in place.

"What's wrong?" a woman's voice asked.

"I'm cold," I replied, behind the gag. The head box was slowly closed and the latches were again locked. Over my exposed body, I could feel a blanket being placed over me.

"Who was this woman? How could she allow such evil to be taking place in her basement? Was she the man's wife? Where was the baby I had seen in the car? Slowly, I drifted off to sleep.

My sleep was interrupted in the early evening hours of the night. Without warning, a hand touched me and I instantly jumped.

This was the start of my third evening in the basement, an evening whose shocking events I would never be able to erase from my memory.

Being released from the rack, a man's voice directed me towards the bedpan. After I had finished, a plate with two egg salad sandwiches and another large glass of water was handed to me. The water tasted good, as did the first sandwich, but a combination of exhaustion and heat from wearing the head box all day had diminished my appetite.

"Thank you, but I'm not very hungry," I said, not knowing the rules. I had broken a prime rule and now I would pay.

"You should be more grateful," the man said, in an angry voice as he took the plate containing the remaining sandwich from my hands.

"I am grateful," I said in a pleading tone, but it was too late.

I was jerked up and marched to the center of the basement where the small chains on my wrists were replaced with the leather cuffs. I knew what was coming next.

"Step up," he said, angrily. The gag was returned to my face to prevent me from screaming. My wrists were once again hooked to the beam above my head and the ice chest under my feet was quickly kicked out. The pain returned immediately to my wrists and down my body to my ribs. This time the whip was used on me with a vengeance. My arms felt like they were going to tear off, and my back burned like fire. Sweat was pouring down my body as I shook out of control.

It was more than I could bear, and I soon blacked out. I had never been unconscious before. I had a feeling of being lost or dead with no control over my body. I was in a total state of euphoria like being lost in space. When I regained consciousness, the pain came flooding back into my body tenfold. It was like the pain had been stored up waiting for me to be revived. A few minutes later, he finally put the ice chest back under my feet. I tried to pull myself back up, but I was too weak and exhausted. My legs wouldn't support my body. I wobbled around and continued to shake until my legs gave way. Once again, I blacked out.

Being out cold, the man assumed I didn't need the box under my feet anymore. When I came to the second time, I couldn't find anything to support my weight. I don't know if it was my weakness, dehydration, or the stress of the pain, but I was unable to stay conscious. As I began to get my senses back, the pain came flooding back into my body again like screaming thunder. I was still gagged and blindfolded, but it didn't matter as I yelled for help and begged for mercy. I threw my legs around as I searched in vain for something solid.

"Shut up and relax. It will be over with sooner," the man said, harshly.

Unable to do much else, I just hung there and cried. Finally, I could feel something firm under my toes. My wrists were released followed by the command, "Step down," which I did. "Now are you going to eat your sandwich?" he asked, sarcastically?

"Yes." I answered, with a weak voice.

I ate the sandwich and was thankful to God the man hadn't killed me over an egg salad sandwich. When I completed the sandwich, I was returned to the rack for another 23 hours.

I was quickly learning, though not fast enough, how this new world worked. Words such as "no thank you" had no meaning. When given an order, I was to obey instantly. I didn't realize it at the time, but I was to be molded into a person different from the one kidnapped three days before. I was becoming a girl who couldn't say "no".

The other primary rule I learned was to be a silent women. I was not to speak unless spoken to by the man. There were never any two-way conversations between myself and my abductor. Sharply worded orders were all I heard. Perhaps my kidnapper didn't want me to have a personality. Conversation would show my personality which, in time, would lead to understanding and attachment. He preferred a silent woman who couldn't say no and did what she was told.

A day or two later, the woman returned to the basement in the middle of the day and once again opened the head box.

"I want you to know you are here to take the pain for me, but don't worry there won't be any sex," the woman said.

I was having a hard time understanding what the woman was talking about. What did she mean, "You are here to take the pain?" I couldn't comprehend, "Don't worry there won't be any sex." What was she talking about? Who were these people?

"Do you know where you are?" the woman asked.

"Yes, I'm in Red Bluff," I said, with direct honesty.

"No, you're not in Red Bluff. What would you do if you were released?"

"I'd go to the police and tell them I'd been kidnapped."

"Stupid," the woman said, as the head box lid slammed shut pinching my neck. The latches were locked and the woman went back up stairs.

"Oh God, how could I have been so dumb," I cried out. Had I missed my chance to be free? I had to be a smart ass and tell the truth. It was too late now because she had gone back upstairs.

What if I had said, "I would leave and go back to my parents?" I will never know what might have happened. On the other hand, maybe her visit was a trick. The man could have been standing behind her. Were they just playing with my mind?

Later in the afternoon, the woman returned. This time she opened the head box and removed the gag. Supporting my head, she gave me a cool refreshing drink of lemonade. I was very thankful and said so. After I finished my drink, she returned the gag, closed the head box, and went back upstairs. She would never visit me alone in the basement again. I heard years later she had a loaded shotgun with her in case I tried to escape. Of course, escape was impossible since I remained chained to the rack.

A routine was forming with 23 hours of isolation, interrupted each evening by the unlatching of the head box. I was then offered the use of the bedpan with the man watching, and a meal consisting of a sandwich or leftovers from the kitchen upstairs. A single glass of water was also handed to me. I knew now to eat "all" that was given to me. This was followed most of the time, but not all the time, by some unpredictable form of sadistic punishment. Being hung by the wrists from the ceiling beam was the most common, usually repeated two or three times a week. Bright flashes of light and the click of a camera, told me I was being photographed. After he was finished with me, I was returned to darkness and isolation of the head box and rack for another 23 hours. I both anticipated and dreaded the unsnapping of the locks on the head box each evening. I knew it meant both nourishment and pain.

I would awake in the darkness behind the blindfold not knowing the exact time of the day or night. I soon learned to judge the time by the temperature in the basement. The mornings were cool and the afternoons were hot. From this, I knew the man usually came down to the basement around 8:00 in the evening. My only other time reference was the loud muffler of a neighbor's car on the street outside. I assumed the neighbor was going to work around 6:00 or 7:00 AM. There were no other clues to tell me the time of day. I would quickly lose count of the days, then the weeks, and finally the months. My next time marker would be the cooling temperatures of the fall season.

The man's anger was unpredictable. Sometimes, I was allowed a word or two without any consequences. Other times, any comment from me would bring on a beating with the whip. Any form of begging, pleading, or crying would arouse his rage. Begging a sadistic person, I learned, just gets them going. If I fought or struggled, the torture went on forever. A sadist, I soon discovered, gains energy from the cries and suffering of a woman. I soon learned to suppress my emotions in order to lessen his "play time." For a sadist, the enjoyment quickly evaporates when his subject shows no emotions. It's no fun beating a limp body. The more I played his game, the better it was for me. I was also intent on not giving him the joy of seeing me cry. In the privacy of the head box was all together different. I cried my eyes out.

I never knew what to expect when it came to his "play time." The man never told me what he had in store for me. He wanted fear of the unknown to work on my mind. My only clues to what was coming were the harsh commands such as, "Step up. Give me your wrists. Turn around." When the diabolical leather cuffs were placed on my wrist, I knew what to expect. Being suspended by the wrists was what I dreaded and what he preferred.

One day while lying face up on the rack, I badly needed to go to the restroom. I started to rattle my chains and scream into the head box. It worked, as the man quickly came down to the basement and allowed me to use the bedpan. After I had finished, the leather cuffs were placed on my wrists and I was hung from the ceiling.

"This is for making so much noise," the man said as a bull whip came down on my bareback time and time again. I soon passed out from the pain of the cuffs and the whip. I learned yet another rule that day. Don't make noise for any reason.

I wanted to escape, but escape seemed impossible. I spent my days in chains or leather restraints. I was released only in the evening when the man was present. At six feet, four inches, he towered 10 inches above my height of five feet, six inches. I knew I couldn't fight him. If I broke free and ran up the stairs, would I find the door locked? Once outside, would I find myself in the country or city? Which way should I run?

With fight and flight out of the question, I was left with survival. Committing suicide was never an option for me, though at times I did want to just give up. I never developed a comprehensive survival plan, but in time three things kept me going.

First, since I couldn't fight the man I would try to understand him. Why did he direct so much anger towards me? Why did the man want to hurt me, yet not kill me? When he tortured me, I felt like I was going to die because the pain was so intense, but he seemed to stop just short of death. Would he someday go too far and accidentally murder me? Was the man a member of some kind of religious cult? I didn't initially label him as a sadist, because I wasn't familiar with the term until much later. I just knew he was evil and enjoyed hurting me. What was the best strategy to calm him? How could I get him to see me as a person? I had 23 hours a day to analyze the man.

Second, during the long hours of isolation I kept my mind busy dreaming about life outside my basement hell. I thought back on the good experiences I had early in life. I created a future world which included a beautiful home and a child of my own. I planned home-cooked Thanksgiving holiday meals around a large table with my family. I had to keep my mind busy. You can go anywhere in your mind and, for a short period of time, be in a really nice place.

During the day I would try to sleep, but nightmares would visit me. I would awake in terror to find I couldn't move my arms or legs. The carpet lining of the head box was directly in front of my face. I realized I had lost everything including my sense of personal privacy and my feeling of safety.

The only thing remaining was my faith in God which was the third element in my survival. What else did I have? My faith in God was the only thing that couldn't be taken away from me. I had lost everything else. As a little girl my grandma, on my father's side of the family, would take my two sisters and I to church. As a teenager, the Lord had been pushed to the back of my mind. I rarely attended church services or read the Bible. I was a free thinking youth doing as I pleased. For me, life was too busy to think much about the Lord.

I still believed in God. How could I not believe in God when I stood among those giant trees in Redwood National Park? Now, I realized I needed the Lord more than ever. I prayed for His help and assistance in understanding what was happening to me. Fortunately for me, God always listens.

Looking back, I'm sure it was God's voice, or one of His angels, that warned me at Paynes Creek. "Jump out the window, run, and never look back. " I misunderstood His warnings because I wasn't close enough to God at the time. I was too rebellious.

In the darkness of my captivity, I started to pray. "Jesus, give me strength and understanding." I wanted to develop a personal relationship with the Lord for the first time in my life. My soul was starving for spiritual growth. None of what I was going through made any sense to me.

The only light in my world of darkness was my faith. I knew someday I would be free. I had to be patient and keep my faith in the Lord.

Chapter 5 - The Box

Approximately a week into my captivity, I heard the sawing of wood and hammering of nails. Something was being constructed. Any building in the basement only increased my anxiety levels. I knew whatever was being built couldn't be for my benefit or comfort.

On Sunday, May 29, 1977, after I had my single meal of the day, I was not returned to the rack as expected. Instead, I was presented with new living accommodations. I knew it was a Sunday because the man had been home from work for two days.

A heavy chain was placed around my neck and secured with a large padlock. The small chains attached to my wrists were then locked to the larger chain around my neck. Now for the first time, I could touch the gag and blindfold covering my face. The heavy chain around my neck ran down the front of my body to the floor.

"Step in," he said with a gruff voice.

I took a high step into a long, almost coffin-like box six and a half feet long, two and a half feet wide, and 20 inches high. Years later, I would learn the house had been rented from Anna Leddy who lived next door. Having a nude woman chained to a rack, with her head encased in a box, might have been difficult to explain if the landlord ever made an unannounced visit to the basement. At the time, of course, I had no idea the house was rented and that the purpose of the box was to provide additional security.

The rack, on the east basement wall, was kept for special torture sessions, but from now on the box was to be my home. The box, on the south wall of the basement, was constructed of particle board which was cheaper than sanded plywood. The particle board was uncomfortable to lie on since it made my skin itch and left splinters in my back. Fortunately, my old sleeping bag lined the bottom of the box. I was soon to learn, however, the sleeping bag could be removed as a form of special punishment.

The box had double-walled construction and a double-top which made escape impossible and provided additional soundproofing. As a concession, I no longer had to wear the head box. However, like the rack, the head box was kept around and periodically used on me. Once, the head box was used on me while I was in the box. It could be said, I was in a box, which was in a box that was in a box (the basement of the house).

The ventilation system for the box consisted of a woman's hair dryer with the heating element turned off. The hair dryer was placed outside the box with a plastic hose connected to a hole through the double-walls of the box. Another small hole allowed air to exit the box. Of course, the air fed into the box came from the musty, dank basement.

"Lay down," was the next command as I stood in the box with my hands chained to my neck. Years later, I would learn the reason behind having my hands chained to my neck.

After lying down, the long chain running down the length of my body was wrapped around my ankles and locked with yet another padlock. Since the chain was not long enough for me to fully stretch out my body, my legs had to be bent or my back arched to be comfortable. The purpose of the chain was to re-enforce the hopelessness of my situation. Even without the chain, I knew I couldn't escape from the box.

As a last measure, the man packed wax into my ears to degrade my hearing and increase my isolation. If anyone came into the basement, I wouldn't be able to hear a thing due to the hair dryer and wax in my ears. I didn't know it at the time, but this was to be my home for the next seven months.

Once in the box, the double-tops were closed one at a time and pad locked. My daily routine quickly returned to what it had been when I was on the rack. Long hours of isolation, followed by the bedpan, a meal with water, and some form of torture. Being hung by my wrists came every three or four nights and lasted 15 to 20 minutes. Like so many other things, I would learn years later why the man never kept me suspended beyond 20 minutes.

Whips were always at hand. Anytime he was angry he would use the whip to beat me. He never beat me with his bare hands. His whips ranging from a bull whip to a cat-o'-nine tails, which I learned consisted of nine strips of leather. The whip would painfully wrap around my body, but never cut or scar my skin. Red welts and stripes, which would stay with me for days, served as a physical remainder of the beating.

The man always avoided cutting my skin with the whips. He knew a cut on my back would leave a scar and could lead to a severe infection.

Without medical aid the infection would possibly result in my death. Of course, I didn't know this and the man never said, "Don't worry; I won't cut your skin." For me death, even accidental death, was always near.

Since I was a woman who couldn't say "no," his demands were limited only by his imagination. His inspiration often came from pictures he found in pornographic magazines. After viewing a photograph, I became his live model to fulfill his fantasies. Once while hanging from the ceiling he placed a heat lamp inches from my skin causing a burn. Another time, he hung me by my wrists and then hung me upside down by my ankles. I was hung upside down to get the blood flowing to my hands again, he explained. This was followed by being flipped over and hung by my wrists again. On another occasion, he touched me with an electrical wire to see how I would react. Once, I was suspended with ropes in a horizontal position with the head box locked on my head. Oral sex was also forced upon me. I also remember the man and woman having intercourse on top of the box with me inside. There was nothing I could do to stop his evil.

One night after being taken out of the box, he handcuffed my hands behind my back and laid me on the rack with my sleeping bag under me. He placed his hands around my neck and slowly started choking me. I panicked as I realized I couldn't breathe, which was followed by a dazed feeling. My body felt as if I was floating freely in space. I soon blacked out. When I came to, my mind was hazy for a few seconds until I realized his hands were still around my neck. The process was started all over again.

This would be the pattern for future sessions. The man would choke, hang, or later, drown me until I was near the point of death. Then he would "rescue" me at the last second only to repeat the process. The session would stop only when the man, not me, had had enough. What was a power trip for him was sheer terror for me.

Once while being choked, I soiled my sleeping bag. This made the man fly into a rage. He pulled me off the rack and rubbed my nose in my own waste, like one would do when housebreaking a puppy. Like so many torture sessions, no words were spoken by the man.

The use of the bedpan, which was kept on top of my box, proved to be a problem. Sometimes I couldn't wait until the end of the day. One day I made a mess in the box to which the man reacted with anger as if I had done it on purpose. I was hung up and beat for not controlling myself. The man cleaned up the mess as I hung and my soiled sleeping bag was replaced with a clean blanket. A week later after another accident, the blanket was replaced with my sleeping bag which had been washed. This process continued as long I remained chained in the box.

After three months, a toothbrush was handed to me. I was expected to brush my teeth. I did as I was told, but was puzzled as to why he would abuse me and then be concerned about my dental hygiene?

On rare occasions an act of kindness came my way. A fresh batch of hot pancakes and syrup, or it may have been French toast and jelly, was brought down one weekend morning for me to eat. I ate twice that day. The reason behind the act of kindness was never explained. To keep me off balance an act of cruelty followed later that evening.

I had not menstruated in months, probably due to stress. That changed in August, 1977, three months into my captivity. When the man opened the box, it became obvious that something had to be done. The man was angry with me because I had caused such a mess. I was taken out and my hands were cuffed behind my back. The man gripped my shoulders and led me across the cold concrete floor to the stairs. Up the stairs I went for the first time in three months. At the top of the stairs I was turned to the left and taken to the bathroom.

I had not had a bath since departing Eugene, Oregon. My head was covered with a cloth, probably a baby diaper, and then my eyes and mouth were duct taped leaving me to breathe through my nose. I was uncuffed and allowed to bathe myself with soap and water while the man and woman watched. My hair was matted and felt like dog hair because of the accumulated filth. The woman tried to brush a tangled mess of knots out of my long hair without success. She then tried hair conditioner and shampoo, still with no success. Next, she went to the kitchen and returned with cooking oil to loosen the knots. Still no success. Finally, she took a pair of scissors and hacked off my waist length hair to above my shoulders. I was brokenhearted and thankful she didn't place a mirror in front of me to see what the scissors had done.

I thought the ordeal was over, but the worse was yet to come. I was placed in a hogtied position with my hands and feet behind my back.

A broom handle, with the broom removed, was placed behind my knees. I was lifted off the floor and placed facedown in the water. The broom handle resting on the edges of the bathtub kept my legs out of the water and forced my head underwater. I was unable to raise my head above the water and started to panic as my supply of oxygen quickly diminished. As I struggled for air, the man calmly took pictures of me in the bathtub. When my last breath of air exhaled from my lungs, he grabbed what remained of my hair and pull my head above the water. As soon as I got a single breath of air, he dropped my head back into the water. This went on at least two dozen times until my lungs were burning with pain.

After two hours the water torture ended, I was guided back down stairs and placed facedown on the rack. My hand and feet were again tied behind my back. While holding what remained of my hair, he forced oral copulation upon me. When he was finished, I was returned to my box. It was all too much for me as a flood of tears and sobs were released in the privacy of the box.

Most people can relate, at least mentally, to the pain associated with being hung, whipped, burnt, electrocuted, drowned, or choked. People often overlook the slow, mind numbing pain of lying in a box or on a rack 23 hours a day. One starts out with nightmare-visited sleep. After eight or more hours of sleep, one's body is wide awake staring into the dark emptiness. Your mind starts exploring every sight, sound, and taste it has stored away over the years. Eventually, one reaches the end of their thoughts and the mind has no where else to go. Time slows to a stop as seconds feel like minutes and minutes feel like hours.

Physically, while in the box or on the rack, your body is restrained and unable to respond to insect bites and itches. You stretch your legs against the sides of the box or the ankle restraints trying to gain some relief. Lying mentally and physically motionless is also a form of painful torture most people overlook.

Also absent from my life were things people take for granted in their day to day lives. Waking up to a beautiful sunrise, eating breakfast, selecting your clothes, driving a car, shopping, watching television, interacting with other people, telephoning friends and love ones, had all been taken away from me. I knew I would never again take these common things for granted.

After my first bath, I was taken upstairs blindfolded and given a bath once a month. I experienced a near drowning experience one other time, but most of the time I was allowed to bathe myself with the man and woman sometimes absent from the room. At least I think they were absent, because I could hear the television in another room and couldn't see anyone through the bottom of my blindfold. During this time thoughts of escape entered my mind.

"If you walk out the backdoor, you might as well put a shotgun to your head and pull the trigger," the woman warned me.

I knew any escape attempt would be dangerous with dire consequences if I failed. Still, my mind searched for a route out of this madness. I considered wrapping a bath towel around my body and smashing through the front window of the house. Once outside I would run for my life. As I examined the odds, I realized the cards were stacked against me. Would the man see or hear me running towards the window? Could I break through the window without serious injury? Once outside, what would I find? Would there be a fence or dog? Were friendly neighbors near? There was too much uncertainty. I finished my bath and was returned to my box.

In time, I learned more about my basement prison. The concrete floor, under the cinder-block walls, measured 14 feet long by 12 feet wide. On the west wall were 14 wooden steps leading to the house above. The basement door was always closed and, I learned years later, locked. The area under the stairs would soon play an important part in my life. To the side of the stairs was an 18 inch square, brick pillar that supported the house. The east wall contained the rack and two small windows high off the floor. The windows were covered with black plastic preventing light or unwanted eyes from entering. The north wall was bare except for the whips which hung from nails. The box was on the south wall. Running north to south in the middle of the ceiling was a 4X6 (4 inches by 6 inches) wooden beam with the hooks used to suspend my wrists seven feet above the floor. An iron pipe, probably gas, ran diagonally across the ceiling. It was to this pipe that my wrist was handcuffed on the first night. The floor of the basement was concrete and the air was rank and dusty. The furniture changed from time to time, but the rack, my box, a chair, the bedpan, and the ice chest were always present.

One of the puzzles in my mind was the woman. After speaking to me during the first days of my captivity, she rarely spoke to me again. Who was she? She and the baby were the reason I got into the car because I thought I would be safe. How could she live with what was going on in the basement? Why didn't she try to help me? I never saw her being hung up, beat, or tortured. Did she enjoy seeing what was happening to me? The answers to my questions seemed far away from my dark world.

I assumed she was the man's wife and the baby, which I never saw, was theirs. Occasionally, I would hear her voice in the corner of the basement when the man was present. One time, when I was suspended from the ceiling, she walked over and sunk her teeth deeply into my side. Another time, she walked over and poked me hard with some sharp object. I also knew her to use the whip on my back while I was defenseless. Was she being told to do these things or did she enjoy doing them?

For months, I had been living in an information void. I had no knowledge of what was going on around me. Life upstairs was a hundred miles away and the outside world was another planet. No one spoke to me and I was constantly kept in a state of sensory depredation where my eyes and ears were almost useless. Oddly, in such an environment my eyes and ears searched for the slightest visual or audio clue. Any information was quickly processed by my brain for any intelligence content. I was starving for news.

"Jan, hand me the whip on the small table," I clearly heard the man say.

Finally, I knew her name, "Jan". I wouldn't be allowed to use it without risking a beating, but I knew it. So Jan was the woman who was in the front seat of the Dodge the day I was kidnapped. I remained stone faced in order to not reveal my new knowledge. Now, I too had at least one secret.

Sometime in the late summer or early fall, I was taken out of the box and walked to the center of the basement and told to sit down. I set down on the hard concrete floor and was chained by the ankle to something. With the blindfold still in place, the man guided my hands over a large piece of wood approximately four feet long and 18 inches wide. He handed me a small block of wood that was covered with sandpaper.

"You will sand the top of this burl all night until it is smooth," he instructed me. "Any questions?"

I shook my head, "No."

The next thing I knew a large head box, different from the one I had worn before, was placed over my head and snapped shut. The head box weighted at least 30 pounds, which was too much for me to support on my neck throughout the night. As a concession, the man attached strings to the top of the head box and ran the strings over the pipe in the ceiling to plastic jugs filled with water. The jugs would counterbalance the weight of the head box. From my point of view I saw none of this, but I could feel the weight of the head box lifted when the man tied the strings to the jugs. This system allowed the head box to move with me as I stretched over the burl to sand the far edges. I'm sure the sadistic man enjoyed watching me extend my bareback over the wood with the awkward box on my head.

A burl, I should explain, is a rounded outgrowth on the trunk or branch of a tree. The growth rings are twisted in interesting patterns. When cut and sanded to a smooth surface, the burl makes a beautiful table top. The completed burl, looking like a work of art when varnished, was popular at the time.

I never knew if the man was behind me or had gone back upstairs. I knew better than to unlatch the head box and take a look around. After a couple of nights the project was completed and the smooth burl was removed without a word of thanks. I'm sure it was later sold at a flea market or yard sale. I was now a captive who could earn cash for the household.

Once the man and woman made money from the sanded burl, they realized I had earning potential. I could at least pay for my room and board. Having me lie around in the box all day was no longer acceptable.

Sometime in November, 1977, I once again heard the sound of hammer and nails. Something was being constructed. This project was bigger and took a couple of weeks to complete. I could hear the man working on it each night as I lay in the box. I was in for another life changing event.

In late November, I was walked blindfolded across the concrete basement floor and guided into what was to become known as "the workshop". Built under the stairs, the front part was tall while the back portion tapered down to the bottom of the stairs. The workshop was long and narrow. The west wall of the workshop was the concrete cinder block wall of the basement. The east wall was made of concrete slabs the man had poured himself. The door was particle board with hinges and a lock. In the workshop was a small chair and, much to my surprise, a bare light bulb. The on-off switch for the light was outside the workshop.

Once I was in the workshop, the man set me down in the chair and locked my ankles together with a pair of handcuffs. The handcuffs were secured to a piece of wood on the floor of the workshop. The particle board door was closed and locked from the outside.

"Remove your blindfold," the man ordered.

I couldn't believe what I was hearing. Remove my blindfold! I had been wearing a blindfold since May. Of course, being trained to obey, I slowly pulled the blindfold over the top of my head. The workshop was completely dark, but I could see some light around the edges of the door.

Without a word, the man turned on the light bulb above my head. I was showered with bright, white light. It had been six months since I had been exposed to any light. Like coming out of a dark theater on a sunny day, my eyes squinted and burned. My eyes started to water and tears formed. The light bulb was of standard size, but for me it was incredibly bright. Slowly, my eyes adjusted to the light.

As I looked around all the colors glowed. The workshop was not especially colorful, but any color was like a neon light to me. My amazement was abruptly interrupted.

"See the burlap sack of walnuts at your feet?" said a stern voice.

"Yes," I answered softly.

"When I come back tomorrow morning, I expect each walnut to be shelled and placed in the empty bowl. Do you understand?"

"Yes."

From then on, I was employed. As the man and woman slept, I worked. All I had done during the previous six months in the box was sleep, dream, and pray. I now had work to do. I knew in eight hours the man would return and the burlap bag full of walnuts had better be empty. I reached down and picked up the nut cracker and went to work immediately.

In the morning I could hear the man coming down the stairs one step at a time. Anytime he approached, anxiety and fear would build within me.

"Put your blindfold back on," he instructed.

I followed his orders and then the light in the workshop was turned off plunging me back into darkness. I could hear the lock on the particle wood door being removed and the door being opened.

A moment later, I knew I had a problem. It was not with the walnuts. They had all been shelled. I had even eaten a few knowing they wouldn't be missed. The problem was with the cuffs on my ankles. During the night the tight handcuffs had caused my ankles to swell. Now the man couldn't get my feet unlocked. His wife came down and tried, but she too was not successful. After many minutes of work, my ankles were finally freed. My feet hurt as I walked across the basement floor back to my box. The handcuffs were not used on my ankles again.

The workshop was a life changing event for me. Now, I would spend my days sleeping in the box until the early evening. The man would open the box, feed me, inflict some pain on me, and then lock me in the workshop for the evening. The bedpan was now in the workshop with me. Various projects were assigned to me each night and expected to be completed by the following morning. Various types of nuts, such as walnuts and pecans, were shelled. I was also assigned crochet and macramé projects.

The woman gave me instructions on how to tie the knots in macramé and how to crochet various articles. Macramé is lacelike webbing made of knotted cords and was used for wall decorations and to hang potted plants from the ceiling. In the morning, the project would be taken from me without a word. I assumed the projects were being sold because no one could eat that many nuts or use that many macramé projects in their own home. Years later, numerous hooks in the ceiling used for torture, would be explained as macramé hooks to hold potted plants.

I was glad to be out of the box and working for at least half of the 24 hour day. I did push on the workshop door in the early hours of the morning, but it wouldn't open. Sometimes, I was left in the workshop all day for some unknown reason. Other times I remained in the box all night. For the man, there were no fixed rules. For me, the rules were always fixed.

During this time, I felt isolated and lonely. I missed human contact and conversation. Through prayer I grew closer to God. I knew God and His angels were near and watching over me. The first night in the workshop, a strange sensation came over me. I could feel my grandma, who had taken my sisters and me to church, praying for my safe return. Her prayers gave me great comfort. Years later, I learned she had indeed prayed for my safe return each night about the same time. I could feel her prayers.

Two other events had a profound effect on me. While in the darkened box, I dreamed the lid of the box was opened and a group of angels were looking down on me. The angels were wearing white robes which were illuminated. Their robes were brighter than anything I had seen on earth.

"Everything will be all right," an angel said.

The angels had been sent by God to protect me. When I prayed, the man would stop torturing me or the pain would decrease. The angels would intercede when things were more than I could bear. A sense of peace came over me knowing God had sent His angels to watch over me. I knew in time, everything would be all right.

The second event was also a dream I had while in the box. My deceased grandfather was sitting in a chair with my head in his lap. I deeply regretted not developing a closer relationship with my grandfather before he died. As a teenage girl, I had better things to do than spend time with my grandfather.

"I'm sorry," I said softly.

"It's all right Colleen," Grandfather replied looking down at me with his hand gently brushing my hair. A warm, secure feeling came over me along with a great sense of relief at hearing my grandfather's words. These dreams were profound and real. They were tangible and spoke directly to my soul. I know God had sent the dreams to comfort and help me.

As winter came my routine varied only slightly. My days were spent in the box and my nights in the workshop. Prior to entering the workshop, my bedpan was emptied and I was given a meal of leftovers with a glass of water. I still brushed my teeth and expected some form of bondage or pain to follow. The only conversation came when an order was given or clarification was required. The whips stood ready to stop any unnecessary talk. The woman remained mostly upstairs and out of sight.

In December, 1977, I was really suffering from the cold, especially at night when the average low in Red Bluff is 37 degrees. Finally, the man gave me my Pendleton jacket. It was the first piece of clothing I had worn in seven months. Much to my surprise, a few days later I was given a dark blue nightgown. The article of clothing was new, not a hand-me-down. The terry cloth gown was trimmed in red with three quarter sleeves. It came to just below my knees and had a slit up the sides just above my knees. The nightgown wouldn't be washed for months. However, since I would be prohibited from wearing the gown most of the year, it would still look new years later. My old sleeping bag, a tooth brush, and my Pendleton jacket were the only other personal items I had.

Looking back, I estimate between May and November I was fed and allowed to use the bedpan once a day, hung up 90 to 100 times, given four baths, and my nails were cut once. I never saw the sunshine, had a conversation with another person, or received any news. My weight, which the man recorded, dropped from 135 pounds to 113 pounds, a loss of 22 pounds. I would lose even more weight later in my captivity.

I knew Christmas was near as the nights grew colder. That year I had no way of telling which of the cold nights was Christmas Eve. Christmas came and went without my knowledge. My 21st birthday followed a few days later with the same results. Most young people celebrate their 21st birthday with a night on the town. I spent mine in the box and workshop none the wiser. New Years Day was the same. The year 1977 ended and 1978 started with no change in my daily routine. My isolation from the world was profound.

However, 1978 would bring dramatic changes in my life. I would soon learn why I had been kidnapped and was being forced to live in an underground dungeon. I would also start to gain information about the world beyond the basement walls. By the end of 1978, I would know my fate.

Chapter 6 - The Contract

January 25, 1978, started out as just another day. I spent most of the day in the box sleeping, dreaming, and praying. As usual, in the early evening I was taken from the box, fed, and given a glass of water. As I set there blindfolded, I still had no idea who the man and woman were and why I had been chosen to fulfill their sadistic desires. My lack of knowledge was soon to change.

After I brushed my teeth, I was escorted to the workshop and locked in for the night. I removed my blindfold and adjusted to the bright light hanging from a cord above my head. I can't remember the project I was working on, but I do remember starting to work immediately.

A little later, I heard someone walking down the wooden steps to the basement and waited for the light to be turned off and the order to replace my blindfold. Suddenly without warning, the door to the workshop was unlocked and swung opened. Shock went through my body as I found myself looking directly into the face of the man who had given me so much pain. The last time I had seen his face was eight months earlier when he placed a knife against my throat. The woman was standing behind him with bandages on her knees.

For a second, I studied his face in frozen fear as the workshop light cast deep shadows across his features. For me, it was like looking into the eyes of the devil. He still had the same dirty, greasy hair I remembered with a part on the right side. Heavy sideburns extended down the front of each ear. His eyes, behind glasses, were repulsive as they squinted slightly. Most upsetting was the smirk on his lips. I couldn't look at his hands which had given me such awful pain. I'm not a person who can judge weight, but I knew I could never overpower him. He was big and strong, towering to a height of about six feet, four inches.

"Here, practice writing your name," the man said, as he handed me a clipboard with a sheet of blank paper and a ballpoint pen. I followed his instructions not knowing, as usual, the reason behind the order. Colleen Stan, Colleen Stan, Colleen Stan, I slowly wrote.

"They know you're here," he said, in a direct voice.

For a second, I was puzzled trying to understand who "they" were. I quickly assumed the police. Somehow the police knew I was in the basement. My spirits soared as I anticipated rescue.

"A man from 'The Company' is upstairs waiting," were his next words.

Now, I was even more confused. What man? What company?

"I don't understand," I said, with a tone of confusion.

"We can't keep the man waiting," he said. "The Company discovered we have you in our basement and is demanding we pay a $1,600 fee and register you immediately. We must make you legal. Here, read this," the man said as he thrust a newspaper titled "Inside News" into my hands. The paper was dated January 1, 1978.

It had been months since I had read anything. Slowly, I adjusted my eyes on the print and began to read to myself. The article, "They Sell themselves Body and Soul when they Sign THE SLAVE CONTRACT," detailed the selling of women into sexual slavery.

"Just out of sight of the general public, young beautiful women are being abducted and sold into slavery in San Francisco to wealthy and powerful men. Once sold, the women become slaves for life and the property of their masters. The process is sealed with an indenture, or slave contract, which makes the transaction completely legal. The Company, a vast underground syndicate, administers the contract and controls the market. Any woman who resisted slavery will be sent to a Rent-A-Dungeon in San Francisco for remedial training. A new slave is given a 'slave name', different from her street name, and a collar permanently fixed around her neck to identify her as a 'slave for life'."

As I read the article, I began to shake. I never knew such things existed. I was still unsure what this had to do with me. The article in itself was disturbing. The text continued with details concerning the purchase of women, establishing their fair market value, and a sample slave contract. I couldn't believe what I was reading.

The man took the newspaper from my hands, turned around to his wife, and retrieved a legal looking document. With his back to me, I could see he was wearing a western-style belt with the name CAMERON engraved on the back. The name Cameron was immediately imprinted on my mind, but I didn't have time to analyze the meaning of the name.

"Now, read this and sign it. We can't keep The Company man waiting," he said, handing me an official looking contract and the same ballpoint pen I had used earlier to practice signing my name.

Type written, on quality paper, the document had an ornately printed title at the top and an official looking seal near the bottom. Slowly, I began to read.

THIS INDENTURE, Made the 25th day of January in the year of Our Lord One Thousand Nine Hundred and Seventy-Eight, BETWEEN Colleen Stan, hereafter known as Slave; AND Michael Powers, hereafter known as Master; WITNESSETH:

That Slave, for and in consideration and in humble appreciation of such care and attention as Master may choose to afford her, has given, granted, aliened, enfeoffed, and conveyed, and by the Presents does give, grant, enfeoff, and convey unto Master:

ALL of Slave's body and each and every part thereof without reservation, every bit of her will as to all matters and things, and the entirety of her Soul,

TOGETHER with, all and singular, every privilege, advantage and appurtenance to the same belonging or in anywise appertaining;

ALSO all the estate, right, title, interest, property, claims, ego, and id of Slave in, of and to the same and in, of and to every part and parcel thereof:

TO HAVE AND TO HOLD, all and singular, the above described body, will, Soul, and premises, with all appurtenances thereof, unto Master and any of His assigns forever.

AND the said Slave does covenant, promise, and agree:

1. She shall immediately, diligently, and enthusiastically comply with and submit her full being to any and all directions or desires of Master or His assigns which He or They may express by word, signal, action, or any other means.

2. She shall at all times afford Master absolute respect, shall address Him only as "Sir" or "Master," shall station herself in a physical position subordinate to His whenever possible, and shall speak to or otherwise distract Him only when granted His permission.

3. She shall constantly maintain her female body parts in such circumstances as will demonstrate and ensure that they are fully open to Him. In particular, she shall never cross her legs in His presence, shall wear no undergarments at any time, and shall cover no part of her body with apparel or material of any description except when the act of doing so and design of the item are expressly approved by Him.

4. She shall preserve her female body parts for the exclusive use of Him and His assigns, which use shall be the sole source of his pleasures, and she shall engage in no self-gratification or any physical contact with any other.

AND Slave does hereby irrevocably declare and acknowledge her everlasting unconditional dedication to serving Master to His full satisfaction; AND she ashamedly confesses that prior indulgence of her intemperate conduct by others may have permitted her to become afflicted with inferior habits that may prove unsatisfactory to Master, from which imperfections she implores Master to free her by retraining with corporal punishment or any other means which He, in His unquestionable wisdom, deems effective toward directing her to her sole ambition and life-destiny of perfectly fulfilling His every desire of her.

IN WITNESS WHEREOF, Slave has hereunto set her hand, and Master has designed to Seal these Presents by permanently affixing His Collar about her neck, on the date first above written.

Signed by Slave, whose Collar was sealed and who was delivered unto Master on the date above-mentioned in the presence of:

Forever Slave Colleen Stan, Master Michael Powers, Witness Janet Powers.

"This is the work of Satan!" I cried out, with tears in my eyes. Up until now, I had been able to maintain my stoic personality. I never showed any emotions or feelings in front of the man. I had not cried in front of him since the first night. However, this situation was different. Everything hit bottom. Now for the first time, I realized there was more behind my kidnapping than just an evil man and woman. The purpose of my abduction, life time slavery, sunk in on me. This explained the isolation and pain I had endured. I couldn't stop crying. I had been abducted to be a slave and the torture was part of my training. It was just too much for me and I couldn't see anyway out.

"What does 'enfeoff' mean?" I sobbed stalling for time and searching for a way out of signing the contract.

"It means...ah...I don't know, just sign it," the man said, with increasing anger in his voice. (Enfeoff is a word from the Middle Ages which means to inherit or freehold an estate of land for life. In this case it's the slave who is inherited or given for life.)

"Why is the name Cameron on the back of your belt while the contract says Michael Powers?"

"Michael Powers is my slave owner's name," the man replied, after a brief pause. "Now sign the contract," he demanded.

"What if I don't?" I asked, softly.

"I will sign it for you and make you wish you had signed it," he said, through his teeth.

"I won't give you my soul," I said. "That belongs to God."

"All right, now sign."

Slowly, I took the pen and signed my name Colleen Stan to the right of the words "Forever Slave." My hand was shaking badly. I tried to distort my signature so it would be evident to anyone the signature had been forced from me.

The man then signed the indenture as Michael Powers and the woman witnessed by signing as Janet Powers. Using the last name of "Powers" must have implied their status over me. The woman, with her bandaged knees, carried the signed contract upstairs to the waiting company representative.

"What's wrong with your wife?" I asked.

"Oh, let me tell you about my wife. She was once a slave just like you. She escaped from her previous owner and flagged down a policeman who, unbeknownst to her, was a member of The Company. After she told the officer her story, he took her to a Rent-A-Dungeon where The Company nailed her up for three days. They wanted her to serve as an example to other slaves. Her knees were badly damaged during the punishment."

"I first saw her at the Rent-A-Dungeon wearing a cross, which indicated she had only a few more days to live. A crucifix would have indicated she was scheduled to die a painful death. A man can pay The Company $10,000 and torture a woman to death in such a place. I felt sorry for her, so I used some of my credit with The Company to purchase her. I had accumulated thousands of dollars in credit with The Company by tracking down runaway slaves over the years. I didn't have a dungeon to keep her in at the time, so I married her. I fixed up her knees, but she still has a lot of trouble."

"What is the company?" I asked.

"The Company is a secret organization run by powerful men who enslave, train, transport, and sells women like you. The Company, completely unknown to the average citizen, maintains a vast underground empire of financial wealth and influence. It's like an omnipotent black market or an underworld crime syndicate. Many men of influence including judges, doctors, police officers, and politicians are members of The Company."

"They also track down and punish any slave who is foolish enough to escape. For an annual fee of $1,600, The Company provides me with security which includes monitoring the house and telephone day and night. I had the fee deducted from my credits with The Company when I registered you tonight. If you try to escape, The Company will find you sooner or later. They will stop at nothing, including harming your family, to get you. Once they have you, they will take you to their headquarters in Sacramento for punishment. You will be nailed to a wooden beam and hung up for five days. After which, if you're still alive, you will be placed on the auction block and sold to the highest bidder."

"Can I pay my way out of slavery?"

"No, The Company sets the rules. Periodically, The Company will require you to under go special punishments to test your obedience. I have no control over what The Company requires. The Company wanted to make you a prostitute, but felt you were too ugly. You will remain a slave for life," the man said.

I had never heard of The Company. I had heard of the Mafia which, among other things, has forced women into prostitution. I also knew of international crime organizations that enslaved women for sexual purposes. I would never have believed in The Company, but the man's sadism and my experiences in the basement convinced me The Company was real.

"Now that you're a registered slave, there are a few rules you should know. From now on you must address me as Master or Sir and my wife as Ma'am. When you speak to us you must kneel down, keep you arms at your sides, and you eyes on the floor. Never look at our faces. You will answer questions with 'Yes Sir or Yes Ma'am.' You must ask permission to brush your teeth, clean your ears, or go to the restroom.

You will never cross your legs in my presence or wear undergarments unless approval is given. You will speak only when spoken to or when it's absolutely necessary. Do you understand?"

"Yes Master," I said, for the first time with my head bowed.

"If you scream or talk too much, I will call in a doctor from The Company who will cut your vocal cords. You'll be like one of those dogs who can't bark. You will be a silent slave. Understand?"

I nodded my head "yes" being too afraid to speak.

"The Company requires you wear a collar to identify you as a registered slave." A metal collar, much like a watch band, was locked tightly around my neck. It had a gold leaf on the front. From the beginning the collar started to itch and corrode, slowly turning my neck green.

"Oh, one last thing," Master said. "The Company has issued you a slave name. From now on you will answer to a single letter of the alphabet, 'K'. The girl previously known as Colleen Stan is gone. K is now your name. Do you understand?"

"Yes, Master."

A couple of weeks later, a laminated card arrived from The Company showing me officially registered as a slave. The card, containing the same official seal I had seen on the indenture or contract, was placed over the door of my workshop. I was now a registered slave for life.

One doesn't automatically accept an incredible story of a brotherhood of slave owners operating in the United States of America. Each night, for years to come, Master told me stories about The Company, reinforcing my status as a slave and the impossibility of escape.

"Let me tell you about the slave who escaped and wrote a newspaper article about The Company," Master told me one night. "The Company tracked her down through her family in three days. Her mother was tortured until she revealed the whereabouts of her daughter. As an example to other slaves, the escaped slave's fingers and toes were pulled off. Her tongue was cut out. Then her arms and legs were surgically removed by a doctor who didn't use any anesthesia. Her eyes were burned out with a soldering gun, and her ear drums were punctured destroying her hearing. Her hair was braided, and she was hung from a hook in the ceiling next to her master's bed. By giving her food and water, she was kept alive for almost a year before she finally died."

From the pain I had experienced, I knew the story was plausible. Yet I still wondered how such an evil organization could exist in a free country? How could law enforcement be so powerless? How could any normal person believe women, such as me, could be held against their will in a small American town? Any person sitting in their comfortable, secure home would find the story ludicrous. For me sitting in my basement dungeon, without any outside information, the story sounded true. Each night another story was told to convince me The Company was real. The stories grew increasingly frightening and soon interrupted my sleep with horrible nightmares.

"One recaptured runaway slave, a beautiful woman, was placed alive in a formaldehyde-filled glass box as a lesson to other slaves. She's on display, along with other women, in The Company museum. Someday, I will take you to The Company museum and show you the "human pickle" in the glass coffin. Anyone foolish enough to believe they can escape the power of The Company should think again."

Supporting evidence of the existence of The Company began to accumulate. The newspaper article, the man from The Company, the signed contract, Ma'am with her badly damaged knees, the arrival of the registration card, the horrible stories about runaway slaves, helped confirm the existence of The Company for me. Most convincing was the evil nature of my Master and the pain I endured at his hands. Most of all, I feared The Company and what it was capable of doing to me.

Master told me he had once taken pictures of me to a private slave auction. He tried to sell me, but the only person who bid on me was the man who had previously owned Ma'am. He didn't want me to fall into his hands, so he decided to turn down the man's $6,000 bid.

One evening, when I was in the bathroom, I came across a letter discussing my poor performance as a slave. The hand printed letter read, "How slow she is, how she better put her heart into it, I could have gotten $6,000 for her and I paid $2,000 for her (sic)." The letter was signed Speed. For me the letter was tangible proof The Company was real.

Fear, a deep fear of terrible pain, a pain that won't stop until death came, was the underlying reason I believed in The Company. Without the horrendous pain I had already suffered, the stories about The Company would have sounded like a bad movie plot. I didn't fear the man or his wife as much as I feared The Company. Law enforcement could deal with two individuals, but not a secret underworld crime organization. My greatest fear was harm would come to my family or I would receive the standard punishment for running away which was having my hands nailed to a beam and left hanging for days. From what I had experienced, being nailed up was not out of the realm of possibilities.

Over time, with continuous daily reinforcements, I became more convinced The Company did exist. I would be betting with my life if I tested the hypothesis that The Company didn't exist. If I was wrong, I would pay dearly and so might anyone else, including my family, who helped me. I accepted the fact that I was a slave for life and escape was impossible. I was trapped in a web of pain, fear, and isolation.

Being registered with The Company, I was allowed upstairs to clean house and wash dishes, but I was not allowed to sit on the furniture or eat with the family. I was thankful to be out of the basement even if for a short period of time. My blindfold and gag had been replaced with The Company discipline and rules. Now, I could see, but I had to keep my eyes cast downward. Now, I could talk, but only when spoken to by Master or Ma'am. In a way, the house just represented a larger box than the one in the basement, where I had been confined.

When upstairs, I was required to wear the nightgown because Ma'am didn't want a naked woman walking around when their child was present. Once the child had gone to bed, the nightgown came off. The doors were always locked and the window shades drawn.

When I had finished cleaning the kitchen, I would knell down before Master or Ma'am and ask, "Is there anything else you wish for me to do?" If not, I would be returned to the basement, where I would be given cold leftovers, and returned to the box or workshop for the evening. Of course, being periodically hung up and other forms of torture never ended.

Slowly, the interior of the house I had lived under for eight months became known to me. However, the exterior of the house remained for the most part a mystery. The house had been built in the 1920's or 30's in the craftsman-style which was popular at the time. With two bedrooms and a single bath, the residence measured 38 feet long by 24 feet wide. I would learn years later, the house had a fenced-in yard and an unattached garage accessible by using the ally. Following the craftsman's design, the interior walls were off-white in color with dark wooden trim around the baseboards, windows, and doors. A small concrete front porch was complimented by a screened-in back porch, which also served as a laundry room.

Front of Oak Street House, 2006

The interior floor plan of the house was ideal for a dog or child because they could run around inside the house from room to room in a loop. Starting in the kitchen there was an air conditioner in the window for the 100 degree-plus summer days in Red Bluff. From the kitchen, one could walk directly into a small dinning room which had a built-in dark wooden cabinet, also in the craftsman's style. Continuing clockwise through the house, the living room came next with a large window facing the street and a door to the front porch. Between the dinning room and the living room was an arched doorway, five feet wide and six feet, seven and a half inches high, which would have a special meaning for me later.

Continuing around the house, the next room was the master bedroom, 12 feet long by 12 feet wide, with two large windows and a small closet. In the closet, a wooden panel could be removed allowing one to see and hear into the basement below. One large window in the master bedroom looked out over the front porch. Also in the master bedroom was a waterbed on a large pedestal. This too would have special meaning for me later.

The next room was the eight feet by six feet bathroom where I experienced my first near-drowning bath. The bathroom along with the kitchen had linoleum floors while the other rooms in the house had wooden floors.

The last room of the house was a 12 feet by 12 feet back bedroom with multiple windows which would have brought in the afternoon sunlight if the shades had not been drawn. This room belonged to the little girl, whose name I would learn was Charity. She was walking, but not yet talking. The kitchen was adjacent to the back bedroom, but first one had to pass the basement door on the right and the back porch door on the left. The basement was directly under the dinning room.

Even with a slave to do the work, the house was a mess with papers lying all around. Master and Ma'am were not neat people. One day while cleaning the bathroom, I found a letter addressed to Cameron & Janice Hooker, 1140 Oak Street, Red Bluff, California. Now I knew the name of my captors and their address.

In February, 1978, Master introduced a new exercise called an "attention drill". When he shouted "attention," I was to quickly strip off my nightgown and run to the arched doorway between the living room and dinning room. I was to then stand on my toes and stretch out my arms until they touched the top of the arched doorway. My eyes were to be closed and I was expected to hold this position until Master said, "At ease." The drill represented being hung up in the basement and was used to reinforce Master's control over me.

Arched Doorway, 2006

"Attention!"

Up on hearing the dreaded words, I ran for the arched doorway as I pulled my nightgown over the top of my head. Once in position, my legs and arms were tautly stretched with my eyes closed.

"You took 25 minutes to do the dishes tonight. (The dishes were not from just the evening meal, but from the entire day.) My wife could have done them in 20 minutes. That's too slow. You need an incentive to work faster," Master said.

With those words, I felt the lash of a whip on my back. Not crying out, I held my position until Master was done with me.

"At ease. Now are you going to work faster?"

"Yes, Master."

No matter how hard I tried, I was never able to satisfy him. Ma'am would tell Master I was sloppy and slow in my work habits. Her words would result in me receiving a beating.

One attention drill stands out in my mind. I had set the dinner table with plates, knifes, spoons, and forks. When no one was looking, Charity innocently removed the fork from her mother's place setting. Ma'am without a word went over to the kitchen drawer and got another fork. After dinner, Charity was put to bed.

"Attention!"

I immediately striped and assumed the position.

"Why didn't you give my wife a fork?"

"Master, I did," I replied.

The whip cracked down on my bare back. Then the whip struck me again and again. My back burned like fire.

"Once again, why didn't you place a fork on the table for my wife?"

"But Master, I did place a fork for Ma'am."

Like in Eugene, when I was asked if I were a college student, I told the truth. Again the whip bit into my flesh leaving long red welts.

Finally, I answered, "I'm sorry, Master. It will not happen again." Weeks later the fork was found under a piece of furniture where Charity had tossed it.

Up until now, I had not been raped. Numerous sex acts had been committed against my body, but Master never raped me. All that changed one evening in February, 1978, when my hands were cuffed behind my back and I was guided up the stairs to the master bedroom. With my eyes and mouth taped, I was tied spread-eagle to the corners of their waterbed. Ma'am lay on one side while Master lay on the other. As they started kissing each other over my body, I wondered, "What kind of sick perverted people are they? "

When Master penetrated me, Ma'am jumped up and ran to the bathroom. I could hear her crying and throwing up. Master quickly ran to the bathroom to be with her. A short time later, I was released from the bed and returned to my basement box. As usual, no words were spoken to me. Like everything else, it would be years before I knew the story behind the events of that night. I was just thankful the rape was of such short duration. Unbeknownst to me, I had now added sex slave to my resume in addition to work and torture slave.

After the rape incident, I could feel a strong sense of anger and hatred directed towards me by Ma'am. She saw me as a threat to the relationship, however bizarre, she had with her man. Suddenly, everything I did was wrong in her eyes. The only words Ma'am directed towards me were sharp commands. I could only speak to her if an order needed to be clarified.

"If my wife is displeased with you, she'll kill you," Master told me trying to reduce the friction between us. Being a slave, all the anger flowed from Ma'am towards me. I was never allowed to talk back or argue. I found it especially humiliating to kneel naked before her, she being junior to me in age, and asking permission to go to the restroom.

On April 28, 1978, I was left in the workshop all day and night. I could hear noise and movement in the basement and in the house above. I missed my evening meal and still no one came down to check on me. Finally, around 2:00 or 3:00 in the morning, I was taken out of the workshop, blindfolded, and handcuffed. I was guided up the stairs and out the back door into the cool night air.

"Where was I going?" I thought. I had learned never to ask any questions. I was scared and concerned. This was the first time I had been outdoors, in the fresh air, in almost a year.

Master placed me in the front seat of a pickup truck with my head on his wife's lap. The pickup proceeded to drive through the dark streets of Red Bluff. After 15 or 20 minutes, we stopped and the engine was turned off. Master guided me out of the pickup and up a set of steep stairs into a mobile home. After reaching the front bedroom, my blindfold was removed along with my handcuffs. In front of me was the same large waterbed I had seen in the master bedroom of the house on Oak Street. The headboard and sides were covered with black vinyl. At the foot of the bed, two panels had been removed revealing the open end of a dark box.

"Get in," he ordered. Down on my belly I went. I worked my way into the box finding my sleeping bag and bedpan waiting for me. It was nice to have the bedpan in the box with me, but the smell of the bedpan also stayed with me until it was emptied. Once I was on my back, the bedpan was kept on the right side of the box near my feet. The air blower, however, was not outside of the box as it had been in the basement. It was now in the box with me on the left side of my head. A hose was attached to a small hole in the bottom of the box to draw in fresh air. Another small hole, one and a quarter inches in diameter, allowed air to exit. The holes were drilled through the floor of the mobile home.

The end of the box was closed and bolted in place with wing nuts. A second panel, part of the base of the waterbed, was then bolted in place creating a double wall between me and the outside. Lastly, a heavy set of steps were placed at the foot of the bed covering the hidden panels. As

I lay in the dark, I surveyed the measurements of the box. It was a little longer then my height of five feet, six inches. Being flat on my back, I had two inches between my hands and the side walls of the box. The height of the box was the distance between the tips of my fingers and my elbow, just barely high enough for me to use the bedpan and roll over. My new box was somewhat smaller than the one on Oak Street. Later, I learned the box was six feet long, 33 inches wide and 15 inches high. The first box was like a crate, the second box opened like a coffin, and now this box was like being enclosed in a tomb. Now I would be kept under gallons of water, inches below Master and his wife, as they slept on the waterbed above me.

What was to become of me now? What did this move mean for me? There were still many questions in my mind. I prayed quietly and slowly fell asleep in the isolation and darkness I had come to know so well.

Chapter 7 - Trailer Life

I was still in a box, just a smaller box than the one on Oak Street. My routine had not changed much, except for the absence of the workshop. There were still many hours of loneliness and darkness to be endured in the box. Each evening, I would be allowed to empty my bedpan, eat leftovers, and drink a glass of water. If no cleaning was to be done or torture endured, I was returned to the box for another 23 hours.

As I cleaned the kitchen and washed the dishes, I learned more about the mobile home. It was a 1977 Sandpointe, serial number 1434. The length of the trailer was 64 feet and the width was 12 feet. Of the 768 square feet of living space, five and a half square feet, the size of my box, was mine.

The mobile home contained a front or master bedroom with the waterbed and my box underneath. The master bath was next to the front bedroom. Adjacent to the bedroom was a combination living room, dinning room, and kitchen. The front door of the trailer, which faced east, was in the living room. Moving toward the rear of the trailer, a small hallway led to Charity's bedroom. A back bathroom, with an exit door facing west, was just off the hallway. The trailer was parked with the front bedroom facing north and the rear bedroom facing south.

The trailer was parked at the end of a short gravel road, known as Weed Court, just off Pershing Road. The mailing address was Route 2, Box 2809. A garden and orchard were soon planted east of the trailer and construction was started on the first of two storage sheds west of the trailer. Other mobile homes and houses were dispersed along Weed Court with the closest trailer being 200 feet to the east. Interstate 5, the primary north-south route on the west coast, was 150 yards to the west. One could hear the noise of the big trucks heading south with Washington apples for Los Angels or heading north with California oranges for Seattle. Of course, for me knowledge of the trailer and its surroundings came slowly. At first, my world consisted only of the front bedroom and bath.

One day in late spring, when the weather was getting warm, I was given a pair of jean shorts, a pink tank top, and a pair of used white tennis shoes. I was to learn that if I wore clothes, Master preferred me in shorts. Underwear was not permitted according to the indenture I had signed. Other than my nightgown and jacket, these were the first clothes I had worn in over a year. Once I was dressed, I was taken outside in the sun which was another new experience for me. The sun felt good on my white skin, but by the end of the day my bare arms and legs were sunburned.

The purpose of my outing soon became evident. Master guided me to a trench behind the newly parked trailer, handed me a shovel, and ordered me to fill in a trench with dirt. The trench contained newly laid utility lines for the mobile home. As Master and I worked together, my unused muscles ached, but I knew better than to stop working.

Suddenly, without warning, a man I had never seen before came around the corner of the trailer and walked right up to me.

"So this is your little rag muffin," the man said, as he eyed me up and down.

I didn't say a word, but kept my eyes down and continued to work. I knew he must have known I was a slave. Anyone could see the metal collar around my neck. Why else would he call me a little rag muffin? I was terrorized by his presence. Master took the man, who I later learned was his brother Dexter, to the front of the trailer where they talked. Finally, his brother departed.

Previously, Master had told me about his family, especially his father Harold and his brother Dexter. They both had close connections with The Company. When his father lived in Arkansas, he had a large dungeon which held 26 slaves which he tortured at will. I was warned not to reveal to either of them that I was a slave.

"If they know you are a slave, they will want to borrow you," Master told me.

"When you're around my family don't kneel to ask permission, don't say Master, and don't parade around naked," Master warned me. Apparently, I was to be passed off as a family friend, housekeeper, and babysitter. Later, I would be referred to as a "live-in" housekeeper and babysitter.

Master had no friends, but there were relatives who visited and neighbors who lived nearby. If word got out that I was a slave, The Company would have to take action. Master would receive the following message:

"Michael Powers. It has come to the attention of The Company that you are unable to properly disciplined and control your slave. Therefore, the privilege of slave ownership is hereby revoked. Slave K will be punished by The Company and sold to another master. You may apply for slave ownership again after three years."

For Master, this would mean the loss of his slave. For me, this would result in me being nailed up for five days and sold to a new master.

A few days later, Master ordered me to dig a hole approximately six feet long, three feet wide, and four to five feet deep.

"Are you having me dig my own grave?" I asked.

"Just keep digging," Master ordered. The next time I saw the ditch, weeks later, it had been filled in with dirt. Years later, I would learn railroad ties had been buried in the hole to support the foundation of a storage shed soon to be built.

My next encounter with Master's family came when his parents arrived unannounced. They were a southern family that didn't believe in calling ahead or ringing doorbells when visiting their son. They just popped in and shouted, "Anyone home?" With those words, I looked up with shock and fear in my eyes. I had been down on my hands and knees cleaning the floor just inside the front door. I was only wearing my nightgown and slave collar. Staring down at me was Master's father who enjoyed torturing women slaves. I froze and couldn't move or speak. Ma'am quickly came to my rescue, escorting me into the bedroom, as Master kept his parents occupied in the living room. Ma'am had me change into a pair of ill fitting pants and an old shirt of hers. The pants were plaid and the shirt was striped resulting in an odd mismatch.

"Dear, isn't it time for you to take Kay back home?" Ma'am said, as we entered the living room together.

"Yes it is," Master said, as he led me out the front door. While Ma'am kept his parents busy, Master locked me in the newly constructed, yellow storage shed outside the trailer. He then drove off in his pickup pretending to be taking me home. After his parents had departed, I was retrieved from the shed and returned to my box under the waterbed.

Later in the summer, I would see Master's father again. His father terrorized me with his eyes. I kept my eyes down, but could sense he was glaring at me and sizing me up. In my mind, he knew I was a slave and wanted to borrow me for torture. How could Master say "no" to his father?

In time, I met the parents of Ma'am. They were an elderly couple who were not, as far as I was told, members of The Company. As with any family member, I kept my head down and remained quiet. Years later, a sister in the family remarked, "I just thought Kay was shy since she never spoke."

During summer nights and eventually during the day, I was taken outside for short periods of time to work in the garden. After being confined in a box for so long, I enjoyed the feel of sunlight in my hair and the smell of fresh dirt between my fingers. Soon, Master's garden was the best kept on Weed Court, being completely weed-free and filled with fresh tomatoes, beans, and corn. While outside, I was always under the watchful eye of Master or his wife. I was seen from a distance, but never introduced to Al and Dorothy Coppa who lived in the next trailer, 200 feet away. They observed how hard I worked in the garden, sometimes starting as early as 5:00 AM.

At night and during much of the day, I was locked in my box under the waterbed. I had ample time to think, day dream, and pray. I slowly reviewed my life starting with my birth in Riverside, California, 21 years before in 1956. My mom, Lynne, and my father, Jack, probably never should have been married.

Lynne and Jack fell in love as high school sweethearts. I guess there's a certain physical attraction between teenage girls and boys in high school. No dating service would have ever matched them together. They were opposites like salt and pepper, oil and water, night and day. After three years, and as many children, the marriage was over. I was three years old.

It was truly a no fault divorce, which unfortunately didn't exist in the 1950's. Mom was an outgoing, gregarious person who loved to socialize with friends and family. Nights were a time to go out on the town and have fun. Dancing and conversation created great times for her. She was a fun person to know and to be with.

Dad, on the other hand was a good, quiet person, who was a hard worker. After high school, from which neither Dad nor Mom graduated, my dad followed his father into construction work. In time, he studied hard and got his contractor's license. He worked hard putting in countless hours, even on weekends. When I was born, he was working on the Riverside Freeway grading and paving, and barely made it to the hospital in time for my birth at 11:46 AM.

Colleen as a Child

At the end of each work day, Dad just wanted to stay home and relax. A good dinner followed by a comfortable chair was his way of enjoying life. He, unlike Mom, was a person of few words. He had friends at work, but didn't care to socialize after hours.

My religion came from my dad's side of the family. Grandma Gertrude took my sisters and I to church when we were children. Dad never darkened a church door unless my grandma made him go which was rare. Mom also avoided religious services. It was Grandma who prayed for me each night after my disappearance.

My parents were both good people, just not good for each other. The family rumor was they had to drop out of high school and get married because a baby was on the way. In the 1950's, young ladies in high school were not supposed to have babies or abortions. They just dropped out of society and had their babies in secret. Sadly, Mom later had a miscarriage.

Mom came from a long line of Southern California women. Five generations had been born and raised in the Riverside area. I'm proud of my family roots on my mom's side, the contributions made to the settlement of Riverside, and the development of the citrus industry. My great-grandfather owned a large portion of land called a block which he developed. The block, in the vicinity of present-day Mary Street and Victoria Avenue, was planted with mostly orange groves as far as the eye could see. He also constructed irrigation canals and built a large house where my mom raised me and my sisters.

My great-grandfather was English and his wife was Argentine. They met when he was in the English Navy visiting South America. Members of my family have either English characteristics, like my mom, or Argentine characteristics, like my aunt. Tall, blue-eyed, red hair and light skin was found on the English side while short, dark-eyed, dark hair and dark skin was found on the other side of the family. Juana, my mom's sister, was the exception to the rule with beautiful, olive skin and blazing red hair. Sadly, she was killed by a drunk driver at age 13. I took on the English characteristics myself and my Irish sounding name, Colleen, came from a nurse on duty at the hospital where I was born. I was almost named Carol, which was the attending physician's first name. I'm glad my parents chose Colleen.

My great-grandfather and my grandfather loved photography and shared a propensity to be pack rats. However, their common interests didn't mean they got along well. When my great-grandfather died, his estate was left to his granddaughters, not his son. My mom and her sister, Gail, inherited the land and a large house that great-grandfather had built with his own hands. Mom purchased Gail's half of the house and moved in with my father when I was a toddler.

My father's roots in California were not as deep. When my father was age 10, his father came to the Riverside area for construction work. Like many others before him, he called his family back in Iowa and told them to join him in the Golden State with its plentiful jobs and warm climate. My father went on to build a moderately successful land grading and construction company.

After Mom and Dad divorced, I continued to live with my mom and visit my dad on weekends. Their marriage produced two other children, my sisters Jenise and Bonnie. Bonnie was born when my parents split up, but my dad always loved Bonnie as he loved all his children.

As a kid, I had a great childhood. My sisters and I played for hours in the orange groves and on our concrete driveway. We bicycled and roller skated each day until the sun went down. Mom had a swimming pool built in the backyard which added to the fun for me and my sisters. When Aunt Gail visited with her five children, the fun really started. In Southern California, rain prevented the outdoor fun only a few days each year. On such rare days, I stayed indoors and played with my Barbie dolls. Television for me was self-limited to a few cartoons on Saturday morning and the Disney Channel on Sunday night. Overall, I was an outdoors girl who loved the sunshine. Being locked in a dark box was especially hard on me.

My mom, to make some extra money, took in a boarder named Ralph. He made his career designing and selling swimming pools. For a hobby he enjoyed sculpturing works of art. The two of them enjoyed each others company and living life to the fullest. In time, Mom and Ralph fell in love and were soon married. The only problem with Ralph was that he didn't like children, especially three little girls from a previous marriage. We found him to be impatient and short-tempered when dealing with us. He believed children were to be seen and not heard. If there was fighting between us, Ralph punished us all. My sisters and I agreed he was a tyrant.

Sadly, my mom always placed Ralph ahead of her daughters. When Mom and Ralph wanted sometime alone, my sisters and I were packed off to church on Sunday mornings. This ended when people at church starting asking, "Where're your parents little girls?" When they wanted to go to Las Vegas for the weekend, a babysitter was hired to watch us.

One event was seared in my mind when I was eight or nine years old. Rebecca, our babysitter, had a newborn baby of her own. When I awoke in the morning, the house was filled with police and medical personnel. My sisters and I were told to sit on the couch in the living room and not to get up. No adult told us what was going on in the house that morning. Years later, when I was older, I learned Rebecca's baby had died during the night of SIDS (Sudden Infants Death Syndrome).

My mother was a beautiful woman who had done professional modeling after she met Ralph. He soon put a stop to my mom's modeling career. In the early 1960's, unlike today, a man could tell his wife to stay home and take care of the house. Mom did everything Ralph wanted including purchasing him several expensive automobiles. All her time was spent with Ralph at the expense of her daughters. When the money from her inheritance ran out, Ralph also ran out. After 10 years, they were divorced.

It wasn't long before Mom had a new boyfriend, Joe. He was a major in the Air Force and Mom wanted to marry him. One day, while Mom was away, Joe molested me by kissing me and pulling off my tube top. I ran upstairs and locked myself in my bedroom. When Mom returned home, I told her what had happened expecting her to defend me. Instead, she wanted to know what "I" had done to provoke Joe. She demanded I apologize to Joe immediately. I refused.

"I'll knock that chip off your shoulder," Mom said, as she hit me really hard on the shoulder with the palm of her hand.

I didn't have any idea what she was talking about at the time, and I still don't know if I understand even today. Mom treated me like my feelings didn't mean anything to her. I found myself in a helpless situation where my feelings were unimportant and ignored by the person who should have loved me the most, my mom.

That night, at age 14, I packed my bags and moved out of my mother's house. I knew ...the....

Suddenly back in the box, I heard foot steps as someone walked into the bedroom. This was followed by the heavy stair steps at the foot of the bed being removed. Then the exterior and interior panels were unbolted and opened, flooding the box with light. Anytime the box was opened, I was gripped with fear about what was to come.

"Crawl out," Master ordered.

I rolled over on my stomach and inched my way out of the box. It wasn't easy because the 15 inch height of the box kept me low to the floor. Once outside, I got on my knees, lowered my head, and awaited orders.

"Come with me," Master said, walking quickly into the living room. I followed him and found myself standing in front of a large rectangular object with sinister looking straps hanging from the top and bottom. The object looked like an empty picture frame. I was to fill the frame.

With the dungeon basement on Oak Street no longer available, a substitute was needed. A couple of months after moving into the trailer, Master had constructed a rectangular frame of wooden 2X4's (boards two inches by four inches) to perform bondage sessions in the trailer. Hooks in the ceiling of the mobile home were used to secure the frame, but not to take my body weight. The frame would bear my weight. Once blindfolded, gagged, and strapped to the frame, I was suspended, spread-eagle, with my feet off the floor. My wrists bore the weight of my body and the pain of suspension. When not in use the frame was disassembled and stored out of sight. The frame was complimented by a later creation, the "X", which worked basically the same. Painwise, there was little difference between the two diabolical devices.

Performing bondage inside the trailer came with risks for Master. The ceiling of the trailer wasn't reinforced enough to support a suspended woman over time. What if someone, like his parents or brother, dropped by unexpectedly? In addition, Charity was getting older and might witness a bondage event in the trailer. Master went right to work on a solution to his problem.

"Put these clothes on," Master said. "Quickly," he barked.

After I dressed, I was taken outside to a pale yellow, plywood storage shed 15 feet west of the mobile home. The shed had been constructed that summer and would be joined by a second adjacent shed the next summer, 1979. The first shed had a gable roof while the second shed would have a slant roof. Once inside the windowless shed the door was closed and locked.

Mobile Home and Storage Shed, 1989

"Strip off your clothes," Master ordered.

I soon found myself blindfolded, gagged, and standing naked on the cold concrete floor. Leather cuffs were buckled on my wrists, and I quickly found myself suspended by the wrist from hooks in the rafters of the shed. The severe pain was no different from what I had experienced in the basement on Oak Street. Being hung by the wrists and whipped is something one never becomes accustomed to over time.

When Master was satisfied, I was let down and told to get dressed. I was escorted back outside and through the back door of the trailer. Anyone seeing us would have seen a young woman, in shorts and tank top, followed closely by a man, larger in size. Once in the bedroom, I was ordered to remove all my clothes and get in the box. A week or two later, the same procedure was repeated, but this time with terrifyingly different results.

The next time, Ma'am accompanied her husband to the shed to watch me being hung and whipped. In the confines of the small 12 feet by 12 feet shed, I accidentally kicked Ma'am in the stomach while suspended by the wrist. Being blindfolded, I didn't see her nor did I know she was pregnant with their second child. Master became very angry, but the punishment didn't come immediately. He did, however, remove the sleeping bag from my box, forcing me to sleep on the splintery particle board for a week.

A week later, I received my special punishment for kicking Ma'am. After being suspended in the shed again, Master poked me in the side with the tip of a ski pole. Then he went back to the trailer leaving Madam to watch me hang. When he returned he had a box of wooden matches. Under my blindfold, I could see a lighted match coming toward my right breast.

"Oh God, please help me," I prayed quietly. God must have intervened, because the fire didn't hurt as Master burned first my right and then my left breast. Since I showed no response to the fire, Master quickly lost interest. I was taken down and returned to my box where the blisters from the 2nd degree burns slowly healed.

When Ma'am was out shopping with Charity, Master would take me out of the box for a bondage session. When finished, Master sometimes wanted a little "cuddle time." I would be kneeling on the floor with my head bowed and arms limp by my sides. Master sat on the couch relishing the power he had over me. On command, I would wrap my arms around him and give him a big hug, while still in the kneeling position.

"K, you have the floor," he said, in a matter-of-fact way. "You can talk about or ask me anything you wish."

After over a year without any meaningful conversation, I was surprised. My opinions, wishes, and thoughts were inconsequential as a slave woman. I did what I was told. Now I had the floor to ask a question or speak my mind. What should I say? I knew not to ask when I was going home. The answer was always the same, "Soon."

"When did you first have these desires to hurt women?" I asked, keeping my head bowed.

"I started drawing pictures of women in bondage when I was five or six years old," he replied, in a calm voice.

How odd it was for Master, as a young boy, to be thinking about such things. Even as an adult, I didn't know anything about bondage or sadism. Sex certainly wasn't part of my life when I was in the first grade. I kept wondering why he was having these fantasies at such a young age. He must have been exposed to pornography or abused, by a family member or neighbor, as a child.

"Master, what if someone did this to your daughter, Charity?"

"I would kill them," he said, without pausing.

"How do you think my dad feels about what you're doing to me?" That question ended the conversation. I was marched back to the bedroom and returned to my box.

On a typical day in the summer, I would awake in the darkness of the box with the air blower whining in my ears. From the heat, I could tell it was late in the afternoon. The temperature in Red Bluff averages 98 degrees in the summer with the daily high well in the 100's. For once, I was glad to be naked. Clothes would have been unbearable in the sweat soaked box.

In the heat, my mind turned to thoughts of water. Cool, refreshing water. I would dream of floating in an inner tube on a large lake. All I could see for miles around was water. I would dip my hand down into the water and take a drink. Then I would splash the liquid over my head to lessen the heat. It felt so good.

Master limited me to one large glass of water a day. I knew better than to ask for more. I never knew if that's all he thought I needed or if it was to keep me from using the bedpan so much. Being a sadist, the lack of water was yet another way he could inflict suffering on me while he was enjoying a cold drink at work.

The woman never brought me anything, after the lemonade I received the first few days of my captivity. Was she also a sadist like her husband? Had she been instructed not to comfort me? Did she care about me? I did learn years later, she kept the door to the master bedroom closed during the hot summer months. Ma'am saw no need to air condition a portion of the trailer not occupied by herself or Charity.

By September, even Master could see the collar I had worn for nine months had to be replaced. My skin had turned green from metallic corrosion and I couldn't stop scratching my neck. Without a word, Master removed the collar and wrapped my neck with tinfoil. Then he soldered or welded a stainless steel ring permanently in place around my neck. The tinfoil was to protect my neck from the hot solder. The stainless steel ring didn't itch as much, wasn't as tight, and didn't turn my neck green like the previous collar. However, it still marked me as a slave girl.

I will never forget September 4, 1978. In the box underneath the waterbed, I could hear what was going on above. I could hear Ma'am going through labor pains and Master coaching her towards childbirth. I soon heard the first small, high pitched cries of life from a baby girl, who would be named Amber. To my surprise, I was removed from the box for a couple of minutes to view the newest life on earth. I couldn't help but cry. All life was a gift from God and here before me was a healthy, beautiful baby. I also noticed no one else was in the room with us. No midwives or relatives were present to assist. Was this from lack of money, fear of hospitals, or to keep the secrets of the trailer in the trailer? Master knew a woman in labor, might say anything.

As I neared the end of the year, an inventory of my life showed some improvement since the Oak Street basement. I was allowed to work outside in the sunlight weeding the garden. I was still required to clean the kitchen, wash the dishes, and scrub the floors. When Ma'am and the children were out shopping or with her parents, the bondage equipment and I came out of hidden storage. Master continued to fill my head with stories of escaped slaves and the punishments they received. I remained in fear of The Company and what might happen to me if I was not a good slave. Most of the time, I just lay on my back in the dark box sleeping, dreaming, and praying to the Lord. There were many secrets in the mobile home at the end of Weed Court and I was one of them.

I spent Christmas, my 22nd birthday, and New Years in the confines of the box, while the other members of the Hooker family celebrated. As I ran my fingers around the ring encircling my neck, I thanked God for my life and prayed to Him for a better 1979.

Chapter 8 - Pseudo-freedom

The year, 1979, started off much the same as the previous year. Long hours in the box, a single daily meal, cleaning the trailer, and bondage were my daily routine. Since it was winter, there wasn't any garden work, but I was allowed to wear my nightgown due to the cold temperatures.

By now, I knew Master worked at a lumber mill owned by the Diamond International Corporation. He worked from 6:45 AM until 4:30 PM and, as his co-workers later reported, at the end of the day he would rush to his car to get home as quickly as possible.

I'm sure while at work he thought about his slave suffering in the dark box under the waterbed, but couldn't discuss it with his fellow workers. As co-workers talked about hunting, sports, and women, Master could only smile. "If only they knew what I knew," Master must have thought to himself. Only he, his wife, and The Company knew my true status.

Money in the Hooker home was tight with five mouths to feed. Large bags of rice and oatmeal were purchased which, for me at least, became the basis of many meals. In April, Ma'am finally took a job as a night cook at Foster's Old Fashioned Freeze, a fast-food business. Most people shortened the name to Foster Freeze. She worked from 5:00 PM until midnight which worked out well since her husband got off work at 4:30 PM.

With Ma'am gone, my responsibilities increased as I was expected to fix dinner, clean the kitchen, and watch the children. I was never alone and always supervised by Master. Once the children were asleep, Master could have his way with me as long as the noise level didn't wake the kids. I would be returned to my box shortly before Ma'am returned home at midnight. The cycle was repeated the next day when Ma'am would take me out of my box late in the afternoon and would tell me what to cook for dinner. No rice or oatmeal for Master. He was a steak and potatoes man. Master also liked to eat rabbit. Just like me, a number of rabbits were kept in a wooden box near the trailer. Master had me skin, clean, and cook the rabbits, after which I too had to eat them. No one else in the family ate the rabbits. I never saw Master torture the small animals like he did me.

Also in April, Master started raping me once or twice a week after the girls had gone to bed and Ma'am was at work. I'm sure Ma'am was unaware of the rapes that went on while she was absent. A condom was always used to prevent his slave from becoming pregnant. Many times my wrists or ankles were tied to the television stand while being raped. Being raped by Master was always painful, gentle and kind he was not. In the evenings, Master would set up the frame and suspend me by my wrists while he watched television. On weekends, Ma'am would join him as they watched both TV and me.

The year would be marked by even more bizarre tortures starting with physical exercises. Master drove me in his Dodge Colt out to Hogsback Road, an isolated dirt road winding east from Red Bluff toward the mountains. I was wearing my short-shorts, pink tank top, and used tennis shoes. Once we were alone, he stopped the car.

"Get out and run down the road. If you stop, I will tie a chain around your neck and drag you behind the car."

My physical condition was poor, since I had spent so much time in the box. My lungs were soon burning as I gasped for air.

"Lord, help me get through this," I prayed. Eventually, I made it to Finley Lake where I was ordered to stop.

"Strip off your clothes and swim 10 laps," Master commanded.

Once again my lungs burned as I struggled for air swimming across the lake. When I had finished, he allowed me to dry off and get dressed. He drove me back to the mobile home and returned me to my box without saying a word. It was painful for me and a power trip for him. This routine was repeated two or three times in the following weeks, once with his two children, ages 9 months and 2 years, in the car.

Soon he had me running down Pershing Road near the mobile home. He followed me in his vehicle and timed me. It took me 15 minutes to complete a one mile circuit and return to the trailer. With the clock ticking, I was soon allowed to jog alone unsupervised.

"You had better be back in 15 minutes or The Company will be notified," Master warned me. Slowly, my physical condition improved and I began to enjoy my 15 minutes of pseudo-freedom.

Evidence of The Company being near, was all around me. I was sure Roger Michael George, a neighbor on Weed Court, knew I was a slave or at least he had strong suspicions. He always glared at me when I walked past his house, and once I felt he released his dog on me.

One day Master was talking to Ma'am about going to Sacramento the next day for The Company meeting. While I was walking past Roger Michael George's house after jogging, I overheard him talking to his father.

"Yes, I'm going down to Sacramento tomorrow," Roger Michael George told his elderly father. Knowing about The Company meeting in Sacramento confirmed in my mind Roger Michael George was a member and could be counted on to watch me anytime I was outdoors.

My jogging days soon came to an end when a friendly neighbor, Al Coppa, stopped me to say hello. I tried to cut the conversation short, but my 15 minutes of allotted time had expired before I could get back to the trailer. Master and Ma'am were furious.

"It's a good thing you got home. We were about to call The Company," Master threatened. My jogging days were over.

Slowly, I gained more access to open doors, telephones, and neighbors. Why didn't I escape? When I had been out jogging, why didn't I just keep running? Why didn't I tell Al Coppa I was being held against my will?

The simple answer was fear, a deep fear of The Company. My fear came from the gruesome stories Master told me along with horrific pain I experienced from torture sessions. Like a prison trusty, I knew I couldn't get away.

Escape would have been easy. All I had to do was walk out the door and go straight to the Red Bluff Police Department. I'm sure the police would have arrested Master and Ma'am, but would they have believed my story about The Company? Would they have placed me in the Witness Protection Program? Would my family have been safe?

I could have walked to Interstate 5 and hitchhiked south to my family in Riverside or I could have gone north to Canada. I could have changed my name, acquired a fake Social Security number, and avoided contact with my family. I could have married and told my husband I was using a false identity to get away from an abusive relationship. Once again, would my family have been safe? Wasn't it hitchhiking that got me in this mess? How long could I stay in hiding? One year? Two years? Maybe three years? The Company, with all its resources, would eventually find me.

I knew how this story would end. Late some night I would be coming home with a bag of groceries in my arms. As I placed the key into the door lock, two men would approach me out of the dark. One man would grab my right upper arm while the other man would catch the grocery bag and my purse before they fell to the ground.

"K, that is your real name, you're coming with us," one of the men would say.

As I instinctively reached for my purse, the other man would say, "You won't need that where you're going."

The fear, the pain, and The Company, were real in my mind. Escape for me was impossible. Death was my only means of escape and I wasn't willing to accept suicide. I still had faith in God and hope for my future. Until I had my freedom, I didn't want to do anything that might endanger my life or end my limited freedom. If I messed up, I knew I would be returned to the box 23 hours a day. Even worse, The Company might want to intervene in my punishment. Being traded to a more sadistic slave owner was also a possibility. I tried hard to be a good slave, a very good slave. I knew I had to return to my box each night.

In addition to runaway slave stories, Master would often tell me about undisciplined bonds women who were sold to masters who knew no limits to their cruelty. One dream that occurred time and time again, while asleep in the box, was of being traded to another overseer.

"K, we are going to a slave owner's party. Put some clothes on," Master announced in my dream.

Once in the car we drove to a large, isolated mansion in the country. Master rang the doorbell as he pushed me forward. A well dressed butler opened the door and at once recognized Master Michael Powers. The butler took Master's coat and led us to a large room filled with people.

"Take off your clothes," Master ordered. "Now, knell down and stay put."

Master proceeded to work his way around the room talking to different men. Other slaves in the room were serving drinks or on their knees like me. Soon Master returned with an older, evil looking man who was dressed all in black.

"She's a good slave, but needs a firm hand," Master said, standing in front of me.

"Stand up K," the older man ordered. "She will learn what a firm hand is under me. It's a deal Michael, I'll take her. She can ride in the trunk of my car."

Fear griped my soul. I was now in the hands of a new master who appeared more evil than my Master.

At this point I would usually wake up from my dream. I knew I had to be a good slave or my bad dreams would come true. The same dream, in different forms, would visit my sleep time and time again.

Everything I did was evaluated both for speed and quality. I tried to do my best, but I found myself in a losing situation. Master gave me an iron skillet that I scrubbed on for hours, but could never satisfy him.

A substitute for the workshop on Oak Street had been found in the mobile home. At night, I was chained by the neck to the toilet in the back bathroom, where I could once again work on macramé projects. Ma'am gave me some cord and printed directions to make a potted plant holder that, like me, would hang from the ceiling. I was expected to complete the project by morning.

Late one night, I discovered I only had 100 yards of cord for a 120 yard project. Thinking ahead, I changed the design to insure it would be finished by daybreak. I assumed a finished project was better than a half-done assignment.

"Why didn't you do the project as designed?" Ma'am asked, the next morning. I carefully explained the situation to her, assuming she would be happy I had finished the hanging plant holder.

"Okay," Ma'am said. She then escorted me to the front bedroom, where I was locked in the box for the day.

A week later, I was taken from the box and suspended by my wrists from the frame in the living room. My feet were off the floor and tied to the sides of the frame. I was gagged and blindfolded. I didn't think I could stand more pain when I realized Master was taping electrical wires to my breasts and the inside of my thighs. The wires were attached to an old lamp switch and plugged into a wall plug. Master and Ma'am, who were seated on a comfortable couch, turned up the volume on the television to drown out my screams.

"This is because you didn't do the macramé project as you were told," Master said, as I received a quick little zap of electricity to let me know what was coming. With his fingers wrapped around the off-on switch, he gave me a hard shock with the 120 volt household current that lasted several seconds. This was repeated again and again every few minutes. Each time the current went through my body, I shook uncontrollably from the excruciating pain. Fear and pain caused me to sweat which made the wires, taped to my breast, fall off. Master and his wife calmly sat watching TV between shocks. When it was over, I had electrical burns where the wires had contacted my skin.

Up to this point, I thought things couldn't get any worse. I was wrong. Evil knows no bounds and Master was pure evil. From my box, I could hear through the air hole, noise outside the trailer. One morning, I heard sawing and hammering. This was never a good sign. "What's Master up to now," I thought. A few days later, I found out.

Ma'am and the children were gone for the day which was never good for me. I was taken out of my box and told to take a shower. I knew from experience this usually signified rape. My body was shaking from fear and anticipation of what was to come. When I finished showering I walked naked into the living room. Before my eyes was a large wooden cross, in the shape of a "T", lying on the floor.

"What the hell is this," I thought.

Leather cuffs were strapped to my wrists and ankles along with a blindfold for my eyes. With out any explanation, I was told to lie down on the apparatus. My wrists were attached to the top of the T and my ankles were locked together and attached to a chain at the bottom of the T. From the bottom edge of my blindfold, I could see a wench on the bottom of the T. As Master started to tighten up the wench my body began to stretch.

"I'm not doing this to punish you," Master told me. "I'm doing this because I like to."

"Oh God," I thought. "This is not going to be good."

The devise would become known as the "stretcher". This invention of his was a modern day version of the stretchers used in medieval times to dismember and torture people to death. A metal rod was used to lock the wench in place when a certain amount of tension was on my body. Master ran his hands up and down my body feeling the tension in my limbs which created great excitement for him. He then ratcheted up the tension another notch. With my diaphragm being pulled tight, I started having trouble breathing. I began to take short breaths and pray for relief as the pain became unbearable. Next, he choked me until I passed out. I thought I was going to die as my air supply was cut off. When I came to, he told me to beg for mercy. I did in a weak voice, because I was unable to fill my lungs with air due to the tension on my diaphragm. Finally, he raped me and forced me to give him oral sex which made breathing even more difficult. I knew I had to endure the pain and suffer until "he" was finished.

From the bottom of my blindfold, I saw him using his entire frame of six feet, four inches to pull the wench as hard as he could. I fiercely prayed for God to help me. Suddenly, the eye hook securing my left wrist broke, freeing my hand, and removing the tension from my body. At last, I could breathe.

Master was mad his toy had broken. He released me from the stretcher and told me to go to the bathroom and fix my hands. After suspension, my hands would feel numb from lack of circulation. I ran hot water over them and flexed my fingers until life returned to my hands. This time was different. The tension produced by the stretcher was far greater than the weight of my body. My back was in such pain I couldn't stand up straight. Draping over the bathroom sink, I slowly massaged my hands.

Back in the box my left shoulder was in constant pain. I cried and prayed for relief. I never told Master about my shoulder because I knew he wouldn't care. After five days, I finally told the Lord, "I can't take this anymore. You've got to help me." While lying flat on my back, I put my left arm up so that my elbow was touching the top of the box. With my right hand, I hit the back of my left arm hard enough it snapped my shoulder back into place. I had been suffering from a dislocated shoulder. I was to visit the stretcher again, but less tension was placed on my body the second time around.

Sometime later, I was taken out of the box and given a bottle of Cold Duck, an alcoholic drink.

"Drink this," Master ordered.

I placed the bottle to my lips and began to sip. I noticed Ma'am was naked and tied spread-eagle on the waterbed.

"I said drink it." Master took the bottle and forced me to gulp the Cold Duck. "The Company has ordered a test. Get on the bed and have oral sex with my wife."

Feeling drunk, I staggered to the bed and tried to comply with orders. After a minute or two, Master stopped me and returned me to the box. I could hear them having sex on the bed above, and they could hear me getting sick below. I empted my stomach into the bedpan and continued to have a series of dry heaves. Master removed me from the box and placed me in the shower with the cold water running over me.

"Lord, please don't let me die like this," I prayed, as the dry heaves kept coming. After 10 minutes, I was back in the box feeling drunk and sick. To this day the thought of drinking Cold Duck makes me sick.

In the fall, another work project came my way. Master told me to get dressed and drove me in his 1970 GMC pickup truck to the vast tracks of forested land near Manton, a small community 25 miles northeast of Red Bluff. I loved getting out, seeing people, and smelling the pine trees.

"See that big man with the beard standing by the junky pickup? He's a member of The Company. You don't want to fall into his hands. I've heard he's hard on women slaves." Master waved to the man and he waved back.

The weather was cold and the work, I soon learned, was hard. Master and I were there to cut cedar post for fencing and firewood. For two days we worked with a chainsaw, wedge, and sledgehammer. Master would later describe these days, working in the woods with his slave by his side, as the best time in his life. I thought otherwise.

On the way home Master ordered me to remove my pants and "play with myself". Under his orders, I penetrated myself with the handle of his whip. Rape with a foreign object became yet another crime committed against me.

Around the same time, Master decided I needed a more private form of slave identification. The stainless steel ring around my neck might cause neighbors to ask questions. With a needle, Master pierced my labia and inserted a gold hoop earring. Nothing was given to me to dull the pain. This along with the electrical burns on my thighs would fulfill The Company requirements for slave identification, Master told me. With a twist of his hands the stainless steel ring, I had worn around my neck for over a year, was gone. I soon learned wearing an earring through my labia could be painful if I was careless when sitting or kneeling.

Before the end of the year yet another work project was started. West of the trailer, under one of the two storage sheds, an underground dungeon called the "hole" was begun. When finished, the hole was to serve as my "new home". Master discussed expanding the hole in the years to come to accommodate four or five additional slaves. It would be my job, as the senior slave, to see to their training and discipline. I prayed to God that day would never come. I knew it would be my responsibility to torture the women until their spirits were broken. I knew this because that's what had been done to me.

We worked two or three hours a night, after Master got home from his job. I would dig the hole with a pick and shovel, then place the dirt in a bucket. Using a rope, Master would pull the bucket from the hole and spread the dirt in the orchard and garden east of the trailer. Other nights would be spent making concrete bricks to line the hole. It would be two years before the hole was ready for occupancy.

Bizarre tortures and work projects did occur during the year, but most of my time was spent in my box sleeping, day dreaming, and praying. I was allowed out to empty my bedpan, eat, and clean the kitchen. I was always watched and supervised by either Master or Ma'am. The isolation and loneliness were hard to endure. I missed having another human to talk with, one-on-one. I pined for someone who truly cared for and loved me as a person.

Toward the end of the year, I was surprised when asked what I wanted for Christmas. I knew immediately what I wanted. Since the day of my abduction, I had been praying to the Lord daily. Why had He tried to warn me in the restroom at Paynes Creek? Why was He sustaining me through all this horror? Why did He send his angels to watch over and protect me? Why had the Lord not given up on me? I was starving for God's word and wanted a closer relationship with Him.

"A Bible," I answered, never expecting to actually see one.

A cold Christmas, my 23rd birthday, and the end of 1979 came and went without any special celebration. I had given up on the idea of receiving a Bible and knew better than to ask about it.

On January 11, 1980, a Bible with a white cover was handed to me.

"Thank you Master and Ma'am," I said with my head bowed. "Don't you think you should inscribe the Bible?"

Turning to the first page Master and Ma'am wrote "a gift to Kay Powers from Cameron and Jan."

From then on, every chance I got, I read my Bible. When I had finished cleaning the kitchen, I would go down on my knees and ask permission to read my Bible before I was put back in the box. When chained by the neck to the toilet in the bathroom late at night, I would read my Bible. I prayed to God for knowledge and understanding, so I could fully comprehend everything I read. Now, for the first time, I was receiving the word of God.

Taste and see that the Lord is good; blessed is the man who takes refuge in Him. Psalms 34:8

Chapter 9 - Limited Freedom

The year, 1980, started out well. I was given three pairs of underwear just before the start of the year. By the end of the year, I would have two pair of shorts, one pair of pants, two tank tops, and one pair of tennis shoes. I would also have my old Pendleton jacket, sleeping bag, toothbrush, and nightgown. All of my clothes, except the nightgown, were used. Dorothy, the neighbor next door, gave me some jeans her husband Al had outgrown and a warm coat when the weather turned cold. Dorothy viewed me as a poor, sad young woman who was in need.

On day while I was in the bathroom, I picked up a pair of nail clippers and started to cut my overgrown nails.

"What do you think you are doing?" Ma'am asked in an angry voice. "Don't you know you must ask permission before you cut your nails, go to the restroom, bathe, or clean your ears?"

"Yes Ma'am," I answered with my head bowed.

Despite this encounter, life was slowly getting better as I was spending more time out of the box. I didn't realize it at the time, but 1980 would be my year of limited freedom or "time-out". Master would see how much freedom he could give me and still maintain control.

Dates on the calendar had little meaning to me. Occasionally, a holiday would mark an event to a certain date in my memory. Such was the case when Master took me on a trip to Reno, Nevada, around the Easter holiday. As usual, no explanation was given for the trip. I was just told to get in the car. He liked keeping me in the dark, both physically and mentally.

"I've made a bet with another slave owner, whose slave begged for money at a rock concert, that you could make more money panhandling. Go up to people and tell 'em you're broke and need money to get home," Master told me once we arrived in Reno. He took me to a Jehovah Witness Convention where I was to approach people and ask for money. The money I received was handed over to Master. That night we ate fast-food and slept in the car at the MGM Hotel parking lot. The next day, he had me panhandling on the Reno gambling strip. I was concerned the police would think I was a prostitute and arrest me. I feared The Company more than the police. Any problems, such as getting arrested for prostitution, might cause The Company to become involved.

That night we started back to California, but were delayed by heavy snows in the mountain pass around Truckee. A set of tire chains were purchased, and back to Red Bluff we drove through the night. Once back home, Master gave his wife a beautiful Easter lily he had purchased before returning home. I was returned to my box.

Master made me panhandle two more times. Once, I begged for money at the Downtown Mall in Redding, a larger town 30 miles to the north of Red Bluff. Surprisingly, the next time I panhandled was in Red Bluff at Raley's Supermarket and Payless Drugstore where the Hooker family did their shopping.

"Young lady you need to move along. Panhandling is not permitted in Red Bluff," a uniformed police officer told me as I stood in the store parking lot. I was both frightened and relieved that the officer had approached me.

"Yes, Sir," I replied not wanting to cause any problems that might draw the attention of The Company. Master wasn't too concerned, but thankfully that was the last of my panhandling experiences. I really hated asking people for money.

Ma'am quit her job at Foster Freeze in January. In May, she started working the swing shift from 10:00 AM until 4:00 PM at Pac-Out, a fast-food business in Redding. For the first time, I was alone with the children from midmorning until Master came home, late in the afternoon. I had now become a trusted slave.

In June, my night time living accommodations were upgraded from the box under the waterbed to the back bathroom where a chain, five feet in length, connected my neck to the toilet. With the chain padlocked to my neck, I could stand up straight. I had been chained to the toilet before, but now I was spending many more nights in the back bathroom.

In July, Ma'am quit her Pac-Out job and started working for JLA Electronics from 7:00 AM until 3:30 PM. This resulted in me spending most of the day alone with the children. Ma'am would tell me each day what to cook and how to cook it. I knew dinner had better be on time and properly cooked or else a beating would follow. Reasons for a beating included not peeling the potatoes fast enough, leaving a little piece of peeling on the potatoes, or lumps in the mashed potatoes. Everything I was told to do was closely scrutinized. Nothing was ever good enough, and my performance was always criticized either by Master or Ma'am. I was in a no win situation.

Most of the time, I cooked meat and potatoes for Master. I ate mostly rice and oatmeal which continued to be purchased in large bags at discount prices. In the summer, garden food would supplement the family diet. I was now eating with the family. However, my place was on the floor next to the table. The only time I was permitted to eat at the table was when other family members, such as their parents, were present. For entertainment Master watched hours and hours of television. As previously noted, television was insignificant to me as a child and nonexistent to me as a slave.

During the day when the children were taking a nap, I had the trailer to myself. I had access to an open door, telephone, and neighbors, but fear of The Company kept me in check. To pick up the phone and call my parents in Riverside would not only endanger them, but would result in painful torture to myself.

Soon, Ma'am was bringing home work from JLA for me to complete. I was given a pile of transistors and a cutting machine. Different pieces of metal, depending on the purpose of the transistor, were trimmed off with the machine. As Master and Ma'am slept, I worked into the night until the job was completed. Then I was allowed to sleep on the living room floor in my sleeping bag. Ma'am would return the finished work to JLA in the morning.

All went well until JLA announced they would not pay Ma'am overtime. That's when she brought home an employment application for me to fill out. From my purse, Master had my Social Security number, date of birth, and my home address. Using this information, he completed the application.

"K, sign this employment application with your pre-slave name, Colleen Stan," Master said. By now, Master felt safe enough to use my real name and Social Security number. It had been three years since my kidnapping, and no one appeared to be searching for me.

The next morning Ma'am returned the application to JLA and I was entered into their employment rolls. My pay check, which I endorsed as Colleen Stan, went directly into Master's bank account. The job lasted about two months before it stopped. I was never told why the job ended.

For me, the stories about The Company never ended. One story told of a man who put his slave on the auction block, but he didn't receive a single bid for her. He was so mad, he took the girl out in the hallway and nailed her breast to a banister. Then he just walked away and left her.

"K, two men from The Company will be visiting us tomorrow. You will be required to serve them and show your obedience. They may want to test your loyalty by seeing you hung," Master said, terrorizing me. Late the next day, I asked Ma'am about The Company men.

"Oh, they couldn't make it," Ma'am said. "They'll come another day."

Master was always thinking of some new way to terrorize his slave. Late one afternoon, he told me to get in the car. We drove deep into the forest, east of town, to an isolated patch of tall pine trees. Master stopped the car and told me to get out. We walked about 30 yards into the forest.

"Remove all your clothes including your shoes," he ordered. "Here's your sleeping bag, a gallon of water, a sandwich, and an apple. I will be back to get you tomorrow morning." He walked back to his car and drove away.

Alone in the woods, I never knew if Master had gone home or was just down the road watching me. I tried to make myself comfortable, but the ants and the cold temperature made the night in the woods miserable. My teeth chattered uncontrollably throughout the night. Early the next morning, I heard hunters firing their rifles. I got down close to the ground not wanting to be hit by a stray bullet or mistaken for a deer. I was fearful as to what the hunters might do if they came across a naked woman in the woods. I kept quiet and waited. By midmorning, Master returned and drove me back to the mobile home. Without a word, I was placed in my box and the panels were bolted shut.

Also during this time frame, Master gave me some sleeping pills to see what they would do to me. I became drowsy, but was too frightened to sleep. I kept thinking about what Master might want to do to me if I went to sleep. He also tried to hypnotize me, without much success. Master knew no limits as to what he could do to me. Later in the year, he ordered me to start a diary listing everything I had experienced in life, including my time in slavery. The writing of the diary would later get me in trouble with Ma'am and be used against me in court.

I was thankful to be spending so much time out of the box. In time, I learned to tell Master what he wanted to hear which improved the quality of my life. On the 3rd anniversary of my abduction, I gave Master a card in which I wrote:

"Sometimes I feel that being your slave has made me more of a woman. But then there are other times when I feel it has made me feel less of a woman. You know how to make me feel good about myself. And I love you so much for it. I only wish that my dreams could be fulfilled with you. Because I fell a strong love and need to be with you (sic). I'll always serve you with singleness of heart. K"

Such words seemed to sooth the savage beast. Torture periods were reduced in time and intensity. Of course, this was all a front and a lie. Telling Master I loved him was a survival strategy not an emotional feeling. I could never have loved the man who had brought me so much pain. When one is held against their will, they often do and say things that they normally wouldn't do or say.

As summer approached, I was spending more time outdoors working in the garden. I worked hard hoeing and pulling weeds. Once again, our garden was the best kept on Weed Court making our neighbors jealous. I was told if any of the neighbors talked to me, I was to be nice and talk only about the garden and animals. I was never to discuss myself. I always obeyed and worked hard. I knew anything less would result in a beating or my quick return to the box.

My most enjoyable activity was caring for Charity and Amber, ages four and two, respectively. They were both innocent little angels. To them, I was their live-in babysitter. Charity, the older one, was reserved and easy going. Amber, the younger one, was feistier and let you know what she thought. I loved them both and never blamed them for my situation. Watching them grow and learn was the only thing that brought a smile to my face during all the years of my captivity. The two girls, now grown women today, will never know how much they helped me keep my sanity during those difficult times.

One day Amber gave me a sticker with a picture of a tennis player. Stickers were popular with young children. The problem was where to stick the sticker. The answer was the only thing I owned in the household, my Bible. Amber was happy seeing the picture of the tennis player on the white front cover of my Bible. The sticker, like me, would remain there for years.

Whereas Ma'am was unaware of me being raped, the children were equally unaware of the atrocities that occurred in the trailer. However, early one Saturday morning before anyone was out of bed, Charity opened the back bathroom door where I was sleeping with my neck chained to the toilet.

"Kay, I'm hungry. Could you get me some cereal?" I don't think she noticed the chain around my neck or the fact that I couldn't leave the bathroom.

"Why don't you ask your mommy and daddy, sweetie. They can help you." From that day forward, Master ordered me to lock the bathroom door from the inside.

Periodically, I would be returned to the box without any explanation. It was during one such time that I experienced one of the strangest events of my captivity. Without a word, I was taken out of my box and told to shower. Ma'am brushed my hair and put makeup on me.

"Okay, what's up?" I wondered, as a pair of jeans and a nice blouse was laid out for me to wear.

"You two are going out," Master told me. This would be my first excursion without Master by my side. Ma'am drove me to The New Orleans, a nearby bar in Red Bluff. She ordered a couple of drinks for us and soon a couple of guys, Larry and Ray, joined us. The men invited us to Sambo's Restaurant for coffee and then over to their apartment. Ma'am who attached herself to Larry, disappeared with him into one of the back bedrooms and closed the door. Awkwardly, I was left with Ray feeling very embarrassed.

Slowly, Ray gently put his arms around me and gave me a few hugs followed by a kiss or two. He did most of the talking about his recent plans and employment prospects. I listened politely without volunteering any information about myself. What was I going to tell him, "I'm a sex slave who lives in a box?" By now, fear of The Company was deeply embedded in my soul.

Later, Ma'am and Larry rejoined us in the living room. We were driven back to the bar where we told the guys good night and then drove back to the mobile home. Off came the nice clothes, the makeup, and back into the box I went. I was taken out on a "date" by Ma'am one other time where I danced with a guy, had one drink, and then returned home with Ma'am.

Like everything else, I never knew why Master had allowed Ma'am to take me to a bar looking for guys. I can only guess they were having marital problems. Master had his slave and Ma'am wanted a boyfriend. Ma'am may have gone out again without me, but I was never again to paint the town.

Discounting the sexual abuse, I was being treated better with more freedom than ever before. My goal was to be a good slave and stay out of the box as much as I could. Despite my limited freedom, I remained a slave who was fearful of The Company.

One hot summer day, I was handed a swim suit, told to put it on, and get in the car. I wondered if this was yet another test mandated by The Company. Instead, I discovered Master's brother had invited all of us to go water skiing in his boat on Black Butte Lake, 30 miles south of Red Bluff. I assumed Master wanted to see me fall on my face, but water skiing was something I had done back in Southern California when I was young. I hated to disappoint Master, but I had little difficulty skiing at ease around the lake.

On June 6, 1980, I was taken to Chico to watch the children while Master and Ma'am shopped. Chico is a university town, 40 miles southeast of Red Bluff. In Chico one of my deepest desires was surprisingly fulfilled.

"I'm going to let you call home," Master said, "but you had better not say anything wrong. If you do, I will cut off the call and make you wish you hadn't." Using a public phone at a gas station, Master placed a call to the home telephone of my dad. When the phone started to ring, he handed the telephone to me keeping his fingers near the receiver switch to quickly disconnect the call. The phone rang three times before someone answered.

"Hello," my sister said.

"Bonnie it's me, Colleen."

"Who is this?"

"It's Colleen your sister," I said, realizing it had been over three years since any family member had heard my voice.

"Colleen! Where are you?" Bonnie's asked, with excitement in her voice. I'm sure I was a voice from the dead to her.

"Oh ..., I'm up north," I replied cautiously, "How is everybody?"

"We're Okay. How are you?"

"I'm fine." I replied.

"Dad's at work, Colleen. He should be back by 6:00 PM. What have you been doing with yourself?"

"I've been staying with some friends," I said.

Our conversation continued for about five minutes as Bonnie updated me on family news. Suddenly, I noticed Master was waving for me to end the call.

"Bonnie, I've got to go. Tell everyone I love and miss them," I quickly said.

"I will Colleen," were Bonnie's last words.

"Bye, bye," I said as Master ended the phone call.

Later, back in the box I thanked God, not Master, for allowing me to live long enough to talk to my family. Bonnie, I would learn years later, immediately went to my dad's work site and told him about the call. Dad was so excited he uncharacteristically shut down the work site for the day. He returned home expecting another telephone call which never came. The telephone company traced the call to a pay phone in Chico, which gave my dad little to go on concerning my whereabouts.

A few months later, I had another chance to communicate with my family. I was given a sheet of paper and pen to write a letter home. No reason was given nor did I ask why. After more than three years, I was being allowed to contact my family. I wrote the letter in general terms discussing my work in the garden and the canning of fresh vegetables. Three times the letter had to be rewritten because Master didn't like this or that. Finally, I was told the letter was okay and would be mailed. Two more letters followed in the weeks to come, each being mailed from Chico with no return address.

One day, I asked Master if I could visit my family in Riverside.

"The Company wouldn't allow such a visit," Master said. "A very large security deposit would have to be paid to The Company for such a visit. In fact, no slave has ever visited their family."

In the late summer or early fall, I was allowed to telephone my dad twice in one day. Both times the calls were made from a pay phone in

Chico with Master monitoring the conversation. At least the people back home knew I was still alive.

Why was I being allowed to call and write home? Was this a reward for being such an obedient slave? What did all this mean? I knew from experience things could change in the twinkling of an eye. One miss step and I would find myself back in the dark box.

Sadistic acts on me alone couldn't satisfy Master. From under their bed, I could periodically hear Master beating his wife. She would cry out, but I couldn't make out any conversations between them. Apparently, one woman was not enough for Master's sadistic appetite.

One event especially stands out in my mind. Master told me to take the children outside the trailer and play with them. The girls were playing on a patch of grass near the front of the mobile home. Through the thin walls of the trailer, I could hear Ma'am crying as Master was whipping her.

"Why is mommy crying?" Charity asked.

"You bastard," I thought to myself, not wanting to alarm the girls.

"No, I don't hear anything. Why don't we play at the other end of the trailer," I told the girls.

During this period, Ma'am never showed any kindness towards me. She probably never liked having a female slave in her household. Anything I did wasn't up to her standards and she was quick to let Master know.

"K was slow again putting the dishes away. I told K to sweep the floor before she started dinner. K was disrespectful to me this morning," Ma'am would tell Master.

One afternoon while Master and Ma'am were at work, I was working in the garden while the children napped. Dorothy Coppa, an elderly woman who lived next to our mobile home with her husband, noticed I was crying.

"Kay, what's wrong," she asked, with sympathy in her voice?

"It's Jan," I said, still softly crying.

"Tell me about it Kay." Dorothy said.

Dorothy was a sweet, old woman who was always kind to me. She saw me as a down-and-out young woman with no money and no place to go. I wanted so badly to tell her my problems, but knew any information about my slave status would endanger her. The Company would visit Dorothy if she became a problem. I didn't want to bring Dorothy into my world and cause her any harm.

"Oh, it's nothing. I don't want to talk about it," I said, trying to dry my eyes.

"I know people at the church who can help you Kay. They can give you shelter and help you get back on your feet. Why don't you let me call them?" Dorothy said, with deep concern for my welfare.

"No, I'll be okay, but thank you," I replied. I wanted to scream out that I was being held against my will, raped, and tortured. I came close to telling this kind, elderly woman everything, but I knew better.

"Why don't we pray together," Dorothy said.

"Yes," I replied.

Dorothy never knew what was going on just a short distance from her mobile home, however she knew something wasn't right in the Hooker household.

In the late fall, the underground dungeon, or hole as it was called, was finished. It had taken two years to complete the project. The hole had been constructed under the floor of the southern most of the two storage sheds, west of the mobile home. Inside the shed was a concrete floor which contained the entrance to the hole. The entryway was 27 inches wide and 34 inches long. A removable ladder extended from the entryway to the floor of the hole, eight feet below. The high ceiling was designed so I could be suspended by my wrists. The floor of the hole measured 10 feet by 10 feet. The walls were made of concrete bricks, handmade by Master and I. On the north wall were two arched niches, 18 inches wide and 24 inches high. They were to allow for future expansion of the hole, under the north shed. Master expected to capture four or five additional women and confine them in the expanded portion of the hole someday. As senior slave, I would be expected to train and punish the new girls.

"Oh God, please don't allow Master to capture more slaves. I don't want to see other women tortured," were my thoughts. Training new slaves horrified me.

"This is going to be your 'new home', " Master said, as I climbed down the ladder into the hole. In the hole were a lawn chair, my sleeping bag, a single electric light bulb, my Bible, and a small battery-powered radio. Master climbed up and removed the ladder.

"If anyone finds you down here, tell them you're down here for peace of mind and to feel closer to God," Master told me before he closed the plywood cover. I climbed on the chair and pushed on the plywood a couple of times, but discovered it was too heavy for me to move. Master must have placed something on top of the cover.

I spent a couple of nights in the dungeon before it slowly started to rain. From November to March, Red Bluff receives on the average over 18 inches of rain. When Master came home late in the afternoon from work, I was standing in knee-deep water. At first we tried to bucket the water out. I would fill a pale and he would host it out with a rope. Next came a pump, but still the water was knee-deep. It would soon became evident to him his underground dungeon was unworkable. Out of the hole I came, after one week, and back into the box I went.

As Christmas approached, the family decorated the trailer for the holiday season. The children and I had been collecting aluminum cans along the side of the roads near the trailer. The money from the cans would be used by the girls to buy Christmas gifts for their parents. On Christmas Eve, I was allowed to telephone my dad from the mobile home, instead of a pay phone in Chico. Master knew The Company would be monitoring the call, and I knew I had better not say anything wrong.

"Colleen, what's your phone number?" Dad asked during the conversation.

"Oh, this is not my phone. I ….. I will give it to you some other time," I said, as Master and Ma'am hovered over me.

"When will you be coming home?" Dad kept inquiring.

"Soon," I answered, using the same answer Master had given me many times before.

Five minutes after I hung up, I started crying. Master allowed me to make a second telephone call to my dad.

Before Christmas, I was allowed to make a baby blanket for Erica. I knew a baby was expected in my family when I was abducted, but it wasn't until I spoke to family members that I learned Erica had been born in September, 1977. I wrapped the blanket in brown paper and addressed it for mailing. When I gave it to Master and Ma'am, they tore open the package and inspected the contents. After I had re-wrapped the blanket in front of them, Ma'am mailed it for me.

As the gifts were being handed out on Christmas morning, I didn't expect to receive anything.

"I believe there's something under the tree for K," Ma'am said. Surprised, I retrieved a large box and slowly removed the wrapping paper. Inside the box I found a practical gift. That year for Christmas, slave K received a new sleeping bag.

"Thank you Master and Ma'am," I said humbly, as I removed the green Coleman sleeping bag with a red lining from the box.

A few days later I turned age 24 in the back bathroom with a chain padlocked around my neck. Next year, 1981, would bring an exciting climax to my limited freedom. I started the year with hopes and prayers.

Chapter 10 - Home Visit

Over time, I proved myself to be a good, trustworthy slave. In February, 1981, I was unchained from the toilet and allowed to sleep on the living room floor in my sleeping bag. However, all was not well in the Hooker mobile home. Ma'am continued to focus her anger and jealousy in my direction. I remained a respectful slave, doing as I was told, but nothing seemed to please Ma'am. She took her complaints directly to Master who soon grew tired of hearing about all my short comings. During this time period, Ma'am may have found the diary Master directed me to write. She read about my so called "love" for Master and the countless sexual encounters (rapes) between us. The straw that broke the camels back may have been Charity calling me "Mom". Tensions had reached a boiling point. Something had to be done.

I was taken out in the forest east of Red Bluff and tied between two trees. With a whip, Master started to beat me.

"I'm not going to take any more of this bickering between you and my wife. I'm the master of this household and you had better start being more respectful towards my wife."

"I'm sorry Master. I will do better," I cried. Truthfully, I was in the dark about what he was talking about. I was showing respect towards Ma'am and had not argued with her. I was the slave.

In February, Ma'am stopped working for JLA Electronics and started staying home with the kids. Unbeknownst to me, big decisions were being made about my future.

In early March, Master had me kneeling before him with my head bowed and arms at my sides.

"The Company has agreed to permit a visit with your family in Riverside. A slave has never before been allowed to visit their family. Of course, an additional $30,000 security fee will be deducted from my account with The Company. They will provide extra security personnel, phone taps, and bugs in your parent's home. If there are any problems, security men will swarm the house and people will get hurt. I hope you appreciate what I'm doing for you."

"Thank you, Master," I said.

"Before you go, The Company will want to test you to see if you're obedient and can be trusted. They may want to hang you up and whip you."

Preparations for The Company testing began immediately. Master took me to his father's farm on Highway 99. His father owned a small farm a few miles south of the mobile home and was not expected home from Klamath Falls, Oregon, until late in the day. Master, Ma'am, the children, Mitzie the family dog, and I drove over to the farm early in the afternoon. Once we arrived, Ma'am took the children inside the farm house. Master took me to a large red barn full of hogs, behind the house. Using a ladder, Master ordered me to climb up to the high rafters in the barn. He tied my wrists to the rafters and removed the ladder. In pain, I dangled several feet above the ground.

Suddenly, Mitzie began to bark. Mitzie was a great watch dog, but a terrible guard dog. He always warned Master when anyone approached the trailer, or in this situation his father's barn.

Master had barely gotten me down when the barn door opened and there stood his father. I was stark naked and not sure if his father saw me in the dark barn. I quickly hide behind a stack of feed bags as Master escorted his father out of the barn. I quickly dressed and calmly walked to the farm house.

"Why are your wrists so red?" Charity kept asking.

"Oh, it's nothing dear," I said, trying to hide my wrists behind my back.

That evening we were invited to stay for a family dinner. All of us were seated around a large table. I kept my head down not wanting to draw the attention of Master's father who kept staring at me. Fear, not the food, was what I remember most about that family dinner.

A week before my visit home, I was taken around the neighborhood to tell everyone, including Dorothy, I was going home to Riverside. Dorothy hugged me and pressed a $10 bill into my hands. I knew Dorothy, who worked as a caregiver to elderly people, didn't have much money.

Even Charity and Amber were told I would be going home and their dad would be driving me to the bus station. Both girls gave me a big hug as they said good bye.

After a sad farewell, I was driven away in Master's pickup truck supposedly to the bus station. Master drove around for a while and then returned to the mobile home with me lying down in the seat. He sneaked me into one of the storage sheds where I stayed under lock and key until dark. After the girls had gone to sleep, I was sprinted into the mobile home, striped naked, and placed back in the box under the waterbed. Master appeared to not want anyone to connect my departure with his later departure. He drove me to the bus station, it appeared, and returned home alone within the hour.

It had been months since I had been locked in the total darkness. Once again the claustrophobic effect came back to me as I couldn't see my own hand in front of my face in the lightproof box. Master told me that the box was necessary to prepare me for whatever The Company might demand of me.

In the coming days, I was hung by my wrists in the frame and beat with a whip. I kept my legs motionless and took the punishment without crying. My final test came a few days later when I was taken out of my box and told to kneel down.

"I want you to put the barrel of this shotgun in your mouth and pull the trigger," Master ordered.

Without hesitation I placed the weapon in my mouth and did as I was told. "Click," the hammer dropped on an empty chamber. Apparently, I had passed the test. I was now ready, but still fearful of The Company test.

Finally, the day came for me to go home and visit my family. Early in the morning on Friday, March 20, I was awaken and told to shower. On that day, I wore a peach colored, V-neck, short sleeve, terry cloth top. I also had on pants and tennis shoes. I packed a few of my things in Master's 1979 Chevy Vega and climbed in the passenger seat. The Dodge Colt, used in my kidnapping, had not been running for sometime and remained parked nearby.

It was a clear, cool day with the sun starting to rise when we started out. I lay down in the seat until we had cleared the neighborhood. Once on Interstate 5, I was allowed to sit up and watch the scenery fly by. Gradually, grazing land turned to orchards and then into cultivated fields as we drove south towards Southern California.

"I have to stop and check in with The Company," Master said, as we pulled off the interstate in Sacramento. "They will probably want to test you before you visit your family."

I was excited about seeing my family, but scared of The Company test. I didn't know what they were going to do to me. We drove to a high rise building near the state capital and stopped. There were no signs on the impressive looking building other than the street address.

"Wait in the car while I see what The Company wants to do to you," Master said.

What would they do to me? Would I be hung up? Given a lie detector test? Shown the woman in the glass coffin? What form of torture would I under go? I was ready for anything because I wanted to see my family. I knew if I didn't pass their test, the trip would end right here in Sacramento. Nervously, I sat in the car praying.

After 15 or 20 minutes, Master emerged from the building with some papers in his hand. He opened the car door and got in the driver's seat.

"This is your lucky day. The Company is too busy to see you today. Here's a permit allowing you to carry the money Dorothy gave you," Master said, as he handed me a card. The card had a seal identical to the one on my slave contract.

"Oh yes, the secretary said to wish you luck," Master said.

We drove south all day on Interstate 5 through some of the most productive farmland in America. On the way down, Master instructed me as to what to say to my family. He also outlined the security measures The Company had in place around my family home in Riverside. In the San Fernando Valley, north of Los Angeles, we stopped at a McDonald's fast-food restaurant where Master bought each of us a small hamburger with fries. Neither of us had eaten all day.

In Los Angeles, we turned east on Highway 60 which ran directly to Riverside. Once we entered the city, I became excited. It had been four years since I had last seen my family. The plan was for Master to spend the night at a local motel while I visited home. As we drove through Riverside, I pointed out various motels where Master might stay. We stopped at a pay telephone where I called my dad to let him know I would be home soon. After a 12 hour drive, there was still some daylight remaining in the cloudless sky.

"Master, may I please stop at my grandma's house and briefly say hello?" I asked.

When we stopped at my grandma's house, I jumped out of the car and ran to her front door. When I saw her, I gave her a big hug. I told her we were going over to my dad's house and would return later. Plans were quickly made to attend church together the next day.

I returned to the car and we drove the short distance to my dad's house on Coolidge Avenue. Full of excitement, I jumped out and ran up the sidewalk to the front door, knocked, and immediately went inside. Master drove away without meeting my family.

Coolidge Avenue House, 1989

Dad's house was on a quite street in a working man's neighborhood with freshly mowed lawns. The house, built in the early 1950's, was a single story, terracotta-colored, ranch-style with a hip roof. The house was small, with a single car garage, and an evaporative air conditioner in the front window. I knew the house well and felt at home.

"Colleen, we're so glad to see you!" In the house were my father, his wife Ruth, Ruth's children, and my sister Bonnie. Jenise, my other sister, and my mom, who lived down the street at the corner of Mary Street and Victoria Avenue, came over soon after I arrived. The house was filled with hugs and kisses as I embraced each family member. In this house I was Colleen, not K.

The conversations were warm and loving, but there was a barrier between us that no one crossed. I wanted to tell my family the truth about the cruel man who had brought me to Riverside, but I couldn't. Fear of The Company and what they would do to my family kept my lips sealed. I knew what had been done to me and didn't want any harm to come to the people I loved.

I'm sure my family wanted to ask, "Colleen, where have you been for the past four years? Why didn't you stay in touch? What's wrong?" These questions and others were never asked because my family was afraid any pressure might drive me away forever. If I was a runaway, the police had told my parents, there was little either they or my family could do. After all, I was an adult.

In addition, my family had recently seen a movie where a young woman had come home only to abruptly return to a religious cult after her family asked too many questions and became too pushy. My family waited for me to say something first about my long absence.

My loss of weight, pale skin, home-made clothes, and lack of money convinced some, especially my sister Bonnie, I was in a cult. Religious cults were prevalent in California in the 1970's and 80's. My sad, tired appearance convinced them even more so of my cult membership.

Colleen's Home Visit, 1981

My family treated me with kid gloves, which was good since any direct questions about my past would have only increased my anxiety. They didn't ask and I didn't volunteer any information. We continued to talk about recent family events such as marriages, new babies, and illnesses in the family. I cherished every moment being with the people I loved so much.

Later in the evening, my sister Jenise brought over a neutral-colored wrap dress, with a V-neck, and ruffled short sleeves. I used the money Dorothy gave me to purchase a pair of panty hose. With a pair of borrowed shoes, I would be ready for church the next morning. I savored the moment as Jenise stood in the doorway of the kitchen watching me press my dress with a hot iron. We talked, as only sisters could, about things of common interest. It was great talking with someone who truly cared about me as a person.

Colleen with her Father, 1981

That night, after everyone else had gone to bed, Bonnie and I stayed up late into the night talking sister-to-sister about family events I had missed.

"Colleen, why haven't you written or called regularly like you did when you first arrived in Oregon?" Bonnie asked, in a serious tone of voice.

"I ...I didn't ...have the money to buy stamps or make phone calls," I answered, hesitantly. "I was too busy working, babysitting, and ...ah...working in the garden."

Bonnie was now convinced I was hiding my cult involvement. Cults were noted for demanding its followers turn over all their money and break all contact with their families. Why else would I have not stayed in contact with my family for almost four years?

I came close to telling Bonnie the truth late that night, but once again I stopped just short. I wanted to stay up all night, but I had to go to church the next morning. At 2:00 AM I finally went to bed alone in the back bedroom of my dad's house.

"Lord, thank you for my family. Thank you for softening my Master's heart and for The Company allowing me to visit home. Thank you Lord for every precious moment I had with my family," I prayed. I wouldn't have traded my visit for anything in the world.

I awoke around 8:00 AM after six hours of sleep. With my borrowed dress, I quickly headed to church with Bonnie and my grandma. Worship services for The Seventh Day Adventist Church are held on Saturday. My grandma, who was deeply religious, had watched the church affiliated television program "The Voice of Prophecy" for years. She had sent in money to the program and had asked them to pray for my safe return.

"We've got to go to church," was the first thing my grandma said to me. In church we all prayed to the same God, but I don't think we prayed for the same thing. I prayed for freedom from slavery. I thanked God for my presence in church with Bonnie and grandma.

After church, all of the family drove to the nearby town of Sunny Mead, which today is called Moreno Valley. We visited my Aunt Jean who was undergoing chemo-therapy for breast cancer. The source of my middle name, Jean, caused me to feel especially close to my aunt. She looked weak and tired with gray hair. The cancer had taken so much from her. Still, I was so glad and thankful to see her sensing her time was short.

We had pizza for lunch, talked, and drank coffee late into the afternoon. Not since Eugene, Oregon, had I talked with close friends over coffee. When we returned to my dad's house, the telephone rang, and a voice asked for me.

"Hello," I answered.

"It's me [Master]. I'll be over in 10 minutes to pick you up."

"Yes Sir," I said, as I hung up the phone. I was upset. Time had gone by so fast and Master was on his way. I was expecting the entire weekend, not just 24 hours.

"Hello, my name's Mike. I'm here to pick up Colleen," Master said, as he entered the front living room. After short introductions to family members, Master announced, "I'm Colleen's fiancé. I've known her for a few months, and we plan to get married soon." Master went on to tell my family he was in the computer business and had just attended a seminar in San Diego. Since we were in the Riverside area, I had asked him to drop me off for a short visit.

"Colleen, we need to get on the road," Master said.

"What's your phone number Mike," someone asked?

"Well …we … ah, we are in the process of moving to Klamath Falls, Oregon. I'll send it to you once we're settled," he replied.

Unbeknownst to me, Bonnie had followed Ruth, my stepmother, to the back of the house to retrieve a camera. An argument quickly ensued between the two women.

"Something's wrong out there [in the living room]", Bonnie declared in a loud voice to Ruth. "I don't like the way Colleen's acting around Mike. With Tim [Stan] she was more affectionate and had a shine in her eyes. I'm not going to let her leave until I find out what's going on. I will block the door with my body if I have to," Bonnie said, with determination.

"Keep your voice down," Ruth said, in a hushed tone. "You're over reacting. You don't want to upset Colleen and drive her away forever do you?" Ruth, with camera in hand, went back into the living room.

"Colleen let's take some pictures of you and Mike before you leave," Ruth said.

With smiling faces, a number of photos were taken of me with various family members. "How about you Mike," Ruth said. "We want a picture of you and Colleen together." I wrapped my arms around

Mike and smiled for the camera. Like an actress on a stage, I was doing my part to keep the show going. Later the photograph would be used against me in court to show I "loved" Mike [Master].

Colleen with Cameron Hooker, 1981

After we had driven away from my dad's house, I begged Master for one quick visit with my mother who lived down the street. He stopped the car, I jumped out, and ran in to tell her good-bye. Once again, I almost lost it. I came very close to telling her the truth about the monster waiting for me in the car. Fearing The Company, I just gave her a big hug, told her I loved her, and returned to the car crying.

"How was your visit?" Master asked, further down the road.

"It was wonderful. Thank you Master. I'm so glad The Company allowed me to visit," I replied. We departed Riverside around 7:00 PM on Saturday, March 21. Not much else was said as we drove through the night back to Red Bluff.

Twelve hours later, the sun was just starting to rise on a Sunday morning as we arrived home. It was a beautiful spring sunrise which I admired from the car window, not knowing it would be my last sunrise for sometime. The trailer was vacant with Ma'am and the kids staying over at her parents.

Master had me vacuum out my box which was something he had me do once or twice a year. The blanket or sleeping bag in the box was also washed once a year. Next, I was told to take a shower which I knew preceded rape. I shook as I showered because I knew sex with Master always came with no foreplay and physical pain. After the rape, I was never allowed to shower. When Master had finished with me on the living room floor, I was ordered to get into the box. The particle board panel was bolted shut and then the end panel of the waterbed was closed. Lastly, the heavy wooden steps were placed at the foot of the waterbed covering the end panel. I was sealed in my tomb.

Throughout my captivity, I was never told what was going to happen next or why. This lack of knowledge was used by Master to maintain a continuous element of fear and control over me. Anytime I was taken out of the box, I never knew what to expect. Fear of the unknown was always with me as I was kept in the dark both physically and mentally.

This lack of knowledge may have been a good thing in one sense. If I had known the length of my entombment after returning from Riverside, I'm not sure I would have survived. Of course, I'm not sure even Master knew how long he was going to keep me in the box.

A few days passed then a few more. Then weeks passed followed by months. Months slowly turned into years. I would spend the next three years of my life (1981-1984) in the box sleeping, dreaming, and praying.

I have to assume my lengthy confinement in the box came about because Master was concerned he had given me too much freedom. Maybe he felt he was losing control of his slave. Too many neighbors had seen me, and questions about my status in the Hooker household were surely to arise. A fast thinking family member in Riverside may have copied down his vehicle tag number. What if the police knocked on his door one day looking for Colleen Stan? What if they searched the mobile home? Would anyone think to look under a waterbed for the girl in a box? Master wanted to keep me out of sight until the heat had passed.

The other reason for putting me into storage was Ma'am. I'm sure she wanted me out of her life, out of her children's lives, and out of her husband's life. Master was not ready to let his slave go. Cloistering was the only answer.

My daily routine soon became predictive as I was allowed out late in the evening after the girls had gone to bed. I emptied my bedpan, drank a large glass of water, and ate cold leftovers in the front bathroom. Sometimes the leftovers were truly leftovers that had been out all day and the family didn't want. Other than leftovers, servings of rice or oatmeal became the norm each night. Meat, fresh fruit, and vegetables were rarely seen. After eating, I was returned to the box until the next evening. My isolation was so great, even Charity and Amber were unaware of my presence in the single-wide mobile home.

I thought the worst was over after my year of limited freedom and a visit with my family, but I was wrong. Regular daily feedings were not always the rule. There were times when I averaged four or five meals a week. I soon became very nervous and anxious as I spent both days and nights without light. Slowly, my hair started to fall out due to a combination of stress, lack of a proper diet, no exercise, and limited human contact. Once after showering, I was told to step on the bathroom scale. My weight had dropped from 135 pounds when kidnapped to 98 pounds.

I soon learned what dehydration and starvation did to the human body and mind. First my body would sweat and my stomach would growl. After 12 or so hours, my body would stop sweating and become cold and dry. My mind felt like I was floating on another plane as I became weaker and weaker.

In the summer of 1981, Master and the family went on a three day weekend trip. They left me locked in the box with a quart size Mason jar of water and chocolate chip cookies. That summer, Red Bluff hit its all time recorded high temperature of 121 degrees. The interior of the box was like an oven. The cookies and water were quickly consumed. By the time the family returned and Master finally got around to letting me out, I was too weak to stand on my feet. I will never know how close I was to death from heat exhaustion and dehydration.

Once I got really angry while in the box. Lack of water and the heat were driving me out of my mind. "I'm getting out of here," I thought.

I scooted down, bent my knees, and kicked the end of the box until something broke.

"Oh my God," I thought. "He's going to kill me when he sees what I've done." I got really scared and stopped kicking the box. I'll never know if I could have kicked my way out since a second panel and the steps blocked my way. The strange thing was when Master came home he fixed the panel with a piece of wood and the repercussions, which I feared, never came.

One more thing about the construction of the box I should mention. I was in a box within a box, which created a double-wall around me. Between the walls was a hollow space about 6 inches wide. In this space, which I could see when I crawled in and out of my box, Master kept my personal items such as my purse, driver's license, and Social Security card. Strangely, in the open space was a wallet size photo of a young woman with long, dark hair and equally dark eyes. I never knew who she was or why she was in the storage space between the two walls. As a slave, I knew better than to ask questions.

The air holes in the box deserve a detailed description since they were of such importance in my life. A hose in the first air hole carried dank air from under the trailer to the air blower to the left of my head as I lay on my back. As previously described, the air blower was a woman's hair dryer with the heating element disconnected. I went through two or three hair dryers during my captivity. Master purchased them at a local discount store. The second hole in the floor of the box was to let the stale air exit the box. The one and a quarter inch diameter hole allowed me a small window to the outside world. During the day, a small amount of indirect light would find its way under the mobile home. Since the trailer had a skirt of panels around the foundation, the light was further reduced. Still this small amount of light allowed me to tell day from night. If I looked into the hole, I could see the dull shadows of the bare ground below the trailer.

As any prisoner of dark, solitary confinement will tell you, small amounts of light and sound take on great significance. Some sound also came through the hole. At night I could put my ear to the hole and hear trucks traveling up and down Interstate 5. During the day, I could hear dogs barking, vehicles starting, and people at the front door. Once the people entered the trailer, all conversation stopped. Each workday morning, Master would start his vehicle and unintentionally fill my box with exhaust fumes. I would place my hand over the hole to keep the smell of the fumes out. When Master was building a torture device, I could hear the hammering and sawing. I could hear foot steps in the master bedroom along with voices, but I couldn't discern the words being spoken.

Even today, it's hard for me to describe to the average person what it's like to be confined in a box for three years. How do I put such an experience into words? How should I describe the long, mind numbing periods of time? How can anyone who has not been a prisoner in a small cell relate to such an experience? How do I convey the total isolation in the box with the constant whine of the small electric motor of the air blower, the smell of the full bedpan waiting to be emptied, the absence of direct sunlight, the lack of human contact and conversation, the sweat drenching heat, the sparse amounts of food, and the limited amounts of water? All I had to survive on were my day dreams, prayers, and faith in the Lord. God was my only friend.

The isolation in the box was so complete it killed part of me. I had to shut down a lot of my emotions and feelings in order to survive. I stopped crying in the box after a year. In such an environment, you have to think good thoughts and remember things that made you happy, such as your family. I sang Elton John's "Your Song" and "Daniel" in the dark box. It was from the song "Daniel," I would someday name my baby. Many Prisoners of War (POW's) did things like this to survive. POW's are one of the few groups I can relate to since, fortunately, there are so few civilian cases like mine in the public domain.

In the box I had ample time to review the details of my life from when I moved out of my mother's house to my arrival in Eugene with Bobby and Alice.

After Joe molested me, I knew I had to move out. My mom chose Joe, her boyfriend, over me, her own daughter. She expected "me" to apologize to Joe.

Brokenhearted and crying, I packed the few things I had and departed. I couldn't live in a house where my feelings were unimportant and ignored. At age 14, I felt rejected by my own mom. Many years later, I vowed never to place my own daughter second to anything or anyone.

Dad was glad to have me move in with him. He was in disparate need of help. His wife, Judy, had just left him for her old high school sweetheart. She told my dad that she wanted to visit a girlfriend up in San Francisco. Dad gave her the money to purchase the airfare. She would be back in a few days, so he thought. They had been married for 10 years and had three children ranging from ages two through 10.

After a week with no word, Dad telephoned the girlfriend in San Francisco to check on Judy. The girlfriend had not seen Judy and knew nothing about a supposed visit. Later, he learned Judy had secretly reunited with her high school sweetheart in Oregon.

Dad was thunder struck. He had no idea Judy would suddenly run off leaving him with three small children. That's when I moved in. For the first couple of weeks he was a mess. He stayed in his room all day and cried. I finally told my cousin Linda we had to do something. She came over and took Dad to her house and gave him some marijuana for the first and only time in his life. They drank and talked things over throughout the night. The next morning, after he had slept it off, he came home and was fine. He went back to work and resumed his normal life. It was funny hearing him talk about all the colors he saw while high on pot.

Now at age 14, I was the woman of the house responsible for three small children, cooking, and cleaning. Hamburger Helper became our main course at each meal until I slowly learned to cook other things. I quickly learned not to wash my father's things with my own. Since he was working with hot asphalt, all my clothes smelled like a California freeway during rush hour.

In addition to my home duties, there was high school. Since I had moved, I also had to change schools even though I was still in the city of Riverside. My old school included grades seven through nine. My new school included grades nine through 12. Since I was in the ninth grade, I went from being on the top of the heap to being on the bottom. Most of the other students were older and more mature then me. During the middle of the year, Dad moved again placing me back again with younger students. Luckily, I had one friend, Collette, who had changed schools in the same way. At the end of the year, Dad moved again to within five blocks of my mom, which put me back in the yet another school, Polytechnic High School or Poly as it was called. Poly included grades 10 through 12. I was now in the 10th grade and had attended four schools in two years. It was a disruptive experience and my education suffered.

When Dad went to court against Judy, his ex-wife, he won everything. The judge criticized her for abandoning her children without any notice. Judy hired a new lawyer and returned to court six months later. The second time, my dad lost everything except his work truck and his construction company. Judy won the house and custody of the children. Dad and I moved in with his mother, and then to an apartment. Later we ended up five blocks from my mom. That's why I changed schools four times in two years.

In the seventh grade, I started experimenting with marijuana or pot as we called it. School soon became just a place to visit with my friends, not a place to learn. During the summer when I was almost 16, I fell in with a group of adults who were not a good influence on me. They were heavy drug users and one day talked me into trying some heroin. They injected it into a vein in the middle of my arm. After I received the injection, I went out in the front yard and sat in a lawn chair. The image before my eyes began to roll just like a television out of adjustment. It scared the hell out of me! Feeling sick I ran into the bathroom and vomited. The next day my body craved more heroin, but for me one bad experience was enough. I'm glad heroin scared me and I got sick, or I might have become a heroin addict from that day forward. I would never recommend heroin to anyone. People use it not for the experience, but because it's so addictive.

A few weeks later, I woke up one morning and found the whites of my eyes had turned yellow. I was really scared. I went to the doctor and discovered I had contracted hepatitis-C from the dirty needle used during the heroin injection. By this time, my dad had married a lady named Ruth who came to us with five children of her own. Everyone, including my friends at school, had to take shots to protect themselves from my hepatitis-C. I was placed on a number of medications and told to stay home away from school.

Even though I was now home-schooled, I soon lost interest in my studies. In addition to being away from my friends at school, hepatitis made me want to sleep most of the day. One friend, Dorothy, did continue to visit me. Even she had to take the preventive shots. The next year when I returned to school as a 12th grade senior, my lack of interest in education continued.

Living next door to me was a guy named Tim Stan, age 22. Tim worked for a local company cleaning swimming pools. He had come to California from Ohio and was living with his sister, Sandy. His current girlfriend, Terry, was also living with him. Tim kept asking me out, but I always said no. In time, I gave in and went out with him. I guess it was his charisma that won me over. I eventually fell in love with him.

During my senior year, before I graduated, Tim asked me to marry him. I quit school and, with a letter of approval from my dad, Tim and I were married in Carson City, Nevada, on December 12, 1973. A letter of approval was required because I was two and a half weeks shy of my 17th birthday and still a minor. We were married in a little chapel with a member of the Salvation Army serving as a witness. I was now Mrs. Timothy Stan.

After we married, Tim and I lived in a beautiful house in Riverside. It was a ranch-style house with a swimming pool in the back yard. We soon acquired a roommate, Sparky, who was a member of The Diablo Motorcycle Gang. Tim owned a Harley Davidson motorcycle, but he was not a member of the gang. However, members of the gang did frequently visited Sparky in our house.

We eventually had a problem with one of the motorcycle gang members. Cajun, a senior member of the gang, asked me to leave my husband and become his girlfriend or "biker mama."

"No," I told him. "I'm married and don't want to leave Tim."

"You will be sorry you said no to me," Cajun said.

One weekend morning the gang, armed with guns, broke into our house determined to teach us a lesson. They beat-up Tim and one member raped me. Other gang members stole Tim's Harley Davidson motorcycle. Tim, being a young and rebellious man, wanted to retaliate, but I knew it would only result in more trouble. I begged him to move away from Riverside.

Tim and I moved back to his home state of Ohio. I didn't care much for Ohio because it was so far in distance and culture from my native California. After a year our marriage was in trouble, but Ohio wasn't the cause. Terry, Tim's old girlfriend, had also moved back to Ohio and Tim started seeing her again. I told Tim it had to be either his wife or his old girlfriend, but not both. Tim told me to leave because Terry wanted me out. It was then I decided to move back to California. Hoping we might someday get back together, Tim and I didn't divorce.

I still liked Terry and didn't blame her for his infidelity. Ironically, as Terry got older she changed her name to Sara. On the day of my abduction, I was traveling to Westwood to visit with the birthday girl Linda Smith, Sandy, and Sara.

Before I returned to California, I discovered I was pregnant with Tim's baby. I moved in with Sandy, next door to my dad, in Riverside. I soon came down with an infection. After taking a medication that contained lye, I knew I had damaged the baby I was carrying. I got an abortion.

Up to this point I had done such a great job of screwing up my life, I decided it was time for me to return to school for my GED (General Education Diploma). I took the test and received my high school diploma at age 18.

I would remain in Riverside for the next year and a half, slowly getting my life back in order. I got a job with Autotronics, a company that installed car stereos. My job included office duties such as answering the phone and receiving money from customers. I lived primarily with my grandma.

One day while out driving around, I spotted a house in an orange grove that had been sold to developers. The house had been vandalized with all its windows broken out. I got an idea and called the developer. I told him that if I could live in the house rent free, I would take care of his property. The developer agreed to the deal, and I moved in immediately.

The house had porches all around the outside and contained two bedrooms, a kitchen, a bath, a living room, and a family room. I went to work replacing broken window panes and cleaning up the place. I planted a little vegetable garden and purchased some egg laying chickens and a couple of ducks. The ducks had a tub full of water and the chickens, on hot days, would try to swim with the ducks to cool off. That's how I learned chickens can't swim. A couple of them drown, but the others kept on laying eggs. I shared the eggs with Mom, Dad, and anyone else I knew. With fresh oranges all around, I was living off the land and loving it.

Sandy, who lived next door to my dad, sold her house to Linda Smith and moved into the spare bedroom in my place with her boyfriend Paul. Smith was a single mom with two children, one of whom suffered from asthma. It was the asthma that caused Smith to move to Westwood with its clean air.

Later, Sandy and Paul married and moved out of my house into a house of their own. David, my new boyfriend, moved in with me. After a short time, I realized David was involved in illegal drugs and other questionable activities. I told him to get out and he said, "Make me." I called the police and they said since he had been living in the house and had paid some of the bills, I couldn't evict him. I telephoned the developer and told him about the situation. I then moved out and eventually rented a room at my mom's boarding house.

I got a job at Sears and met a new boyfriend named Eric. That's also when I met Alice and Bobby who were also renting a room from my mom. It was with Alice and Bobby that I traveled to Eugene, Oregon.

Chapter 11 - Into and Out of Darkness

While in the box, 1981 turned into 1982, and then 1983. Christmases, birthdays, and news from the outside world were all lost. Once during this period, I contracted strep throat. Ma'am had the same illness for which a doctor prescribed medication. Some of her drugs were shared with me. Perhaps all the time I spent in the box reduced my exposure to communicable diseases. During my captivity I was only sick two other times: once after the "Cold Duck" experience and another time with a urinary infection. Going to the doctor was out of the question, so Master told me to drink lots of water for the urinary infection.

During my long confinement in the box, the fear, torture, and rape never ended. When Ma'am and the children were out of the trailer, I was removed from the box for bondage. Master would bring out the frame and whips which were often followed by a shower and rape. During one such event around April 1981, I was taken to the bathroom where the lower part of each leg was tied to the back of each thigh. Then my legs were placed on each side of the toilet. My hands were handcuffed behind the toilet and a rubber gas mask was placed over my head. The eyes and air holes of the gas mask had been taped shut, except for a tiny breathing hole which Master would place his finger over. Master left me in this position as he went out for a bit to eat. After two hours, I was released. My legs were numb due to lack of circulation.

Between April 19 and 23, 1982, Ma'am was in the hospital for surgery on her knees. The children were at her parents, which gave Master an opportunity to have his way with me. The X was set up in the bedroom from which I was hung by my wrists and ankles. A chain was tied around my waist. I was having a hard time bearing the pain so Master choked me to help take my mind off the pain. Master wanted to leave me on the X all night, but after my arms went numb I was taken down. Master then tied my wrists to the corners of the waterbed with my back to the foot of the bed. As I set on the floor, Master went to sleep. Early the next morning my legs were falling asleep due to lack of circulation. Suddenly, I saw something move out of the corner of my eye. When I turned my head, I saw a snake had slithered out of the bedroom closet. A cold chill went through my body at the sight.

I knew better than to wake Master. Eventually, thank goodness, the snake turned and fled. The snake was probably heading for the kitchen where I could hear mice squeaking. When Master woke up I told him about the snake, but he didn't seem too concerned.

While in the box, I had another animal encounter. A small field mouse came through the air hole in the bottom of the box and ran down the length of my naked body. Fear gripped me as the small creature explored the box then exited the same way he entered. The mouse was probably as frightened as I was.

At another time, I broke off a portion of my big toe nail while being hung on the frame. Master was angry at me for bleeding all over his carpet. My personal grooming opportunities were limited resulting in uncut nails and tangled hair. I'm sure with pale skin due to lack of sunlight, lose of weight, lack of vitamins, hair falling out of my head, and going without daily exercise my body looked like a shadow of its former self.

In October, 1983, Master decided to put me in the hole again. The previous time proved to be a disaster with the hole flooding with knee-deep water. This time would be different, Master thought. Late at night, I was given clothes to wear and transferred from the box to the hole. I had not worn anything since 1981.

The hole was better than the box. I had an infrared lamp that gave off some heat, a jacket to fight off the cold, a single light bulb hanging from the ceiling, a lawn chair, my sleeping bag, and my Bible. I also had a small electric clock radio that I was allowed to play as long as I kept the volume down. I tuned the radio to KVIP, a local Christian radio station.

Master tried again to make the hole my "new home" again, but this time the results were different.

Charity and Amber were unaware of the hole under the floor of the storage shed. They were also unaware that Kay, their babysitter, was still living in the mobile home. They had been warned to not go near the shed or the master bedroom. The Hooker children followed instructions, but when a six year old niece came over to visit things changed.

The children were playing around the shed when the niece opened the unlocked shed door. Suddenly, I looked up and saw little angel faces staring down at me from above. I'm not sure they saw me in the dark hole, but Master and Ma'am weren't taking any chances. They quickly removed me from the hole and returned me to my box. I had been in the hole only one week. That was the last time Master tried to keep me in the underground hole. I'm sure Master was disappointed because his dream of an underground dungeon full of slaves had come to nothing after four years.

Late in 1983, things started to slowly change. Master must have felt safe, and Ma'am no longer felt threatened by my presence. I was gradually becoming an accepted member of the family, i.e. a trusted family slave. About this time Master stopped raping me. I never knew the reason behind this change and I wasn't about to ask Master why there was no sex between us. I can only speculate that Master was looking towards the future and was seeing me as more of a co-wife, second class of course. With the girls getting older, Master knew he couldn't keep me in the box forever. Something had to be done. I did nothing to encourage this second wife idea. In my mind, I was still a slave and The Company was still to be feared.

A relationship also slowly developed between Ma'am and I. This new relationship was based on the Bible. Perhaps Ma'am was searching for something from the Lord? Perhaps a sense of guilt had overtaken her? I was the only person she could talk things over with, outside her husband. I knew the secrets behind the locked doors at the end of Weed Court. I wanted to maintain this growing relationship because it was much better than what I had in the past. Whatever the reason, Ma'am was soon removing me from my box so we could read and study the Bible together. This was the first conversation I had with Ma'am since my abduction in 1977. Previously, I had received only orders and commands from Ma'am.

Master not only allowed, but encouraged us to read of the Bible. He especially liked the parts dealing with master-slave relationships and how a wife should be obedient to her husband.

"A wife who doesn't obey her husband will go to hell according to the Bible," Master told his wife. Ma'am didn't question what her husband told her.

Master especially liked the story in the Bible about Abraham (Abram), Sarah (Saria), and Hagar found in Genesis 16. Abraham's wife, Sarah, was unable to give him any children. Therefore, she presented their slave girl, Hagar, to her husband to have his child. Master twisted the stories in the Bible to fit his own desires. Ma'am and I were expected to play our roles. After I had cared for Ma'am while she was sick, she sent me some flowers with a card that read, "To Hagar from Sarah."

"Women should have their heads covered when reading the Bible as a sign of submission and respect towards God," Master ordered. From then on, Ma'am and I would don knit caps like the ones worn on cold winter days before opening the Bible. My cap was grey while Ma'am's cap was red, white, and blue in color. Even though we were having face-to-face discussions about the Bible, Ma'am and I never developed a close person-to-person relationship. As a slave, I still addressed her as Ma'am with my head bowed, but at least we were talking.

"God wanted you to be here," Master told me one day. Drawing the letter "Y" he went on to say, "One path leads to righteousness and the other to hell. You were going the wrong way before I got a hold of you. Now you are at a crossroads and you have to decide which path to take." I said nothing.

Surprisingly, about this time I had the second of two open conversations with Master where I was allowed to talk freely. The first had been five years before when Master told me I could ask him anything I wanted.

"K, read something from the Bible to me," Master said. Slaves don't get many choices. I was always being told what to do. Now I had a choice as to which passage of the Bible to read to Master.

"Maybe this will grab his attention," I thought as I opened my Bible.

"And I saw the dead, great and small, standing before the throne, and books were opened. Another book was opened, which is the book of life. The dead were judged according to what they had done as recorded in the books. The sea gave up the dead that were in it, and death and Hades gave up the dead that were in them, and each person was judged according to what he had done. Then death and Hades were thrown into the lake of fire. The lake of fire is the second death. If anyone's name was not found written in the book of life, he was thrown into the lake of fire...." Revelation 20:12-15

I continued to read from Revelations and when I had finished there was no discussion. I don't think Master ever believed in God, and I know he didn't fear the Lord. For him, the Bible was just another instrument, along with the whip and The Company, to keep his slave and wife obedient.

When I passed my 27th birthday in late December, 1983, I was presented with a birthday cake which was the first acknowledgement of my birthday in six years. At age 27, most young women have completed their education, married, had a baby, and were enjoying life. I too had done the same, at least in my dreams. In the darkness of the box, my mind was free to explore and dream about my future. I could see the house I would one day live in, and the family I would one day have. I planned each and every aspect of my house right down to the white fence out front. I always had faith in the Lord and knew freedom would come someday.

In January 1984, I asked Master to allow me to do something with my life. After years of lying on my back in a box, I wanted to go out in public and work. A month later, Master told me, "God said you can get a job." Master talked about using some of the money I earned to purchase a small trailer. My trailer would be parked in the backyard behind their mobile home. After almost seven years, Master knew I was a trusted family slave. Working a public job was not out of the question. Plus the family could always use the extra money.

I started spending more hours during the night out of my box. Meals started coming with more regularity and quantity. Somedays I would be feed twice, once in the morning, and once in the evening. Soon I had gained 25 pounds and was starting to look presentable to the world. I had to gain weight or else people would have been shocked at my emaciated appearance.

I didn't know it at the time, but in May, 1984, I would spend my last night in the box. It had been more than three years since I had "departed" and now I was ready to "return". I was given cloths to wear and a story to tell. I was returning to be a live-in babysitter once again and was happy to be home. Charity and Amber remembered me and were excited to see me again. I was surprised how much they had grown. The girls had gone from being three and five to ages six and eight.

"Hey look, Kay is back," the neighbors were told, as I was escorted around Weed Court.

I was thankful to once again be out under the sunshine and in the garden. Now, I was allowed to sleep in the back bathroom without a chain around my neck. I was instructed to stop saying Master, but to start saying Cameron. However, after so many years, I didn't feel comfortable calling him Cameron. I usually didn't use any name when I talked to him. If I had to use a name I called him Sir. I didn't want to do anything that might return me to the box, so I tried hard to be the best slave I could.

On May 21, 1984, Ma'am drove me around Red Bluff looking for employment. We visited 20 different business establishments before I finally landed a job. I was hired as a housekeeper or maid at Kings Lodge Motel where I listed Ma'am as a character reference and used my true name, Colleen Stan. Kings Lodge was located where Antelope Boulevard crosses the Sacramento River near downtown Red Bluff. The motel was a couple hundred yards from the Highway 36 overpass where I was picked up hitchhiking seven years before. I had now come full circle, geographically speaking.

Ma'am would drive me three and a half miles to my new job each morning around 8:00 AM. After five hours, when I had finished cleaning, Ma'am would pick me up and drive me back to the mobile home. Sometimes, I would ride her bicycle to and from work. On hot summer days, Ma'am would bring the girls over to swim in the motel pool. I was paid $200 every two weeks. Except for $20, which I was allowed to keep, all the money went into Sir's bank account. At night, I was now allowed to sleep on the living room floor in my sleeping bag.

California Highway Patrolmen had coffee at the Denny's Restaurant next to the motel and the Red Bluff Police Department was a short distance up the road in downtown Red Bluff. For me, The Company was still much closer. Any attempt to cry for help would result in The Company becoming involved. Painful torture and death were never far from my mind. Sir's stories about runaways convinced me escape was not only dangerous, but impossible.

My slave training made me the ideal person for the motel job. I worked fast and efficiently, never wasting time talking with the other housekeepers. When I completed my assigned rooms, I would help the other maids with their work. Motel guest never complained about my work to managers Doris and Rock Miron. I was friendly with everyone, but never volunteered any information about my life with the Hooker family.

Lenora Scott, another housekeeper at the motel, invited me home with her one day after work. I checked with Ma'am for approval first, and then told Lenora yes. We went to her apartment where I met her husband. The three of us then went to the Palomino Room, a bar in Red Bluff. After an hour they drove me back home to the trailer. I had not experienced such freedom for over seven years and didn't want to do anything to lose it.

"Colleen, would you like to work behind the front desk a couple of hours each day after you finish cleaning your rooms?" Doris asked me after a few weeks. "My husband Rock and I need to get some shopping done and want someone like you to watch the front desk and answer the telephone while we're gone. It's a simple job and we can show you how to do it."

"Yes, I would love to, but I need to first check with Mrs. Hooker," I replied. They knew I was living with the Hookers and Mrs. Hooker, I don't think they knew her first name, dropped me off and picked me up each day. Ma'am had no objections to me working a few extra hours, since my pay check went directly into their bank account, and I was glad to stay away from the mobile home for a few more hours.

The job behind the front desk was not difficult. The guests were always nice to me as I worked during the slow period of the day, between 1:00 and 3:00 PM. If something came up that I couldn't handle, like a broken air conditioner, I simple told Rock when they returned from shopping.

One Monday morning in May, 1984, as I was cleaning a motel room I found a note from a guest.

"I wanted to thank you for doing such a great job each day cleaning my room. You have made our stay more enjoyable," the note read. Enclosed was a $20 bill. Boat races are held at the Red Bluff Diversion Dam on the Sacramento River each year. The guest had spent the weekend attending the boating event and apparently had a good time. I took the money and purchased a pair of blue and gray tennis or running shoes for myself and some flowers for Ma'am.

My relations with Ma'am were the best it had been since I got in the backseat of the Dodge Colt on the day of my abduction. We continued to study the Bible together and discussed God's part in our lives. Ma'am even allowed me to drive the car one day to K-Mart. Sir had told me I could get a drivers license soon. I had a good relationship with Ma'am and wanted to maintain the good feelings between us.

One weekend in July, I was included in a family trip to Burney Falls, a popular landmark 100 miles northeast of Red Bluff. After a family picnic, Sir took a picture of Ma'am, the children, and me. Later the picture, like so many other things, would be used against me in court. Granted the photo looked like one big happy family, except I was not there of my own free will and the Hooker family was not my family.

Colleen (on the right) and Jan Hooker with the Girls, 1984

One Sunday, I asked Sir if I could go to church. Since religion had served him well up to this point, he had no objections. The children and I went to the First Church of the Nazarene on the church bus. Later we were joined by Ma'am and once even Sir joined us. Pastor Dabney must have noticed two women in the congregation praying especially hard and sometimes crying. Ma'am and I took part in "alter call" which was an invitation to go to the front of the church, pray, talk to Pastor

Dabney. We told him of our troubles at home, but avoided the gruesome details concerning sadism and slavery. He prayed for us and advised us to get out of the house. I was thankful for having a chance to worship the Lord.

One day, while alone doing the dishes, Pastor Dabney paid the Hooker house a friendly visit. When he knocked on the door, I was so surprised I dropped and broke a dish. I talked nervously with him for a few minutes before he left. I was grateful for the visit, but even more grateful when Pastor Dabney left.

By 1984, Ma'am had changed, but Sir remained the same. He was not willing to give up bondage or his sex slave. The Company was still there, but more and more Sir used God as his weapon of choice.

"God wants you to have sex with me," Sir told me one day. "You need it to be normal." I thought otherwise. It had been over a year since I had last been raped. Sir kept putting pressure on me to have sex with him and when Ma'am backed him up, I finally said yes.

Sir explained to me that I could become his second wife and someday all of us would move to Lake Tahoe. He would own 1,000 acres of beautiful forested land and I could have my own cabin. I could live in the cabin with his baby and he could acquire additional slaves. He showed me a wedding announcement in the newspaper and told me the couple, who were getting married, were master and slave.

"Someday you can have my baby," he told me, knowing how much I wanted a baby.

"Are you telling me or asking me?" I asked.

"I'm asking you."

"No, I don't want to have your baby," I said.

"What if I didn't give you a choice?"

"Well, then I wouldn't have a choice," I replied. I knew it was out of the question to bring a baby into this environment.

About this time, Sir discussed what he called "an alternate night plan" for sex. He would sleep with Ma'am for two nights, with me for two nights, and be by himself for three nights. Sex was not mandatory, so he said. Ma'am and I never really liked or understood how this plan was to work. However, rapidly moving events overtook the plan before it could be implemented.

Thursday, August 9, 1984, started out as just another work day for me. Sir was 31, Ma'am was 26, and I was 27 years of age. The weather was typical for the time of the year, hot and clear. The thermometer was climbing to a forecasted high of 100 degrees. Unknown to me, my Capricorn astrological forecast for the day read in part, "Cycle moves up, long distance communication could relate to travel or educational opportunity. Lunar position highlights individuality, originality, and willingness to pioneer a project."

Kings Lodge Motel, 1989

I was working hard to get the motel rooms clean before noon. I was on my last room when Ma'am walked into the room around 11:30 in the morning.

"We need to talk," Ma'am said.

"Okay," I said, as I continued to make the bed.

"I have something serious to tell you."

"Okay," I repeated, still not anticipating the impact of her next words.

"Cameron is not part of The Company, but there is a Company and you should fear them. I'm sorry Colleen, I hope you can find it in your heart to forgive me."

I stopped cleaning and stood in shock for a few seconds. I couldn't believe what my ears were hearing. I didn't have to ask her to repeat the statement. I knew what it meant. In a split second it all came back to me. The years of torture, darkness, depredation, abuse, and humiliation ran through my mind. If Master, or Hooker from now on, was not part of The Company then he was acting alone. The stories about runaway slaves, Company meetings, Company permission to see my family, even the Indenture Contract I signed were all lies. I didn't think anyone was capable of creating such distorted lies over so many years.

At this point, I fell on the bed and literally broke down in tears. Ma'am, or now Jan, was also crying.

"Oh God, how could I have been so stupid?" I said aloud through my tears. "What a fool I have been. How could I have believed such a lie all these years?"

To this day, I never found out why Jan decided to tell me the truth on that particular August morning. I can only guess she must have feared Hooker was about to kill both of us. Jan has never told me what released her long pinned up conscience. Was it guilt? Something she read in the Bible? Was it to protect Charity and Amber? Did she feel her marriage was threatened and wanted to send me home, far away from her husband? The camel's back may have been broken by the straw of poor planning. Hooker never established an agreeable plan for the sexual relationship between the three of us. He had not calculated the impact of his "alternate night plan" on Jan.

I can only guess why Jan told me, "… there is a Company and you should fear them." Perhaps she was concerned I would go to the police, and this was an attempt to persuade me otherwise. She was willing to give up some power, but not all the power she had over me.

"We need to get out," Jan said, as she sat crying on the edge of the bed.

"Okay," I replied. I was thinking, "Why has she waited all these years before saying, 'We need to get out.'"

Jan started to become upset because she didn't know what to do next. I'm not sure who suggested it, but a decision was made to consult Pastor Dabney at the Church of the Nazarene.

I quickly finished my house cleaning duties and departed work early. Before I left, I told Doris I wouldn't be coming back, and I would send a forwarding address for my last pay check. She was concerned that her best worker was departing so abruptly. Doris could clearly see I was upset.

Jan and I drove to the church and found Pastor Dabney in his office. We sat down and started telling our story. Jan did most of the talking which portrayed her husband as abusive and having an affair with me. Jan avoided most of the gruesome details of torture and humiliation. However, she did mention I was being held against my will as a sex slave.

"Yes, Colleen Stan is my real name," I added.

Pastor Dabney was a small town minister who couldn't fully comprehend a world of bondage and sexual slavery. Later, I would find no one could believe what they were hearing, not even the police. Pastor Dabney placed the story in the only context he knew and was trained to deal with, marital problems and an abusive husband. He said we were living in sin and needed to get out of the mobile home.

"Do you have any place to go?" he asked.

"I guess, I could move in with my parents," Jan said.

Suddenly, a new problem arose. Jan remembered she was scheduled to pickup Hooker from work around 4:00 PM. It was already 3:30 PM and Hooker would know something was wrong if Jan didn't arrive on time.

Pastor Dabney suggested we get Hooker and drive him home like we would on any other day. The next day, after he had departed for work, we could put the children on the church bus for Vacation Bible School and start packing our things. We could pick the girls up at noon and drive directly to Jan's parents. It sounded like a good plan.

Once we got back in the car, Jan had a panic attack. She knew her husband always demanded the truth from his wife. Jan was afraid she would tell him what had happened. She kept no secrets from him.

"I not sure I can go through the whole night alone with him," Jan cried. Both of us were afraid he would kill us both if he knew what she had done.

Now I started to panic too. "Oh God," I thought. "We're going to die." I knew she would probably tell him I knew The Company was not part of his life.

"Why don't you tell him your feeling sick and don't want to make him sick by sleeping with him. Tell him you will sleep in the living room this one night." I suggested.

All night, after we picked up Hooker, I prayed Jan wouldn't have another panic attack and spill the beans. We didn't even tell the children what was going on. We bedded down on the living room floor in our separate sleeping bags, neither of us sleeping well that night.

The next morning, Friday, August 10, Hooker got off to work at 5:00 AM. The children were loaded aboard the church bus for Vacation Bible School. Jan and I worked hard and fast gathering up clothes and personal items for us and the kids. Among other things, Jan packed two photos of herself in bondage. I guess she wanted proof in case someone didn't believe her story. By noon the kids were back, and we were ready to go.

At 1:00 PM we arrived at the home of Jan's parents on Dove Street in Gerber, about nine miles south of Red Bluff. Her parents were surprised to see us bag and baggage with two kids in tow. Jan asked them if we could stay a few nights. They must have assumed Jan and her husband were having a little marital discord.

Once we were safely in their house, I knew I had to go home to Riverside. I thought about staying and helping Jan with the kids, but God was telling me to go home. Jan had to make it by herself. Jan agreed I should go, but begged me not to go to the police. At this point I wasn't thinking of justice or revenge. I only wanted to get away from Red Bluff. Anger, guilt, and other emotions would come later, but first I just wanted to go home to my family.

I telephoned the bus station in Red Bluff and asked about a one-way ticket to Riverside, California. The clerk informed me a bus would be leaving early tomorrow afternoon and the charge would be $150. I knew I needed money fast.

"Hello," my dad said, on the other end of the telephone line.

"Dad, it's Colleen. I want to come home and need you to wire me $150 bus fare."

"Colleen! I'll send it today, but don't you think you might need more money. Why don't I send you $200?" Dad said. It had been more than three years since he had heard my voice. "No, maybe I should send $250," he added.

"No, Dad. I only need $150," I answered.

"Well let me make it $175 so you will have a few extra dollars to get something to eat," he said. I think he would have sent me a million dollars if I had asked.

I told Dad to wire the money to the Western Union office in Red Bluff. I would arrive home August 12, on the 7:00 AM bus. I also told him I loved him.

I'm sure Hooker had no idea what was coming when he went off to work that morning. When he came home, late in the afternoon, the mobile home was empty. His wife, two girls, and slave were gone as was most of their clothing.

Hooker knew where to find us. Just before dusk, he showed up in the driveway of Jan's parents looking for his family. Jan told me to keep the girls in the back bedroom and not, under any circumstances, to let them out. She went outside to talk with him. Their conversation, which I couldn't hear, went on for about 30 to 45 minutes. The girls wanted to run to their dad, but I told them Mommy and Daddy wanted to talk. When the conversation ended Hooker got in his car and drove away.

While talking to Jan, Hooker must have promised to change his ways if they would return home. I assume he must have begged for a second chance. Jan probably told him she would think about it, but in the mean time she and the children were going to stay with her parents. Jan never told me what was said between the two of them.

When Jan came back inside the house, she took her parents outside away from the children to explain why she had left her husband. I was present when she told her parents about my sex slave status, the confinement, and the torture. Like Pastor Dabney, her parents found the story too difficult to fully comprehend. They saw the situation as a marital disagreement. I believed they hoped the two would get back together soon for the sake of the children. As for me, I believe they were glad to see me go back home to Riverside. Having a single, 27 year old woman living in the trailer couldn't be viewed as helpful to the marriage. The children probably knew something was wrong, but remained isolated from the turmoil.

Around mid-morning, on Saturday August 11, Jan drove me to the Red Bluff Western Union office to pick up the money my dad had wired to me. She then drove me over to the bus station to purchase the ticket. Since there was some time before the bus departed, we went to a city park and talked.

"Please don't call the police. We need to give Cameron a chance to change," she implored me. At the time, I was only thinking of going home. Jan then dropped me off at the bus station and drove away.

I was wearing the new running shoes I had bought with the motel tip money, a pair of jean shorts, and a pink tank top. I had a small bag with another change of clothes, my tooth brush, and my blue nightgown I had in the basement on Oak Street. My departure from the mobile home was fast. I left behind many personal items such as my purse and Bible. My original clothing and shoes either remained in the trailer or had been sent to the trash years before. My expired driver's license and Social Security card remained in my purse under the waterbed in the space between the double walls.

Right before I boarded the 1:00 PM bus, I did one last thing. I wanted to tell Hooker something. I dropped a coin in a payphone at the bus station and dialed 527-9216, the Hooker mobile home.

"Hello," he said, in a toned down voice.

"I'm leaving you and you can't stop me. I'm getting on the bus and going home and there's nothing you can do about it," I said to him in a determined voice.

He knew immediately who was on the other end of the phone. I could hear Hooker was emotionally upset. In 24 hours, his whole world had come crashing down. Everyone had left him. He cried like a baby which was something I had never heard him do before.

"Good bye," I said, as I hung up the phone.

Once on the bus, the door closed, and the bus driver started the diesel engine. I was now on my way home. What were my emotions at this time? Fear, apprehension, guilt, anger, and sadness were what one might expect. However, at this moment, and throughout the bus ride south, my only emotion was pure joy. I was so happy and excited to be going home. Other emotions and feeling would come later, but for right now I was full of joy. God was right, "Everything would be all right." The Lord had answered my prayers. I was going home after 2,634 days in captivity.

Chapter 12 - Home at Last

As the bus sped south through the night, I couldn't sleep. I was too excited about going home. Just north of Los Angeles, everyone else on the bus was asleep, including the driver. Suddenly, the bus started drifting across the multilane highway. A car honked its horn which woke the driver, who quickly corrected his mistake. The other passengers on the bus woke up and looked around for a minute or two, then returned to their dreams.

While changing buses in Los Angeles, I phoned Dad to let him know I was almost home. Around 7:00 AM on Sunday, August 12, 1984, the bus pulled into the Riverside bus station where I could see my dad Jack, his wife Ruth, my mom Lynn, my sisters Jenise and Bonnie, and Linda my cousin. I stepped off the bus into the waiting arms of my family. I was home at last.

The first thing I told them was that I had to go to the restroom. As I walked into the restroom, Mom and Jenise followed me. Inside the restroom, they grabbed my arms and pinned me against the wall.

"You're going to tell us where you have been, and you're going to tell us now," Mom demanded, with Jenise backing her up.

"I have every intension of telling you, but I can't tell you right now. I promise, I will tell you over breakfast," I replied.

They let me go into the stall and close the door, but stood in the restroom waiting for me. They escorted me out of the restroom and back to the other waiting family members. All of us then went to breakfast at a nearby Denny's Restaurant. Over bacon and eggs, with a side order of pancakes, I told them what had happened to me over the past seven years.

"I was kidnapped and held against my will by a man and his wife in Red Bluff. They didn't allow me to call or write to anyone. I was made to clean house and watched their children. The man who abducted me was the same man who was with me when I visited you in 1981. I didn't stay away from Riverside because I wanted to, but because the man wouldn't allow me to visit. Now, thank God, I'm home." Not wanting to hurt my family, I avoided the painful details of my story which included the torture, the box, and my slave status.

"You should go to the police," someone said.

"Not right now." I said. "His wife begged me not to go to the police, but to give him a chance to reform. He promised her, he would change his ways. I want to give them a chance."

My family was relieved my absence was not due to my own decision or something they had done. I had been kidnapped and held against my will. As my family thought about what had happened to me, their anger grew, and they insisted I go to the police. Since it was Jan who released me, I wanted to give her a chance to reform Hooker. Perhaps it was Christian forgiveness on my part that caused me not to go directly to the police. I was just glad to be home, and my fear had not yet transitioned to anger. Deep down, I still probably feared The Company. "… There is a Company and you should fear them," Jan had told me in the motel room. Perhaps after so many years in captivity, I couldn't convince myself I was truly free.

"You don't understand everything, and I would appreciate it if you would let me take care of this," I told my family. "I promise, I will not leave again, and if I feel any danger from those people, I will go to the police." I think they were still afraid of pushing me too far. They too were just happy to have me back home.

I learned my family had conducted an extensive search for me. After I failed to return, Alice and Bobby called Smith in Westwood and discovered I had never arrived. They then called my dad in Riverside who called my mom. Dad and Mom, even though they had divorced years earlier, drove to Oregon together. They filed a missing person report with the police on May 23, four days after I had disappeared.

They collected my few belongings and placed my old Saab automobile on the back of Dad's work truck and drove back to Riverside. On the way home, they stopped at police departments along the way, including Red Bluff, and reported me missing. The police filed the reports, but had no information to give my parents. I had just vanished in thin air somewhere between Eugene and Westwood.

Mom did tell me Mark, my boyfriend in Eugene, was upset I had vanished. He regretted he had not tried harder to stop me from hitchhiking on Interstate 5.

"Colleen, he really loved you," Mom told me.

I telephoned Mark after I had been home for awhile. I wanted him to know I had returned home safely. I told him about my ordeal and he was thankful I had survived. I learned he had married and was the father of a son. I thanked him for all the good times we had together. We had each gone down separate paths in life, and we were never to see each other again.

Back in Dad's home on Coolidge Avenue, I started catching up on the family stories I had missed. Family members who had just married in 1981, now had new babies in 1984. I spent many hours going over family history, and looking at wedding and baby pictures. My extended family, not already mentioned, included two half-sisters, one half-brother, along with cousins, nieces, and nephews.

In the afternoon of my first day back, I went to Jenise's condominium where I met her husband Randy and their 3 year old son Nicholas. We had a barbecue and then swam in the community pool. It was good to be back with the people I loved.

Colleen Back Home, 1984

The next day, I told Dad I didn't have anything to wear. I needed new clothes, underwear, shoes, and cosmetics. I had to rebuild my life starting with the basics. With a few of his dollars, I headed for the local shopping mall. Linda, my cousin, went with me since I really didn't want to go out in public by myself. A day or two later, I received more shopping money from Dad. The third time I asked for money, his answer was short and to the point.

"What do you think I'm made of money?" Now, I knew I was truly back home at last.

As soon as I got home, I used a calling card to phone Jan at 8:16 AM to let her know I had arrived safely in Riverside. Over the next three months, I placed 29 telephone calls back to Red Bluff for a total 500 minutes. An equal number of calls were made to me, mostly from Jan. Later, I had to explain and justify these calls in court.

I had spent over seven years with the Hooker family and found it hard to simply cut the ties. I wanted to know if Hooker was changing as promised, or if he was on Interstate 5 coming after me. They wanted to know if I had gone to the police. I asked about the children and was told they missed me. I can't remember the content of each conversation, but one call from Hooker I remember well.

"Could you tell me how to make a tuna sandwich?" he asked, in a sad voice.

For the first time in his life, he was home alone without his mother, wife, or slave to do things for him. I told him how to make a tuna sandwich and quickly hung up. It was obvious the power had shifted from him to me. I no longer feared him as much now, knowing he was not part of The Company. At this point, I even felt a little sorry for him, but not in a good way. He was pathetic.

The telephone calls to Red Bluff were odd in another way.

"Hello," the person in Red Bluff would say as they answered the phone.

"This is Colleen."

"Who is this?"

"Colleen…I mean Kay."

"Kay, how are you?"

In Red Bluff, people still knew me as Kay.

On August 18, I wrote a letter to Jan and Hooker in which I cited a passage from the Bible. The passage explained how I felt.

Hear me. O God, as I voice my complaint; protect my life from the threat of the enemy. Hide me from the conspiracy of the wicked, from that noise crowd of evildoers, they who sharpen their tongues like swords and aim their words like deadly arrows. They shoot from ambush at the innocent man; they shoot at him suddenly, without fear. They encourage each other in evil plans, they talk about hiding their snares; they say, "Who will see them?" They plot injustice and say, "We have devised a perfect plan!" Surely the mind and heart of man are cunning. But God will shoot them with arrows; suddenly they will be struck down. He will turn their own tongues against them and bring them to ruin; all who see them will shake their heads in scorn. All mankind will fear; they will proclaim the works of God and ponder what he has done. Psalm 64:1-9

On September 19, I wrote a letter to tell them I was thinking about returning to Red Bluff with Ray, my half-brother. We were going to visit the land my father owned north of Red Bluff. My father had purchased the land as a future retirement site without knowing I was alive in a box, just a few miles south. In the letter I wrote, "But, I do not want to play God and forgive you and Cameron for all these things -- it's done." I planned, but never made the trip.

A few days later, my cousin Linda, came over to visit. I was staying in the spare bedroom in the back of Dad's house. His wife Ruth and Erica, their seven year old daughter, were also living in the house. Linda and I were in the house alone since everyone else was either at work or school. I could tell Linda was angry.

"What's the bastard's phone number? I'm calling him right now," Linda said, with determination. Linda was always the drama queen and fireball of the family. Hooker was still in the mobile home by himself when he picked up the phone.

"What gives you the right to do what you did to Colleen, you filthy bastard? I should go to the police right now you ...I hope you rot in hell. You're nothing but a ....(expletives deleted)." When Linda was finished she hung up. I don't think Hooker got a word in edgewise. I'm sure Linda made his day, I know she made mine.

In October, I experienced something I had never felt before or since. I'm talking about true love. As soon as I walked into a Circle K convenience store our eyes met. I knew it was love at first sight. His name was Mohammad and he was a Moslem from Iran. He had a dark complexion and equally dark eyes. We talked for a while and exchanged phone numbers. We soon became close friends, and in time he would become my soul mates as we talked about love, life, and religion. Our souls were so strongly connected and I'm not sure exactly how to describe this connection in words. I have never felt so close to anyone before or since. Mohammad did everything with great passion and never half-heartedly. I admired his zest and love for life. Mohammad spoke directly to my soul.

Mohammad worked as a clerk at the Circle K. Soon, we were taking long walks, riding bicycles, and discussing the Bible and Koran. We realized the message in both books are the same, God wanted people to love one another. The message was simple and clear, but people are always trying to complicate the message and make it difficult.

Mohammad told me as a boy in Iran, his father was a man of wealth and influence in his small town. People respected and looked up to his father. Mohammad entered the United States on a student visa and attended college in Florida. Life was good to Mohammad with his father sending money to him periodically.

In the late 1970's, Iran experienced an Islamic revolution. When Mohammad asked his father for money, he was told it had all been taken by the government. Soon after that, Mohammad dropped out of school, moved to California, and began working for a living. That's when I walked into his life and our eyes met.

After I got to know Mohammad well, I told him about my enslavement by Hooker and his wife.

"In Iran, Hooker would have been taken out and killed. There wouldn't be a trial," Mohammad said.

My family didn't like Mohammad, but I didn't care. I loved him, but our relationship was soon to end. Mohammad's father had become seriously ill and was expected to die. Mohammad knew he had to return to Iran to see his father one last time. Mohammad knew once he departed the United States, he would never be allowed to return.

Once back home, Iran would not let him depart and the U.S. would not allow him to enter.

The obvious answer for me was to marry Mohammad and go to Iran with him. I loved him deeply, but knew our cultures were too far apart. He promised he would treat me the same in Iran as he treated me in the United States. In public however, I would have to cover myself by wearing a chador with my face behind a veil to hide my blue American eyes. I knew once he was with his family, I would be expected to convert to Islam. Moving to Iran was just too much for me. I had been a slave once and didn't want to become one again.

"Mohammad I love you, but I know it won't work. You should go back to Iran by yourself to be with your father."

Mohammad sadly returned to Iran without me. We stayed in touch for several years, exchanging letters and phone calls on a regular basis. His father soon died and his mother, finding it an embarrassment having a 30 year old unmarried man at home, proceeded to find him an Iranian wife. His mother would bring home a group of women and line them up.

"Now Mohammad, pick one to be your bride," his mother would say.

"But Mother, I love American women not Iranian women," Mohammad would tell his mother, making her furious at him.

"Mohammad, don't say such things," I told him during an overseas telephone call. "It shows disrespect towards your mother."

In time, Mohammad built a house in his hometown and remained single. We continued to communicate regularly until Ray, my future husband, intercepted a call from Mohammad one day.

"Colleen is a married woman and I'm her husband. Don't ever call or write her again," Ray told Mohammad.

I was angry with Ray for what he said to Mohammad. He was my friend, living on the far side of the world, and Ray had no right saying what he did. I will never forget Mohammad.

On Sunday, November 11, I suddenly received a short, cryptic telephone call from Jan.

"Someone's going to call you. You need to talk to them," she said before hanging up. Her voice was filled with tears and panic.

"Who's going to call me? Talk to them about what?" I asked myself. I quickly dialed back Jan's phone number.

"What the hell are you talking about?" I asked.

"I told the police everything, and they are going to contact you soon," Jan said, still crying.

It turned out on Friday, August 17, Jan returned to Hooker with the children. Back in the mobile home, they went to counseling with Pastor Dabney where Hooker promised to change his ways. Pastor Dabney referred to his bondage equipment as a "false god" and told Hooker to get rid of everything. One night, Hooker and Jan burned most of the pornography and sadistic paraphernalia he had collected over the years. They also burned photographic slides of me being tortured. They burned a lot, but not everything.

On Friday, September 28, Jan could see Hooker was not changing so she and the kids once again left Hooker. On Thursday, November 1, Jan returned to the mobile home to find a statue of a nude woman Hooker had created with his own hands. (Hooker had a natural artistic ability to work with his hands.) On Wednesday, November 7, Jan told Connie Fleming, a medical receptionist in a doctor's office in Redding, about Hooker. Connie told Jan she should consider the safety of Charity and Amber. On Thursday, November 8, Jan told Pastor Dabney about her fears that Hooker was going to harm her or the children. Pastor Dabney, with the permission of Jan, called the police. Jan was granted immunity on November 9 in exchange for her truthful and complete testimony in the developing case against her husband. A short time later, I received a call from the Red Bluff Police Department.

"I'm Detective Shamblin of the Red Bluff Police. We have been talking to Janice Hooker and want to meet with you to hear your side of the story."

"Okay," I said.

"How about Monday, November 12, at your home in Riverside?" the officer asked.

"Okay, that would be fine," I answered.

I'm not sure what caused Jan to suddenly go to the police. My guess is Hooker failed to reform his ways or was talking about getting more slaves. Perhaps she feared for her life and the future safety of their girls.

A guilty conscience may also have been a factor. The crime had now ended and the police investigation had just begun.

I knew Hooker was not part of The Company, but as Jan said in the motel room, "The Company does exist and you should fear them." I still feared The Company even though I was at home in Riverside. I still didn't trust anyone, especially men who said they were from the Red Bluff Police Department. I asked my mom and dad to be at home with me when the men came the next day.

Two men in business suites knocked on the door early Monday afternoon. They flashed their badges and identified themselves as Detectives Al Shamblin and McCall of the Red Bluff Police Department. I invited them into the living room where we all sat down. The officers told me they had talked to Janice Hooker and now wanted to hear my story. With a small tape recorder and note pads, they asked me to start from the beginning. I slowly told my story starting with the events of that warm May afternoon in 1977. The interview, which lasted three hours, covered a seven year time frame. I gave the detectives the blue nightgown I had brought home with me from Red Bluff. They took pictures of the scars on my body from the torture.

For the first time, Mom and Dad heard the disturbing details of my day to day life with the Hookers. Previously, I had avoided the stories about painful torture, beatings, being stretched, electrocuted, and raped. I also told the police about the box, lack of water, and limited human contact over the years. I knew it was hard on my parents to hear the details and I couldn't look at my dad's or mom's face as I talked. I remained calm and told my story in a detached, businesslike manner. The two detectives, like Pastor Dabney and Jan's parents, had a hard time comprehending the bizarre details. It was out of their realm of experiences and training.

"You came here [to Riverside]," Detective Shamblin asked, with a tone of shock in his voice.

"Yes, I came home in 1981," I replied.

I also told the detectives the knife used in my abduction was probably still under the front seat of Hooker's Chevy Vega. I had seen the knife as I vacuumed out the floorboard of the Dodge Colt and later saw the same knife in the Chevy Vega.

At the end of the interview, the detectives asked to speak to my parents alone. In private, they told my parents my story matched Janice Hooker's account except for one important event. They wanted to know if I was strong enough to hear what Jan told them in Red Bluff. My parents said yes.

"Colleen, did the Hookers ever talk about the woman kidnapped prior to you?" Detective Shamblin asked.

"No," I replied.

"Well there was a young woman abducted off the streets of Chico about 16 months before your kidnapping. Her name was Marie Elizabeth Spannhake or Marliz as her parents called her. She was 19 years old and was walking home on January 31, 1976, when Hooker and Janice spotted her. They offered her a ride, but she refused. They kept asking until she finally said okay. She got into the same Dodge Colt they were driving when they picked you up on the Highway 36 overpass. When the car arrived at Marliz's destination, she thanked them and was about to depart the car. Hooker grabbed Marliz by the hair and physically overpowered her. He tied her up and locked her in the head box, according to Janice. They drove to a park, waited until it was dark, and then returned to the Oak Street house."

"Hooker took Marliz down into the basement and did to her what he did to you. The only difference was Marliz wouldn't stop screaming and kicking. Hooker took her up to the kitchen, pulled a knife from a drawer, and tried to cut her vocal cords. We understand he always wanted a silent slave. A slave who could hear, but not talk," Detective Shamblin said, without emotion.

"The procedure did not go well. Marliz lost a lot of blood and probably had a sucking neck wound through which air entered and exited. Hooker realized he had gone too far, and Marliz would probably die. Releasing her was out of the question, as was a trip to a hospital emergency room. At this point Marliz motioned for a piece of paper and a pen. She wrote a note saying her parents would pay any amount of money if he would release her. However, money for Hooker was not the motive behind the crime."

"After talking with Janice, Hooker returned to the basement and attempted to kill Marliz with a pellet gun. He fired a number of rounds into her abdomen which only brought her more pain. Finally, he choked her to death with his bare hands. Her body was wrapped in a blanket and carried her to the trunk of his Dodge Colt. Janice accompanied Hooker on a midnight drive into the hills east of Red Bluff. They stopped in an isolated wooded area off a logging road. A shallow grave was quickly dug in the frozen January soil. She was dropped, unceremoniously, into her final resting place and covered with a layer of earth. The Hookers then drove back to Red Bluff as the sun was rising.

"Does her death bother you?" Janice asked her husband.

"Nope," Cameron replied. Hooker was only disappointed his new captive had died on him. Now he would have to find a replacement. Detective Shamblin now turned to me.

"Colleen, do you have any knowledge of these events?" the detective asked.

"No, I never heard of Marliz, but I always knew Hooker was capable of murder. He did tell me once, in the basement on Oak Street, to go ahead and scream. 'I will cut your vocal cords. I did it once and I can do it again,' Hooker told me."

The detective went on to tell me that Hooker wore Marliz's wristwatch to work and how workers at the lumber mill thought it odd for him to be wearing a woman's watch. Janice said, the watch was lost when it fell off Hooker's wrist into a wood chipper. Hooker buried the woman's purse somewhere in Red Bluff's Dog Island Park. The police made an effort to locate the purse, but were unsuccessful.

As I set thinking about Marliz, one thing did come to my mind. When I crawled into the box under the waterbed, I remembered seeing my purse in the space between the double walls. I also remembered seeing the picture of a beautiful, young woman whom I couldn't identify. I described her as being Italian-looking, with a dark complexion, a large nose, and long black, wavy hair.

"That's her," Detective Shamblin interrupted. "That's Marie Elizabeth."

It appeared that Hooker didn't throw away everything after he murdered Marliz. He kept a souvenir photo of Marliz which was burned, along with much of his other pornographic material, late one night.

Jan, as part of her immunity deal struck with the District Attorney, tried to help the police find the remains of Marliz. She guided a search party out to an area 35 miles northeast of Red Bluff, between the communities of Shingletown and Viola, where Marliz was buried.

"I can't remember," Jan told police. "It was dark, cold, and so long ago."

To this day, I'm not sure if Jan couldn't remember or if she didn't want to remember. Perhaps she didn't want to look at the remains of the woman she helped murder eight years before. Without any physical evidence, the District Attorney, or DA, chose not to bring murder charges against Hooker. The DA only had Jan's word and no physical proof. Allegations of murder remained only allegations. They considered the case to be weak, whereas my case was much stronger. If for some reason Hooker was found not guilty in my case, the DA could still bring murder charges at some later date. There is no statute of limitations in a murder case.

I still hope and pray Marliz will someday receive her day in court and Hooker will receive justice for what he did to her. Marliz's blood and DNA are still probably under the floor boards of the kitchen on Oak Street.

After hearing the detectives interview me, my parents had a better idea of what I had been through. Now they knew how dangerous and evil the man was who kept me as his prisoner for so many years. They knew how lucky I was to be alive.

When the police returned to Red Bluff, they believed the incredible story Jan had told them about me being kept as a slave. Hooker was arrested Sunday morning, November 18, and taken to the Tehama County Jail where he was charged with a number of felony counts ranging from kidnapping to rape. Various forms of torture such as being confined in a box, chained to a rack, stretched, burned, electro-cuted, dunked in the bathtub, and hung or crucified were not against California law at the time. I understand today the law has been changed to include such acts of torture.

People in Red Bluff were shocked when they opened their news-papers Monday morning. Those who knew Hooker described him as a low key, quiet guy who was a hardworking family man. Lacking close friends, he was more of a nerd than a slave master. Hooker's parents couldn't believe the charges against their son. How could Kay be a slave? She didn't even wash dishes after the family dinner at the Hooker farm.

Dorothy, the next door neighbor, always knew something was wrong in the Hooker household and now she knew the truth. The wheels of justice slowly began to turn.

After being home for several weeks, I wanted to get my life going again. I wanted to get a job, an apartment, and a car. However, my dad became emotional when I talked about moving out. He wanted me to continue to stay with him in his home. He didn't want to lose me again. For a car, Dad loaned me a Volkswagen diesel pickup he used in his construction business.

I was glad to be home and my heart was filled with joy. Feelings of guilt, anger, or revenge wouldn't enter my life until later. I still had some fear, but didn't want fear to control me. I wanted to get out into the world and on with my life.

For a job, I went to the nearest Circle K convenience store and applied for a cashier or clerk position. (It was not the same Circle K where I met Mohammad.) The manager hired me, but specified I was to only work during daylight hours. He didn't want me in the store by myself after dark. I never told him I had already been a victim of a violent crime. It was none of his business.

After a couple of months my sister Jenise, who worked at Riverside Community Hospital, heard about a job in Environmental Services, better known as housekeeping. The position was better than the job at the Circle K, and I knew I had the skills to do well at housekeeping, thanks to the Hookers. On the application was a large blank space for previous job experience. I wrote "personal housekeeper for the Hooker family." What else could I write? I couldn't write that I was a recently freed slave who had been forced to clean house during the day and kept in a box at night. The "personal housekeeper for the Hooker family" would be used against me in the upcoming Hooker trail.

I got the job and started to work immediately. While at the hospital I got to know one fellow worker well. Her name was Lynn Sherman. She was an African-American woman who had a couple of children from a previous marriage. As we worked together, we talked about everything under the sun. One day she asked me what I did before coming to the hospital. I told her I had worked at a Circle K for a couple of months.

"What did you do before the Circle K?" Lynn asked.

"Well, I was abducted by a man and his wife in Northern California and held as their slave for over 7 years," I answered. I went on to tell Lynn about the torture and being locked in the box. Lynn was surprised and shocked. Then she asked the single question I receive from almost everyone who hears my story for the first time.

"Colleen, how can you be so normal after all you went through?"

Many people can't understand how I could lead a normal life after Hooker. People assume such events would scar a person's soul, leaving them unable to function. I gave Lynn the same answer I always give to the question.

"I was normal before I was abducted, so why shouldn't I be normal now? It was Hooker, not me, who was abnormal. He may have stolen years from me, but I'm not going to let him steal everything from me. He's not going to prevent me from living and enjoying life."

Lynn later married a serviceman, had another baby, and moved to Texas. We wrote for years, but in time we both moved on and lost contact with each other. I still consider her a friend and hope she's doing well.

Lynn was the first person, outside my family and Mohammad, I told about my abduction. Only after I have gotten to know a person well, over a long period of time, will I tell my story. Most people I meet and do business with don't know and don't need to know my past. It's my story and I will decide when, if ever, the time is right to tell my story.

One thing I did when I returned home was to go to church to worship the Lord. My faith in the Lord remained strong, because I knew He had seen me through my darkest days. Living in the sunshine now, I wanted to give thanks for what He had done for me. "Everything will be all right" was the answer I had received to my prayers while in captivity. My many prayers, in the darkest of days, had been fulfilled. I was alive and safely back home.

I tried a number of churches to find one where I felt comfortable. I went to a non-denominational Christian Church near my mom's house. After a couple of visits, members of the congregation tried to pair me up with a young man they were sending off to ministerial school. He was a nice guy, but I was looking for a church, not a husband.

I went to the Adventist Church and the Church of the Nazarene a couple of times, but found neither right for me. After a few visits, the members kept trying to draw me into their church politics and gossip. I didn't care to hear which member was sleeping with whose husband. I only wanted to worship God.

I felt like a returning POW (prisoner of war). I found myself thankful for the simple things in life. Getting out of bed in the middle of the night for a glass of cold water was an experience I relished. Being able to wake up in the morning and fix breakfast was heavenly. No more rice or oatmeal for me. It was now eggs, toast, and orange juice. It bothered me when people, who had so much, never appeared to be happy. Their houses were too small, cars too out of date, and husbands or wives too dull. None of them knew, or appreciated, their abundant blessings. Everything, for them, was taken for granted.

I was also bothered by how people rushed through things. No one wanted to slow down and enjoy life. People were in a hurry to get to the shopping mall, get supper on the table, and get in front of the television for their favorite show. I was amazed and disheartened at the fast pace of life surrounding me. People weren't taking time to watch beautiful summer sunsets followed by the appearance of uncountable evening stars. Perhaps it was the difference between Red Bluff, a small town, and Riverside, a large city. Whatever the reason, my years of isolation had taught me to slow down and appreciate the simple gifts of life.

At first, anger was not part of my emotional repertoire. As a slave, I was not permitted to express anger. Over the years, I have talked to many victims of violent crime and they all share one thing in common. They could not experience fear and anger at the same time. Fear has to end before anger can begin. That's why so many rape victims don't initially go to the police in anger. Instead, they go home in fear and often take a shower destroying vital evidence. Only later do they become angry and report the crime or too many times the crime never gets reported at all.

During the first three months, I was somewhat depressed and anxious, especially when it was necessary to leave home. Only after I learned of Hooker's arrest did my fear change to anger. I started to realize what he had stolen from me over the years. I wanted him to pay and never be able to hurt another woman.

Soon, my life would enter a new phase. Slowly the wheels of justice began to turn. I was to learn the worse was yet to come. News reporters, defense attorneys, and court rulings would cast me as a willing participant. Photographs of me smiling with Hooker, love letters I was forced to write, even my telephone calls from Riverside, would be twisted and turned against me. Soon, I would wonder who was on trial.

The only silver lining in the dark clouds surrounding me was the light being cast by the investigation. I would finally learn the answer to questions that had plagued me for years. Who were the Hookers? Why were they so evil? Why was I chosen to become their victim? After years of being out of range of their husband and wife conversations, I was now learning the reasons behind their actions. For years, asking a question out of turn would have resulted in a beating. Now asking a question would result in an answer. With the trial procedures starting, I was ready for answers and the truth.

Chapter 13 - The Preliminary Hearing

As soon as the story of Hooker's arrest hit the news, the media circus began. Reporters converged on my dad's house seeking a personal interview with what they called "The Girl in the Box" or "The Sex Slave." Both of these titles were products of the media. For weeks, at least a half dozen members of the press, with cameras ready, staked out my dad's front yard.

I had no interest in talking with the media. I quickly moved in with my boyfriend Mohammad, who had not yet departed for Iran. I told him to speak Farsi if any reporters inquired as to my whereabouts. None did. Staying at Mohammad's apartment was convenient, since my job at the hospital was within walking distance.

"Colleen, we have already missed too many Thanksgivings without you. I'll be damned if I'm going to let these reporters keep you from spending Thanksgiving with your family," Dad said.

After he picked me up at Mohammad's apartment, I ducked down in Dad's pickup truck as we approached a group of reporters outside his house. It reminded me of the times I would duck down in Hooker's pickup to avoid being seen by the neighbors. Once my dad drove through the reporters, he stopped behind the house out of sight of the media. Ruth closed the drapes, allowing the entire family to have a peaceful dinner without being hassled. It was the Thanksgiving dinner I had dreamed of in the box. I was truly thankful to God for allowing me to be with my family.

"It's sad all those reporters aren't at home with their families enjoying dinner," Dad commented during the meal.

My phone conversations with Jan quickly dried up after Hooker's arrest. Previously, Jan had called me to report on Hookers progress. He was going to church, attending counseling, and had burned much of his pornography and bondage equipment. She also wanted assurance I had not gone to the police. After his arrest, there was no reason for us to communicate.

After Hooker's arrest, I felt a great sense of relief. I knew with him in jail, he couldn't hurt me or any other woman. He had told me he wanted more slaves, therefore I knew he would abduct another innocent woman sooner or later. Now with my fear of Hooker gone, I started to feel anger towards him. He had stolen over seven years of my life for his own vile purposes. Seven years when I should have been completing my education, getting a job, and starting a family.

I was angry now, but other emotions soon entered my life. How could I have been so stupid? How could I have believed he was part of The Company? How could I have believed in The Company? Should I have attempted an escape? Should I feel guilty for being such a good slave? Why did I do what I did? I needed answers fast, since I would soon be on the witness stand in court testifying against Hooker. I needed to know not only what I did, but the reasons behind my actions. I needed confidence in myself and my actions. Did I do the right thing while in captivity?

The preliminary hearing was scheduled in early December, 1984. Dad didn't want me to travel back to Red Bluff alone, fearing I might disappear again. The two of us drove north on Interstate 5 through a heavy seasonal rain storm. As I was driving across a bridge the Volkswagen pickup began to hydroplane. Skidding out of control and turning 90 degrees, Dad and I exchanged glances as we thought, "This might be the end!" Once over the bridge the pickup straightened out and we went on our way with a feeling of relief. One can only think about what might have been if I, the primary witness against Hooker, had been killed in a car crash. Perhaps once again, a guardian angel interceded on my behalf.

The prosecuting attorney didn't want us to spend the night in Red Bluff because of all the media attention. Anderson, a small town between Red Bluff and Redding, was selected for us to spend our first night. Wanting to look my best for the preliminary hearing, I purchased a nice dress the next morning. The dress was navy blue with small yellow and red decorative dots. The straight skirted dress extended from my neck to my knees and looked professional. For shoes, I had a pair of black pumps with one inch heels. Overall, I felt the dress was conservative and would make a good impression at the hearing. I would later learn the dress made me look like a promiscuous woman in the eyes of one important person.

I had an appointment with Dr. Michael Vovakes on Tuesday December 4, to document any visible medical evidence for the upcoming trial. First, a nurse weighted me and took my height.

"Your five feet, seven inches," the nurse said, as she filled in a medical form.

"No, I'm five feet, six inches," I said. "I've always been five feet, six inches all my life."

The nurse looked a little irritated, as she looked up at me. She knew she had recorded the numbers correctly.

Dad, who was sitting in a nearby chair, broke the tension when he said, "Cameron must have stretched you an inch."

"Oh Dad, shut up," I said, trying to suppress a smile on my face. It had been a long time since humor had been part of my life.

The doctor noted and carefully recorded each and every scar on my body. He knew his report would be used in a criminal trial. He found a small discolored scar on my left wrists, two white scars on my right wrist, and another scar on one of my ankles. My labium was pierced where I had worn a ring.

"Those are electrical burns," the doctor said of the scars on the insides of my thighs. "Regular scars are flat whereas electrical burns are raised and bumpy."

The doctor noted the thinning hair on the top of my head, and the damage to my shoulder from the stretcher. My eyesight had also decreased from years of darkness, and I was physically exhausted. I had also not seen a dentist in years and calluses were on parts of my body from the years of sleeping on the hard bottom of the box. The marks on my body matched the story given to the police by both Jan and myself.

Dad and I stayed in a Redding motel on December 4, the night before the hearing. The next morning, we ate breakfast at Annie's Restaurant, next door to the motel. As we were sitting in a booth enjoying a cup of coffee, we could hear the conversation in the next booth.

"I hope to get an interview with Colleen Stan today for my paper," an apparent reporter said to the person across from him. "Try to get a good picture of her for the front page. No one has published a photo of her, and I'm not sure what she looks like."

It took all our will power to keep from laughing out loud, as Dad and I sat in the next booth. Dad put his index finger to his mouth as he indicated for me to be quiet. We both cracked up once we were outside the restaurant.

Before the hearing, scheduled for Wednesday, December 5, I met with Detective Shambin and the prosecuting Deputy District Attorney Christine McGuire. The purpose of the meeting was to go over the statement I had given to Detective Shamblin in Riverside a month earlier. They would also go over what I should expect during the hearing. They were not allowed to tell me what to say, but they could refresh my memory as to what I had already said.

Christine would become an important person in my life during the trial. It was her job to represent the State of California and to achieve a conviction of Cameron Hooker. I will always be grateful to her for working so hard to put Hooker behind bars. She was an outstanding, 28 year old attorney, who knew her way around in the courtroom.

However, Christine and I never saw eye to eye on anything. Many times, in my personal opinion, she was like a brilliant medical doctor who lacked good bedside manners. She was an outstanding attorney, who viewed me as just one of the tools at her disposal to prosecute Cameron Hooker. My human and emotional needs were not her concern. I supported her goal of getting Hooker convicted, but often felt she viewed me as a juvenile in need of close supervision. In her hands, I once again felt like a victim.

As soon as Christine saw the new dress I had purchased, she was furious. The dress was too tight and didn't present me well in the eyes of the court. The color, dark blue, was all wrong. She wanted me in white, but saw only red with her eyes. The shoes, with their one inch heels, were stilettos that made me look too sexy to pass as a victim. Later when the actual trial began, Christine purchased an appropriate courtroom dress for me. It was baby blue and I wore a pair of beige Mary Jane flats. I looked like a little school girl in the costume. I know her purpose was to make me appear sweet and innocent, but it made me feel like a puppet on the end of a string. Christine wanted to control everything, even my wardrobe.

The preliminary hearing, case number 13961, took place on Wednesday, December 5, at 10:50 AM in the courtroom of Judge

Watkins. The purpose of the hearing was to determine if there was enough evidence to turn Cameron Hooker over for trial. Judge Watkins, not a jury, would make the final decision. At the end of the day, Hooker would be ordered to stand trial or he would be set free.

The hearing in Red Bluff took place in the Tehama County Courthouse with its Greek Ionic columns and a red tile roof. Jan, Detective Shamblin, and I would testify. The court was packed with reporters, including the two from Annie's Restaurant. I was not allowed to be in the courtroom since I was scheduled to testify. My dad sat in the back row of the spectators section. Later, Dad told me what I had missed.

Jan, who testified first, presented a disheveled appearance before the court in her faded jeans and sweatshirt. The DA had granted her full immunity in exchange for her cooperation. On the stand, Jan was under the influence of two drugs to prevent depression and panic attacks, Xanax and Desyrel. She was listless and responded poorly to the questions.

"I don't ...ah...remember, well...I don't know, and I can't recall," were her answers to many questions.

Preliminary hearing testimony:

Question by Ms. McGuire: During the period of time that you lived at the house on Oak Street, did you ever see the Defendant hang Colleen from the rafters?

Answer by Jan: The rafters of what?

Question: The rafters of the basement.

Answer: On Oak Street?

Question: Yes.

Answer: Yes.

Question: And approximately how many times did you see the Defendant hang Colleen from the rafters of the basement?

Answer: On Oak Street?

Question: On Oak Street.

Answer: I think only once.

After Jan had testified, Christine took her aside.

"Your immunity was granted to you to tell the truth and the whole truth." the Deputy DA chided her. "Before you testify again, you had

162

better pull yourself together and start remembering or else your immunity will be revoked. Do I make myself clear?"

Now, it was my time to testify. I entered the courtroom, was sworn in, and took my seat on the witness stand. Hooker was directly in front of me wearing an orange jumpsuit, issued by the jail, along with a smirk on his face.

"This isn't going anywhere," Hooker appeared to be saying through his smirk. "I know I'll beat these charges and then I will beat you."

Hooker, who had pleaded not guilty, had a good defense attorney. Attorney Rolland Papendick had practiced law in Red Bluff for years. He knew the territory and was a good match for Christine. He had ample evidence to present to the court in favor of his client. If it came to a trial, Papendick felt Cameron would walk free.

I testified for two and a half hours. It was difficult with all the reports staring at me. Testifying in court required me to go into greater detail about the tortures and humiliation I endured at the hands of Hooker. I felt sorry for my dad who was hearing many of the painful details for the first time. Like in the living room on Coolidge Avenue, I couldn't look at my dad's face while testifying. He was the only man I trusted, and I didn't want to hurt him. Afterwards, I asked my dad what he was thinking during my testimony.

"I wanted to go up there and kill him with my bare hands," Dad said, with an angry voice.

Judge Watkins ruled enough evidence existed to warrant a trial and Hooker's bail should remain at $500,000. Hooker's bail was later reduced to $150,000, but he remained in the county jail.

People of California vs. Hooker would start in nine months. On April 18, 1985, the trial was moved to Redwood City where a jury pool, untainted by all the press coverage, could be found. Redwood City was a continuation of the urban sprawl from San Francisco, 20 miles to the north. This time there would be a jury and Hooker would learn his fate.

Before Dad and I returned to Riverside, we visited Burney Falls. Previously, I had visited the falls in the summer of 1984, with the Hooker family. Now I was back in the winter with my dad. Rather than water, the falls was now an art work in snow and ice. I loved the beauty of the falls and the freedom I now enjoyed.

Back in Riverside, I quite my hospital job after eight months. On my first day working in the Medical and Surgical Intensive Care Unit a nurse walked up to me and said, "Have you ever seen a dead body?"

"No," I said.

"You will," the nurse, said before abruptly turning around and walking off.

She was right. I have a lot of respect for people who can work in a hospital environment, but it was too depressing for me.

My third job was with a manufacturing company. We made rubber parts for pharmaceutical products and lawn irrigation systems. My boss, Betty, ruled with a firm hand. Conflict arose when I had to take time off for official court business. Betty felt I was spending too much time away from the job, even after I showed her an order from the court. I had recently bought a Honda Accord and didn't want to lose both my job and car. Christine was upset with me because I was so concerned about being fired from my job. I was caught between a rock and a hard place, Betty and Christine. All of this added more stress to my life.

Linda, my cousin, came to my rescue by calling the George School of Law in Sacramento. They put me in contact with the Victim Witness Program run by California. I needed help because I didn't feel anyone was watching out for my interests. What if I needed legal advice or had a question? Christine worked for the state. I needed someone to be there for me. Today, they are called victim advocates. In 1985, the Victim Advocates Program was just getting started.

The Victim Witness Program put me in touch with Marilyn Barrett, a Santa Monica tax attorney, who was with the Los Angeles Commission on Assaults on Women. Marilyn became my advocate and friend. She was never my attorney and never charged me a fee. She was a life saver in helping me find my way through the legal labyrinth of an archaic court system. I could always count on Marilyn to be a phone call away, and I soon needed her.

On June 4, Christine telephoned me at work to inform me a plea bargain would be arranged with Hooker in six days. The DA's office had been instructed to seek a plea bargain by the Tehama County Supervisors because of a severe budget crisis. Tehama County, which included Red Bluff, had announced layoffs of up to 50 county employees beginning in July. The Chairman of the County Supervisors vehemently denied the budget and trial were linked, but everyone knew the trial would cost $261,000. The state government could advance funds to a county to prosecute a homicide, but not for other serious felonies such as kidnapping and rape. A plea bargain would result in Hooker pleading guilty to a lesser charge and receiving three to five years in prison.

Upon hearing the news over the telephone, I broke down in tears as I ran for the woman's restroom. Betty followed me asking, "What's wrong?"

"He will kill me," I said, between sobs. "I testified against him, and I know he will come after me."

"Is there anyone you can call?" Betty asked.

"Yes, I can call Marilyn Barrett."

"Don't worry," Marilyn said, after I told her about the plea bargain. "I have friends in Sacramento. "

Marilyn went to work on the problem knowing six days would soon pass. She called California Assemblyman Richard Katz, a Democrat from the San Fernando Valley, who contacted California Attorney General John Van de Kamp.

"He [Hooker] would have been out in less years than he held the woman captive and that's absurd," Assemblyman Richard Katz told the news media.

Before the deadline, Tehama County was told it was "unethical" to plea bargain away a high profile case due to a lack of funds. A bill by Assemblyman Stan Statham, a Republican from Redding, went to the California Assembly authorizing the state to pay Tehama County $120,000 toward the expenses of the trial. The plea bargain was cancelled and Hooker was told to prepare for trial. A California law was later passed preventing DA's from plea bargaining solely due to a shortage of county funds. Credit for this victory belongs primarily to Marilyn Barrett, Richard Katz, and John Van de Kamp. Others in Tehama County tried to falsely take credit for this action.

Before I testified in the trial, I needed answers to the questions still plaguing me. I knew what I did while with Hooker, but I didn't know why I did it. A sense of guilt still overpowered me. Why had I been such a good slave? Why had I been so stupid? Should I have tried to escape? Why had I written those "love" letters to Hooker? Why had I smiled with my arms around his neck when pictures were taken? I lacked confidence in myself and expected to be shredded by Hooker's defense attorney once on the witness stand. Marilyn had come forth to help with legal questions, and now another person came forward to help me with questions I had about myself.

Dr. Chris Hatcher, Ph.D. was an Associate Clinical Professor of Psychology at the University of California, San Francisco Medical School. He had been tasked by Christine to produce a report on me and testify in court. Dr. Hatcher had spent years studying hostage behavior, predatory kidnapping, violent behavior, and abusive relationships. He had extensively studied the People's Temple in Jonestown, where 909 people died, and years later Polly Klaas, a young girl who was kidnapped and murdered. Marc Klaas, Polly's father, described Dr. Hatcher as a "lifeline in a sea of fury and rage." He went on to say, "His [Dr. Hatcher] overall contribution to the understanding of the mind and fragility of victims cannot be overestimated and will never be fully appreciated."

With most people, I have to explain my feelings and justify my actions when I tell my story. With Dr. Hatcher, he knew my feelings and actions before I told him. It was like he had been in captivity with me. He could tell me how I felt at different stages of my confinement. He knew my reactions to the brutal torture and the endless periods of loneliness. I was talking to an expert in the field of hostage behavior.

Being a gentle and caring man, I found it easy to open up to Dr. Hatcher during my interview which lasted for hours. I told Dr. Hatcher about the questions that had been plaguing me.

"Colleen, you didn't do anything abnormal," Dr. Hatcher said. "A lot of people will tell you they would have done this or that, but they don't know. They haven't been in your situation. If they had done these things, they probably would have been killed. What you did was the right thing, because in the end, you came out alive. You're a survivor. You did the right thing."

Dr. Hatcher helped me understand the things I did were normal for a person in my situation. I had not done anything wrong. I had made the correct decisions under the circumstances and had come out alive. I was a survivor. I was now ready to testify in court against the man who had taken so much from me. I can't thank Dr. Hatcher enough for giving me confidence in myself before I took the witness stand.

On March 26, 1985, I traveled once again to Red Bluff to meet with Christine to prepare for the trial. This time my mother accompanied me. Christine spent a lot of time going over a timeline of my captivity which would prove invaluable to the jury. A timeline was needed because of the numerous crimes that took place over such a long period of time.

"What religious denomination are you?" Christine asked.

"None," I answered.

"Are you a Christian?"

"I'm trying," I answered.

Christine placed a tape measure around my neck to see if the neck hole in the head box would fit me. She didn't want to ask me to place my head in the box again.

"Cameron said he was a sadist," I told Christine. Jan questioned herself, "Am I a masochist?"

"Are you [a masochist]?" Christine asked.

"No," I replied emphatically.

As I looked over the physical evidence which would be used in the trial, I was surprised by one piece of prosecution evidence. During the interview on Coolidge Avenue, Detective Al Shamblin asked me to draw some of the torture items used on me such as the frame and the stretcher.

"I would be glad to, but I can't draw," I told Detective Shamblin.

"That's okay, Colleen. No one will ever see the drawings other than me," he assured me.

I proceeded to draw a number of stick people on various pieces of equipment. The drawings looked like the work of an elementary child with no art ability. Now in Christine's office, I was standing in front of my drawings after they had been enlarged for all the court to see. I slowly shook my finger at Detective Shamblin, as he had a sheepish look on his face.

Chapter 14 - The Slave Owner's Wife

The trial started on Tuesday, September 24, 1985, in the Superior Court of California in and for the County of San Mateo. Jury selection was the first order of business in case C-14661, People vs. Hooker. Sixteen felony counts were charged against Cameron including one count of kidnapping with the use of a knife, seven counts of rape, one of forced oral copulation, one of penetration with a foreign object (a whip handle), one forced sodomy, three of false imprisonment, and two of abducting to live in an illicit relationship. The multiple counts of forced imprisonment and abducting to live in an illicit relationship were due to the law changing during my long captivity. Keeping a person in a box, hanging from the ceiling, partial drowning, stretching, and electrocuting were not against California law at the time. The law was later changed to cover various forms of torture.

Judge Clarence Knight was selected to preside over the trial. Five men and seven women, on the jury, would sit through five and a half weeks of high courtroom drama. CNN (Cable News Network) wanted to televise the trial, but Judge Knight refused. Reporters were permitted to observe the trial and pictures were allowed when the court was not in session.

Hooker's defense was anchored on two assumptions. First, the seven year statute of limitations for kidnapping had passed. Therefore, Hooker could not be convicted of kidnapping. Second, the defense claimed I was a "willing participant" and I was free to leave anytime after early 1978.

The prosecution countered the Hooker defense by arguing the kidnapping was continuous from 1977 to 1984. The statute of limitations period didn't start until 1984. They also claimed I was not a willing participant and could not leave anytime I wanted. My willingness to stay or not stay with the Hooker family couldn't be proven in court. It came down to Hooker's word against mine. The jury had to decide who was telling the truth. In this trial, expert witnesses for both the prosecution and defense would play a vital role.

The 140 pieces of physical evidence in the trial was shocking to the public. On display in the courtroom were leather straps, whips, chains, head boxes, the frame, the stretcher, bondage photographs, and numerous pornographic publications. A quarter-sized mockup of the underground hole was also on display. Reporters had a field day photographing the torture items for their newspapers. The jury had to decide if these items were used to torture me or used in a consensual relationship between adults.

The box under the waterbed deserves special mention. The box had been reconstructed in the courtroom with the top removed for all to see where I had spent six years of my life. Natural body oils and sweat had left an imprint of my body in the bottom of the box where I had laid. Only the area to the left of my head was stain free. That's where the hair dryer, which provided air to the box, set. With the bedpan in the lower right, I always laid diagonally in the box as the imprint showed.

Early on, Judge Knight ruled that the alleged kidnapping and murder of Marliz was not to be brought up in court. Hooker had not been indicted or convicted in her disappearance and death.

The primary witnesses for the prosecution included Jan, my sister Bonnie, Dr. Hatcher, and myself. The defense would rely mostly on Hooker and Dr. Donald Lunde, a noted psychiatrist. Other witnesses also testified including the detectives, the medical doctor, my employer at the Kings Lodge, the landlord on Oak Street, neighbors, and Hooker's relatives including his children.

Since I was a witness in the trial, I was not permitted to be in the courtroom except when called to testify. I followed the proceedings in the newspapers and on television. The conviction of Hooker was not a forgone conclusion. I knew it took only one juror to deadlock the trial. A mistrial could result in a plea bargain with the charges being reduced, or Hooker being released.

For over a month, I was a nervous wreck during the trial. The newspapers were filled with headlines such as "Slave Girl Chose to Stay" and "Girl in Box Wrote Love Letters to Her Master." My step-mother was misquoted in the papers as saying, "[Colleen] was free to come home." The error was corrected the next day, but the damage was done. Who would the jury believe? How would they interpret the evidence? Would Dr. Hatcher or Dr. Lunde win over the jury? Hooker's smirk told me he believed he would soon walk out of the courthouse a free man.

Throughout the trial, I began to slowly understand the minds of Cameron and Jan Hooker. After years of being kept in the dark, I was now learning the reasons behind their actions. Why was I kept naked most of the time and given the name K? Why were my wrists chained to my neck when first put in a box? What was the story behind the first rape, when Jan ran out of the room? Things that made no sense at the time, now became clear. Unlike when I was with the Hookers, I could ask questions without fear of receiving a beating and I was now receiving answers.

Janice Hooker, or Jan as she was called by her family, was the first witness called to testify. Sitting in the witness chair, as I would soon learn, is a nerve racking experience. All eyes and ears in the room are focused on everything you do and say. Hooker, the father of Jan's children, sat 10 feet away staring at her. Many times, Jan continued to say she couldn't recall certain facts, conversations, or dates. To her credit, the police have told me her story has not changed over the years, which indicates she was telling the truth.

Her testimony in court was not a continuous flow of coherent words. Like any courtroom testimony, her statements were interrupted with questions, legal objections, and rulings from the bench. I will condense and paraphrase her testimony while maintaining her feelings and points of view. As far as I know, Jan has never given a complete summary of the events of her life outside legal circles. The following is not the voice of Jan. It's my voice attempting to convey her thoughts and feelings.

Jan was sworn in and took her place on the witness stand. She began her testimony by stating her name for the court record. I'm Janice Annette Hooker, age 27, born in February, 1958, in Los Gatos, California. I attended Red Bluff High School and, like any young teenager, I had doubts and insecurities about myself. In 1973, at the age of 15, I met Cameron Hooker through a mutual friend. He was nice, tall, good looking, and most importantly, showed an interest in me. Cameron was four years older, had a job, and his own car. We started dating and grew closer together with time. Eventually, I fell in love with him.

I knew early in our relationship that Cameron had some bizarre sexual interest. He was fascinated with slave women, horror movies, and

Halloween. Six months into our relationship, he asked me if he could hang me by the wrists from a tree. He told me other girls had allowed it. I was hesitant and scared, but didn't want to lose him. Finally, I said okay. It was painful, but afterwards Cameron hugged me and treated me with tender loving care. I tried to blot out the pain from my mind and only focus on the nice aspects of Cameron. He was the only guy who treated me special.

I was both fascinated and repulsed by Cameron. He was a nice guy, but he came with disturbingly strange interests. I knew he won't hurt me, because he never forced me to do anything against my will. To gage his love, I said the two words that will test any man's attachment to a woman, "I'm pregnant." To my delight, Cameron asked me to marry him.

Before the wedding, I was concerned about his bondage interest, but believed I could handle it. We were married in Reno, Nevada, in 1975. I was 16 and Cameron was 21. Of course, the baby never came. I later confessed, in 1979, that I had lied to him.

"I knew," were Cameron's only words in response to my confession.

We moved to a small house in Red Bluff for a short time, but eventually moved to the rental house at 1140 Oak Street. The bizarre activities grew more frequent and painful. Cameron began to collect large amounts of pornography and bondage equipment. In 1975, he made the first of two head boxes. He called me down to the basement when the small head box was finished to check the fit on a woman's neck. I placed my head in the box which was quickly closed and locked. The experience was terrorizing. A second head box was too large and heavy for a woman to support on her head. It had to be suspended from the ceiling. I never wore the smaller head box again or tested the larger head box.

Of special interest to Hooker was the book, or in his case the movie, *Story of O*. The story dealt with a young, beautiful woman who was so in love with a man, she would do anything for him including becoming his slave. Cameron drew inspiration from the movie and later used many of its techniques on Colleen. Her slave name K, having her wrists chained to her neck, the slave collars, not being allowed to wear underwear, calling him Master, and kneeling naked to ask permission, all came from the *Story of O*. Of course, O was a willing participant, whereas K was not.

Cameron was also interested in a June, 1976, article in "Oui" magazine titled "Brainwashing: How to Fold, Spindle and Mutilate the Human Mind in Five Easy Steps" by Dr. Timothy Leary. ("Do not Fold, Spindle, or Mutilate," was a common warning printed on computer punch cards. To do so would have resulted in problems with the computer card reader. Such cards are obsolete today, having been replaced by soft copy and magnetic storage media.) Since Cameron had dyslexia, he was not a good reader, and I had to read the article to him.

The steps included:

1. Seize the victim and spirit her away.
2. Isolate the victim and make her totally dependent on you for survival.
3. Dominate the victim and encourage her to seek your recognition and approval.
4. Instruct the victim and re-education her to think and act in terms of your ideology.
5. Seduce the victim and provide her with a new sexual value system.

Cameron used these five steps to control and brainwash Colleen. (Dr. Leary intended for his article to educate people, not serve as a roadmap to evil. The article was written during the Patty Hearst controversy.)

In time, I began to fear what Cameron would do to me next. He hung me by the wrists, which was the most painful, and whipped me regularly. My greatest fear was a rubber gas mask with the air holes taped shut. I couldn't take the pain anymore, so I accepted a proposition Cameron made to me in 1975.

"You can have a baby, if I can have a slave girl."

The slave would take the pain, humiliation, and torture. Cameron's love, kindness, and tenderness, were to be reserved for me. There also was to be no sex with the slave.

I finally got my baby, Charity, later the next year, but Cameron still didn't have his slave. Then late one afternoon, we spotted a young woman hitchhiking on the overpass above Interstate 5. We offered her a ride which she accepted. As we drove into the mountains, Cameron and I communicated between ourselves as only a husband and wife can. At Paynes Creek, Cameron moved the head box from the trunk to the backseat of the car. When the young woman returned to the car from the restroom, she had no idea her last chance to escape had passed.

After pulling off the main road, I and the baby went down to a mountain stream while Cameron kidnapped the woman. Within five minutes, we were back on the road returning to Red Bluff. We stopped for some hamburgers at the Jolly Cone, drove to the nearby Diversion Dam, and waited for it to get dark. Returning to our Oak Street house, Cameron took the woman down to the basement while I put the baby to bed. I stayed upstairs with the baby while Cameron hung the woman up in the basement. I was terrified.

After 45 minutes, Cameron called me down to the basement where I saw the woman hanging naked from hooks in the ceiling. She was thrashing around, moaning, and was in great pain. Her eyes were blindfolded or taped and she had a ball gag in her mouth. (A ball gag is a rubber ball with a leather thong passing through the middle of the ball. The ball is inserted in the mouth and the thong is tied behind the head.) Cameron placed a pillow case over her head and we had intercourse in the basement. After which, I went back upstairs and Cameron remained with the woman. I later learned her name was Colleen Stan.

(Note: After eight years, some details of Jan's story differed from mine. I remember wearing what became evidence item number 31, which was a leather strap head harness. The harness had straps, when pulled tight, prevented my mouth from opening.)

The next day, after Cameron had gone to work, I heard Colleen rattling her chains and making a lot of noise. With a shotgun, I went downstairs to check on her. She was naked on her back wearing the small head box. I opened the head box and found her blindfolded and gagged.

"What's wrong?" I asked.

"I'm cold," Colleen answered, from behind the gag.

I placed a blanket over her, closed and locked the head box, and went back up stairs. Cameron came home after work, fed her, and allowed her to use the bedpan. Colleen ate and used the bedpan once a day.

From the very first night, I took no joy in having a woman in the basement of our home. I was riddled with guilt and sick with fear. I stayed upstairs and focused my attention on the baby while Cameron focused on his slave. Between August and September, 1977, I worked at Exatron, an electronics company in Sunnyvale near San Francisco. During the week, I stayed with my sister who took care of my child while I was at work. On the weekends, I would go home to Red Bluff. Colleen didn't realize I was gone because her isolation in the basement was so profound.

"It's not fair for her to be here," I once told Cameron. "Let her go."

"No," he replied.

After a week or two, Cameron built a box to keep her in during the day. Her hands were chained to her neck, she was naked, and she wore the head box while confined in the box. The box itself was closed and locked. After two weeks her hands were unchained and the bedpan was placed in the box with her. I was too scared to open the box while Cameron was at work. Colleen stayed in the box for five months. (Note: Jan said the bedpan was placed in the box with me. I remembered not having free access to the bedpan until after I was removed from the box.)

After about three months, Colleen was taken upstairs for her first bath. Her eyes, mouth, and head were covered with cloth and duct tape. She was placed in the water, facedown, with her hands and legs tied behind her back. A rope, taped to her hair, was used to pull her out of the water. I couldn't comb the tangles out of her hair, so I used scissors to cut off large portions of her hair. Photographs taken of Colleen were later burned in 1984.

The workshop was build by Cameron under the stairway in 1977. The workshop had a wooden latch and light switch on the outside. A chair and bedpan were in the workshop with Colleen. She was kept in the workshop at night and the box during the day. Colleen worked seven or eight hours at night while we slept upstairs. She shelled nuts or worked on projects such as macramé or crochets which I taught her to do. The shelled nuts and projects were sold at flea markets.

In January, 1978, I found a slave contract in one of Cameron's underground newspapers. I later helped Cameron by typing the slave contract, on a rented typewriter, while he added the title in old English lettering. Colleen appeared really shook up after reading the contract. She didn't want to sign it, but Cameron told her she would be sorry if she didn't. Once Colleen signed the contract, she became slave K.

Colleen asked about the bandages on my knees. Cameron told her an elaborate story about how I was once a slave of The Company. After an escape attempt, I was captured and tortured by The Company. My damaged knees were a result of the torture. The Company would torture or sale Colleen if she tried to escape, and her family would be killed if she went to them for help.

Truthfully, I had arthritis in my knees and underwent surgery in January, 1978, October, 1980, and April, 1982. I was also in the hospital in September, 1976, for the birth of our first daughter, and March, 1977, for tonsils. In fact, the bedpan Colleen used was from one of my hospital stays.

After Colleen became slave K, she was allowed upstairs. In the next three months, she ate with the family six times and cleaned up the kitchen about 25 times. She wore a blue nightgown during the winter and nothing during the summer. Anytime she wanted anything, she had to go down on her knees, bow her head, and address Cameron as Master and me as Ma'am.

In February, 1978, I wanted to test Cameron's love for me and see if he would keep our agreement that there was to be no sex with the slave.

"You can have sex with K," I told Cameron. He smiled and immediately went to the basement to retrieve Colleen from the box. She was naked, handcuffed, and her eyes were taped. He laid her spread-eagled on the bed with her wrists and ankles tied to the corners. After I saw him penetrate her, I ran from the bedroom to the bathroom and vomited. Cameron, who had failed the test, tried to comfort me. I was pregnant with our second child at the time.

We moved into the mobile home for more privacy in April, 1978. Colleen was kept under the waterbed in a box with all the doors, including the bedroom door, locked because Cameron had a lot of things he didn't want anyone to see. Throughout most of 1978, Colleen was only allowed out of the box for short periods of time during the night to eat and empty her bedpan. Both Cameron and I would let her out of the box. Amber, our second daughter, was born on the waterbed above Colleen on September 4, 1978.

Cameron developed his own film producing 35-millimeter slides. He also had a large collection of magazines and paperback books. Some of the titles included: "Alphabet of Pain, Roped, The Tutor, Punishment, and Love French Style." Since Cameron was a poor reader, I read many of the articles and books to him. I also used a whip on Colleen's back as Cameron watched.

To bring in extra cash for the family, I worked at the Foster Freeze between April, 1979, and January, 1980, as the head cook. My hours were from 5:00 PM to 8:00 PM in the winter and 5:00 PM to 12:30 AM in the summer. Cameron came home from work at 4:20 PM and would take Colleen out of the box to cook dinner and clean up. On January 11, 1980, she was given a Bible with a white cover as a late Christmas gift.

Starting in June until July, 1980, I worked at a fast-food chain called Pac-Out from 10:00 AM to 4:00 PM most of the week. It was during this time, Colleen started to care for the children. She was allowed to sleep in the back bathroom with her neck chained to the toilet.

I worked at JLA an electronics plant as an assembler from August, 1980, until February, 1981. My hours were from 7:00 AM to 3:30 PM. Colleen continued to care for the girls while Cameron and I were at work. I brought some of the JLA work home at night, but since my boss didn't want to pay overtime, Colleen was signed up as an employee. She used her real name and her pay checks were deposited into our bank account.

Twice, Colleen and I went out to the New Orleans Bar where we drank and met men. We were invited to the apartment of two men to listen to music. I followed one of the men into a spare bedroom where we kissed. Colleen also accompanied the family on a water skiing trip and to Burney Falls. She ate Christmas dinner with both his and my parents.

In early 1981, Cameron told me he was going to put Colleen back in the box. He didn't want anyone else babysitting our children. Colleen and I didn't get along well together, which was another reason for putting her back in the box. She was allowed a visit with her family before going back in the box. From 1981 through 1982, Colleen was let out of the box one hour each night. In 1983, she was out from one hour to most of the night. By 1984, she was out of the box all night on a regular basis.

My emotions towards Colleen ranged from anger, to feeling sorry for her, to jealousy. I didn't like her raising my children or being around my husband. In 1982, Cameron admitted having sex with Colleen. He even let me read a diary written by Colleen which outlined her love for, and sexual activities with, my husband.

Colleen had not brought the relief from torture I had expected. Cameron continued to perform painful sadistic acts on me on a regular basis. I was hung up by my wrists, even in the late stages of pregnancy, experienced baths with my arms and legs tied behind my back, placed on the stretcher, and wore the rubber gas mask. I was also placed in the hole and told to expect more slaves. I was choked to the point of unconsciousness, and told not to eat or drink anything for three days. I was only spared time in the boxes and electrical torture. Colleen sometimes heard, but never saw the things Cameron did to me. I too was a victim just like Colleen. The only difference was Colleen feared The Company, whereas I feared Cameron.

It's hard to comprehend, but I still loved Cameron. He was a good provider and the father of our daughters. We had been married for nine years and had many good memories in common. I knew I couldn't make it alone in the world with my limited job skills. If what Cameron did became public, I might go to prison and lose my daughters. My only hope was that Cameron would change his ways, release his slave, and abandon his sadistic habits.

Cameron had me read the entire New Testament to him paying special attention to the duties of a wife and slave, which Cameron viewed as basically the same. Both were to be totally submissive to the husband or master. I believed that if the wife and slave were not submissive, as the Bible said, they would go straight to hell.

In late 1983, I began to discuss the Bible with Colleen. By the next year, I would take Colleen out of the box and we would study the Bible together for hours. Colleen was the only person, other than Cameron, who knew my feelings of guilt and pain. Who else could I talk to? Following Cameron's instruction, we both wore ski caps on our heads as a sign of respect towards God when reading the Bible.

Colleen slowly came out of the box and back into the world. She was reintroduced to our children and even allowed to seek employment. She worked under her real name, Colleen Stan, and was permitted to keep $20 from each paycheck she earned at the Kings Lodge Motel. Sometimes she rode my bicycle to work and back. Life for Colleen was getting better. The same couldn't be said for me. By July, 1984, Cameron had changed his relationship with Colleen. She was no longer a punishment and humiliation slave, but a co-wife.

"I'm going to sleep with K whether you like it or not," Cameron told me. He also told me, "You're possessed by the devil and this [sadism] is a way to get it out."

I was to accept Colleen as his "slave wife" like Hagar in the Bible. Cameron talked about getting Colleen a small house trailer that would be parked behind our mobile home. He also talked about Colleen bearing him a son. Someday, all three of us with our children would move to a cabin in the Lake Tahoe region. Finally came "alternate sex nights" where Cameron discussed sleeping with me for two nights, Colleen for two nights, and then resting for three nights. I was very confused and distressed. If I disobeyed, Cameron would make me feel bad.

Previously, I had used denial and compartmentalization to keep my mind from going crazy. I denied what was going on in my own house and never told anyone what Cameron was doing, not even my own parents. Now, things had become too much for me to handle. I asked Cameron to choke me to death. I couldn't take it anymore and wanted to die. Cameron did choke me to the point of unconsciousness, but I didn't die. My life was falling apart.

By this time, Colleen had asked Cameron for permission to go to church. Since the Bible had served him well, Cameron granted her request. The children and I joined Colleen in church where we met Pastor Dabney. When we confided in Pastor Dabney, he told us to get away and send Colleen home. I was still unsure and hesitant.

On August 9, 1984, I took Colleen to work and met with Pastor Dabney. Later in the morning, I went to the Kings Lodge and told Colleen, "Cameron was not a member of The Company." She cried, got angry, and quit her motel job. We then returned to Pastor Dabney for advice. The next day, we moved in with my parents and Colleen called her dad to let him know she was coming home.

On August 17, I returned to Cameron because everyone insisted it was the right thing to do. I was told to forgive Cameron. We went to church, and I asked Cameron to seek counseling. We destroyed much of his bondage equipment, and burned most of his magazines.

On September 28, I moved back in with my parents, suffering from panic or anxiety attacks. On November 1, I returned to the mobile home to see if Cameron had gotten rid of his bondage items. I found slides of myself in bondage and a sculpture Cameron had done of a naked woman. I talked with Pastor Dabney again, but still didn't want to turn Cameron in to the police. My life was a mess, and I didn't know which way to turn.

On November 7, I met with Connie Fleming, a medical assistant to Dr. Tillman, a physician I was seeing in Redding. I confided with Connie and told her everything. Connie told me I should turn Cameron in to the police because he might harm my girls. I then went back to Pastor Dabney and told him I was afraid Cameron would hurt the girls. Pastor Dabney, with my permission, called the police.

My world, which I had been trying to save, was now destroyed. The father of our children had been arrested, and my nine year marriage was over. Red Bluff would soon know what had happened in the trailer on Weed Court. I too faced possible charges. More panic attacks were followed by guilt and depression. I went under the care of a doctor and was heavily medicated.

I too was a victim of Cameron Hooker. Even after he had his slave, the physical torture never stopped for me. I feared for my life and wasn't able to escape from Cameron, anymore than Colleen was able to free herself. We are both survivors from a horrible situation.

With Jan's courtroom testimony completed, she was dismissed by Judge Knight. Jan quickly departed the courtroom. Now, it was my turn to testify.

Chapter 15 - The Slave

Christine wanted the strongest possible case against Hooker. I can understand why she granted immunity to Jan. I just wish Jan had been held accountable for some of her actions. I'm grateful she finally came forward in 1984 with the truth. I just wish she had taken action earlier and saved herself, Marliz, and me from a lot of pain.

Now, it was my time to testify in court and tell the world what Hooker did to me. I was ready, but scared. This time, there would be a jury. This time, I would have to go into even greater details about the painful events. This time, Papendick, Hooker's lawyer, would challenge each of my words. The stress was overwhelming. If just one jury person felt that I was lying, Hooker could go free. The testimony would go on for three and a half exhausting days.

Mom had accompanied me to Redwood City to testify at the trial, but Christine decided not to place my mom on the witness stand. Mom, who I loved very much, had a way of saying things that just came to her mind. I believe she had an undiagnosed personality disorder. Sometimes her words, even to me, could be quite hurtful.

Years later, when I was planning a visit to Riverside, I told Mom over the phone that I wanted to stay at my Cousin Amy's house because she had an extra bedroom and bath. Mom, who still operated a boarding house, only had a communal bath. Mom was upset I was not staying with her because of the communal bathroom.

"Well, the 'box' was good enough for you," Mom said, sarcastically.

I hung up the phone.

While I was in captivity, Mom had been abducted and raped by a man with a gun. She was released after a couple of hours, but the trauma continued for years.

"Don't let me die like Colleen," Mom thought during the rape.

Later, when I told her the details of my ordeal, Mom asked me to stop talking about it.

"Colleen, I've heard enough. I can't take anymore," she would say. She had her own ghosts and didn't have room for mine.

I can understand why Christine didn't want her to testify. Mom went back home to Riverside leaving me to face the trial alone. This may have been a good thing, since I needed private time to recharge after each day of testimony.

Testifying in court is not like one sees on television. Many times, I was restricted to answering the question with a simple "yes" or "no." If I tried to explain, a lawyer would object, and the judge would tell me to just answer the question.

"Did you tell Cameron you loved him?" Hooker's lawyer, Papendick, asked.

"Yes, but …"

"Did you write love letters to Cameron?"

"Yes."

"Did you put your arms around Cameron and kiss him?"

"Yes."

Only when Christine had a chance to cross examine me, did I have a chance to explain.

"Why did you tell the defendant you loved him?" Christine asked.

"Because I felt forced to say I loved him. He wouldn't hurt me as much if I expressed love towards him," I replied.

"And did you love him?"

"No!" I said, emphatically.

After hours of testimony, I wondered if I had set the record straight and the jury was accepting my explanation. I would glance at the jury to see if they believed me. Their blank expressions gave me no comfort. The only reaction in the courtroom came from the reporters who would gasp, or shake their heads, when I would cover an especially graphic scene.

Most disturbing was Hooker sitting 10 feet in front of me. He had changed his orange jail uniform for a business suite, but his sarcastic smirk had not changed. He still seemed to be saying, "I going to get off and then I'll get you." In his mind, the jury would see it his way and he would soon be on his way home. His lawyer had a lot of evidence to use against me, such as people who saw me jogging unescorted around the neighborhood and my visit home.

Papendick was always trying to trip me up in front of the jury by using my own words against me.

"What did the defendant say to you about your family?" Papendick asked.

"He told me if I contacted my family they would be hurt," I answered.

"Now, Ms. Stan, during the preliminary hearing you testified the defendant "might" hurt your family and now you're saying he "would" hurt your family. Which of the two versions is the correct version?" Papendick asked.

Papendick also tried to portray me as a "biker mama" because of the incident with the motorcycle gang after Tim Stan and I were married. I tried to explain to the jury that I was never a motorcycle gang member, much less a biker mama. The jury remained stone-faced during my denial. I prayed that my testimony was getting through to the jury members.

After my first day of testimony, I walked to the elevator and found Jan waiting for the same elevator. We were suddenly standing face-to-face.

"Someday, I want to tell you the whole story," Jan said to me.

"Okay, some other day," I said and then looked straight ahead at the elevator door. I was tired and exhausted after a long day on the witness stand and didn't want to talk to her.

Years later, while passing through Red Bluff I stopped at the same trailer on Weed Court where Jan and the girls were still living. I never understood why she continued to live in the same mobile home in Red Bluff after the trail. I would have moved far, far away.

I walked up to the trailer door and knocked, looking for "the whole story." Jan came to the door and quickly escorted me back to my car, out of hearing range of Charity and Amber. Then she started a verbal attack.

"You were the cause of my broken marriage. All these problems were your fault," she said, in an angry voice. "You could have ...."

I was surprised and shocked. This is not what I came here for, I thought. "I'm out of here," I said, as I got back in my car and drove away never to see or speak to Jan again. I'm still waiting for the whole story.

My testimony during the trial was difficult. The details were painful to express in front of Hooker and a gallery of reporters I didn't know. During the breaks, I would go into the hallway and cry.

"Why can't you cry like that on the witness stand?" Christine badgered.

"I'm not an actress. I can't just turn it on and off," I told her.

The truth is I didn't feel comfortable crying in front of a room full of strangers. Plus, after years with Hooker I had learned to shut down my emotions and not show them in front of others. After the first year of captivity, I had stopped crying even when alone in the box. I had hardened myself for what was to come. Most importantly, I never wanted Hooker to see me cry, even during the trial. Not withstanding the lack of emotions, the pain still hurt right down to my soul. I was determined to testify so Hooker would never hurt another woman.

I answered each question in a flat, businesslike manner. I tried to be clear, objective, and truthful. I'm sure Christine thought my testimony sounded like a dull shopping trip story. How could anyone talk about being repeatedly raped and not cry? Even today, people wonder how I can talk about such horrible events with such detachment. I guess my personality remains hardened, but not as hardened as I thought.

Near the end of a long day, Papendick started a line of questioning about the time Jan told Cameron I was not following directions. Hooker tied me to the frame and attached electrical wires to my body.

"Where did the electricity hurt?" Papendic asked. He assumed the voltage would cause my leg muscles to painfully contract. He wanted to show the jury either, I was not seriously shocked, or I was lying.

"It hurt all over," I replied in a calm, detached voice. "The pain radiated throughout my body."

"Yes, but where on your body did it hurt?" he asked again in an irritating voice.

"All over," I said, starting to lose my composure.

"Yes, I know it hurt all over, but where exactly did it hurt the most?"

"I told you it hurt all over," I said, crying my eyes out. Christine finally had her request that I cry on the witness stand in front of the jury. The judge could see I was clearly upset by this line of questioning and called for a 15 minute recess.

I reported to the court I had been hung up by the wrists 90 to 100 times during the first six months of captivity. I was always whipped when hung up. When asked to rank the order of my pain, from most to least, I said burning, shocking, hanging, and stretching.

I also told the jury, "I really tried to be a good slave."

After three and a half days, I had covered all aspects of my abduction from the knife being placed against my throat to my bus ride back home to Riverside. I was finally excused from the witness stand. I thanked the judge and departed the courtroom exhausted and concerned how the jury would view my testimony.

A series of witnesses next testified for the prosecution. First to take the stand was Dorothy Coppa, who lived 200 feet east of the Hooker mobile home. She told the court how she had seen me walking, babysitting, bicycling, and jogging, but admitted we didn't talk very often.

"One time, Kay did come over. She was upset and crying," Dorothy stated. "Kay, what's the matter?"

"It's Jan," Kay replied, not going into any detail.

Dorothy went on to tell how she gave me $10, a lot of money for her, when I went home to Riverside in 1981 and a warm jacket when I returned in 1984. Dorothy talked about how hard I worked in the Hooker garden. A key moment in the testimony came when Judge Knight asked Dorothy a question.

"Did Kay seem to be a servant?"

"I remember saying to someone she worked like a 'slave'." The word slave rang throughout the courtroom.

The next witness was my sister Bonnie Sue. She discussed the telephone calls, letters, and late night talk we had when I visited Riverside in 1981, but that's not why Christine had put her on the witness stand. Christine had Bonnie testify so the jury could not just hear what Hooker had done to me, but to see what he had done to me. Bonnie was a beautiful, young woman full of life. Her skin was healthy, and her hair was thick and flowing. I, on the other hand, looked weak, my teeth needed dental work, and my hair was very thin on the front of my head. Seven years with the Hookers had taken its toll on me as anyone could see.

Al Coppa, Dorothy's husband, testified next. He told the jury how I wore the same clothes most of the time. On cross examination, he discussed my swollen feet which were seen on more than one occasion.

"Yes she worked hard in that garden," Al told the court. "I wish I could get my wife to work that hard."

"After the trial you can get a copy of the transcript [to get your wife to work as hard as a slave]," Judge Knight said from the bench. Laughter filled the court. Papendick later tried to get Judge Knight removed from the case for the remark, but was unsuccessful.

Another neighbor, Cathy Devers, was sworn in to testify. Once, while in the shed next to the Hooker mobile home, Cathy asked Jan what the hole in the floor was for. Jan bypassed the question. On another occasion, she asked me how much I got paid for babysitting and house cleaning? My answer, according to Cathy, was that we were good friends, and I just wanted to help them out. I also told Cathy, any money I made went to Jan.

Next to testify was Pastor Frank Dabney. He conveyed how Jan and I had come to his services and appeared quite upset. A few days later, he made an unannounced visit to the Hooker trailer. Kay was so shocked and nervous she dropped a kitchen dish. Later, Jan asked him about Sarah giving Hagar to Abraham to bare his child. Pastor Dabney told them the Old Testament story was wrong then and is wrong now. She then asked him about sections of the Bible regarding wives obeying their husbands.

"My husband is using passages in the Bible to make me submit to unnatural acts," Jan said.

Upon hearing the details, Pastor Dabney advised Jan to go back to her parents and to send me home. Later in counseling, he advised Hooker to get rid of his pornographic magazines and paraphernalia. When Jan told him she feared for the lives of herself and her children, Pastor Dabney called the police, with Jan's consent.

Al Shamblin of the Red Bluff Police testified after Pastor Dabney. Detective Shamblin showed a video of the Hooker mobile home taken as evidence was being collected. Bruce Palmer and James Weidgan assisted Detective Shamblin in collecting evidence from the trailer and the house on Oak Street. For three hours the three men detailed each item taken from the two locations. Hooker and Jan had burned much of the evidence, especially things connected to me, late one night. Still, many items including hundreds of magazines, photographs of Jan in bondage, the box under the waterbed, the workshop on Oak Street, the hole under the shed, the frame, the X, the stretcher, the blue nightgown, the Bible, and various hooks, whips, straps, handcuffs, and gags were found. All of these items, except the hole and the workshop were on display in the court for the jury and press to see. However, a quarter-size model of the underground hole was constructed and a diagram of the workshop was drawn for the court.

The head boxes were found in the dusty rafters of the shed and were shown in court as found, with the small head box inside the larger head box. I never wore both head boxes at the same time.

During the search, a roll of undeveloped film was found. The film, an older style no longer in use, was sent to the FBI in Washington, D.C. for processing. On the film were pictures of me naked, blindfolded, and being hung from the frame by my wrists. Jan, showing signs of pregnancy, was also pictured being hung up. Both pictures were enlarged and displayed in the courtroom. Most importantly, a photographic negative of the slave contract was found among Hooker's papers. The contract which was dated and signed by Michael and Janet Powers along with me, Colleen Stan.

Nine year old Charity Hooker was next on the stand. She told how I had been her babysitter, slept on the floor, and had few clothes. Charity said she and her sister were not allowed to play in the master bedroom or around the shed behind the mobile home. When asked about her ninth birthday a few weeks earlier, Charity admitted she didn't receive any gifts. The financial strain on the family, along with the trial, prevented the celebration of the child's birthday.

Next on the stand was Charity's sister, seven year old Amber. She spoke of going on walks with Kay and how she loved Kay. Both girls had been shielded from what had gone on, but no one could shield them now with their Dad on trial. I wasn't the only victim in this crime.

Roger Michael George, another neighbor of the Hookers, talked about his dogs and how his father, a disabled veteran, had to travel to Sacramento often. He was not The Company member traveling to the Sacramento headquarters as I had assumed.

Doris Miron, Kings Lodge Motel's owner and manager, told the court I was the best worker she ever had. When asked if Colleen was suntanned, Doris said, "No."

Connie Fleming, a medical assistant for Dr. Tillman in Redding, met Jan during an office visit. Connie turned out to be the one person Jan trusted and talked with freely. All the secrets of so many years finally came out.

"Are you afraid of Cameron?" Connie asked.

"Yes," Jan answered. "I'm afraid he will kill me."

"You should go to the police," Connie advised.

"I'm afraid."

"Then go to Pastor Dabney."

Loretta Hutton, former wife of Dexter, told about meeting Kay. Loretta commented to her daughter that it was odd that Kay worked in the garden, but didn't have a suntan.

Dr. Michael Vovakas discussed my December, 1984, medical examination. Small scars were found on my ankles, wrists, and breast. Also there were raised scars on the inside of my thighs from electrical burns. My right labium was pierced. Dr. Vovakas did remark that the scars were larger on my right wrist and ankle because people move their dominant side more vigorously.

The final prosecution witness was Dr. Hatcher. Now that the jury knew "what" had happened, it was Dr. Hatcher's job to explain "how" it had happened. He started by telling the court he was a Professor of Psychology at the University of California, San Francisco. It took half an hour for him to cover his qualifications.

Cameron Hooker, according to Dr. Hatcher, had followed a 15 step procedure to control a human being. Hooker may not have known about each of the steps, but his actions indicated that he knew what he was doing. These steps would work on anyone, but would require a little more time on an older person who had military or police training. In time, anyone and everyone would break. The 15 steps Dr. Hatcher described which applied to me included:

1. Violent abduction, followed by removal of clothes and isolation.
2. Physical and sexual abuse, to shock victim.

3. Removal of normal daylight and nighttime patterns.
4. Control bodily functions and destroy sense of privacy.
5. Control and reduce food and water.
6. Punish for no apparent reason.
7. Require victim to constantly ask permission to do anything.
8. Establish a pattern of physical and sexual abuse.
9. Become the only source of food, water, human contact, and information.
10. Present a new model and goals for future behavior.
11. Threaten victim's family.
12. Threaten to sell captive to a worse master.
13. Beat and torture at irregular intervals.
14. Use irrelevant acts of kindness to keep victim off balance.
15. Sign a contract to become a slave for life.
16. Incorporate new behavior goals.

The last point was the most important and difficult. The victim would be taught a new way of acting, behaving, and responding. They must willingly accept new rules for the world in which they now lived. If they did not, then the captor would repeat items two through 14. Constant reinforcement was necessary to keep the victim under control.

The prosecution rested once Dr. Hatcher completed his testimony. The defense called Cameron Hooker to the stand to give his side of the story.

Chapter 16 - The Slave Master

Roland Papendick, Hooker's attorney, called his first defense witness, Cameron Hooker. I can only speculate why Hooker took the stand in his own defense. With two women testifying against him, and all the bondage equipment displayed in the courtroom, Hooker and his attorney must have felt they didn't have a choice. Hooker had to testify.

Hooker, dressed in an Ivy League jacket and gray slacks, took the witness stand and was sworn in on Friday, October 18, 1985. The spectators in the courtroom had heard from the slave and the slave owner's wife. Now they would hear from the slave master himself. All eyes were on Hooker, as complete silence gripped the courtroom. He would be on the stand for three days. As with Jan, the following is not the voice of Hooker. It is my voice in an attempt to convey the reasoning and feelings of Hooker.

My name is Cameron Michael Hooker. I was born in Canby, California, on November 5, 1953 and I'm 32 years of age. From a young age, I've been fascinated with BDSM (bondage, discipline, sadism, and masochism). Between consenting adults, such activities are completely legal and I believe normal. Many people keep slaves and many people are willing to become slaves. Consent is the key word in this arrangement.

In April, 1973, I met Janice or Jan as I called her, when she was attending Red Bluff High School. She was 15 and I was 19 years of age. We dated for a short time before I told her of my interested in BDSM. She was interested and allowed me to try a few things on her. Jan liked and enjoyed it because it brought us closer together.

In time, Jan told me she was going to have a baby. I was excited and asked her to marry me. We were married in Reno, Nevada on January 18, 1975, but the pregnancy turned out to be false. Later, Jan and I struck a deal in 1975, she could have a baby and I could have a slave. I had a fantasy of practicing bondage on a girl who couldn't say "no".

On September 27, 1976, Jan gave birth in the hospital to a baby girl who we named Charity. She had her baby, but I still didn't have my slave. We considered placing an ad in the newspaper for a bondage model, but we lacked the money to pay her.

On May 19, 1977, we were on our way to the mountains east of Red Bluff to practice bondage. We saw a young woman standing on the side of the road, with her sleeping bag at her feet, and her thumb out seeking a ride. Her name, we later learned, was Colleen Stan. We offered her a lift and she accepted. As we drove towards the mountains the idea came to mind to make Colleen my slave. She acted spacey and appeared to be on illegal drugs which made the decision to kidnap her easier.

While gassing the car, Colleen went to the restroom which gave me time to move the head box from the trunk of the car to the backseat. When she came out, we were ready. Once we were off the main road, I kidnapped her. I was age 23, Jan was 19, and Colleen was 20 years old.

I admit kidnapping her. However the California statute of limitations for such a crime is seven years which ended in May, 1984. Therefore, I shouldn't be charged with kidnapping under the law.

(Note: Christine claimed the kidnapping was a continuous event until I went home in August, 1984. Therefore, the statute of limitations for the crime would not expire until May, 1991.)

Once we got back to our home on Oak Street, I took Colleen to the basement and hung her by the wrists for five minutes until she started crying. Jan and I had sex after which I lost all interest in bondage. I put Colleen in a crate and placed the head box on her to keep her quiet. You couldn't hear her yelling if the head box was on her head.

The next day I felt really bad about what we had done. We couldn't release her, so I staked her out on the rack. We were not sure what to do with Colleen.

On the third day, I told Jan to get Colleen dressed, and we would take her where she wanted to go. Jan went down to the basement, came back a few minutes later, and told me Colleen wanted to go to the police. Jan and I were both worried about what might happen if Colleen contacted the police.

I went downstairs to talk with Colleen. I found her sweating, shaking, and sick. She kept asking for some little white pills from her purse. I could tell she was going through drug withdrawal and refused to give her the pills. Over the next two weeks, Colleen became depressed and sicker. I stayed with her, sometimes all night, holding her hands and hugging her. She did most of the talking, and I listened. Illegal drugs had been pervasive in her life, and she had come from an abusive family background. Colleen remained blindfolded as we talked, but there wasn't any bondage or sex.

(Note: Fearing rape, I was asking for the birth control pills in my purse not illegal drugs. I didn't have any and wasn't on any drugs.)

During the next two weeks, Colleen started to improve as the illegal drugs drained from her body. Jan and I wanted to free her, but we couldn't figure out how to do so without her going to the police. We didn't want to go to jail.

After the first month, Colleen started feeling much better and her attitude improved. Jan and I realized we were stuck with Colleen. We built a double-walled box to keep her in. We couldn't keep her out on the rack, and we didn't have the money to sound proof the basement.

While in the box, Colleen was not chained because restraints were not necessary. She was out of the box for four to six hours each night at which time we talked. The other hours of the day she slept a great deal. There was no bondage or sex. After the first couple of weeks, Colleen had a bath once or twice a week. Once again, there was no bondage or sex.

"When are you going to let me go?" Colleen asked.

"Soon," I responded.

After three months, Colleen and I had become close and she started talking to me about my interest in bondage.

"Why do you like bondage," Colleen asked?

"I don't know," I answered.

The first time Colleen had been hung up, the night of the kidnapping, was not a good experience for her. I took her down after five minutes when she started to cry. When I told her Jan could be hung 15 to 20 minutes, Colleen thought we should try it again. The second time, Colleen was hung 15 minutes and never cried. The longest anyone was ever hung was 20 minutes, because I knew a tourniquet should never be on more than 20 minutes.

Incidentally, during this time I continued to practice bondage on Jan. We also dunked Colleen once in the bathtub and Jan cut her hair. Colleen's hair had become gummed up from the duct tape.

Between the third and fourth month, Jan and I built a workshop for Colleen to shell walnuts. She spent all night and sometimes all day in the workshop. She liked to macramé so we purchased some cord for her to make plant hangers. Jan also taught her to crochet.

About this time, Jan wanted a guarantee I wouldn't have sex with Colleen. I agreed and Jan told Colleen there would be no sex between us.

"Why no sex?" Colleen kept asking me.

After six months, Jan went to San Jose for two months to stay with her sister and work. During this time, Colleen and I talked for hours. There was no bondage or sex.

One day, after Jan had returned, she found a copy of a slave contract in the "Inside News" an underground paper. Jan was the first to realize the slave contract, combined with fear of The Company, might allow us to release Colleen. Jan typed up the slave contract.

"Don't look up," we advised Colleen as she sat in the workshop. I showed her the contract and told her The Company was a powerful organization which was everywhere, possibly international. There was no escape. I went on to tell Colleen that the damage to Jan's knees were a result of her days in a Rent-A-Dungeon.

Colleen believed our story and was scared to death. I was upset it disturbed her so much, but happy we had succeeded. I selected the letter "K" as her slave name. The letters "B" and "D" were also considered, but rejected. That night Colleen came upstairs and ate at the family dinner table. From then on she would come upstairs a few hours each night.

An attention drill, where Colleen would drop her clothes and stand with her hands over her head, was used to remind her The Company was more than just an article in a newspaper. About this time, Colleen got the idea my father and brother were members of The Company.

Before the contract, Colleen had a sweet attitude and displayed a great deal of affection towards me. After the contract, Jan treated her like a slave and her spirits dropped. Any harsh words or raised voice would bring Colleen to tears. Colleen couldn't understand why I wouldn't have any sexual activity with her.

Jan had trouble with sex during pregnancy, therefore I told Colleen I was going to have sex with her to get Jan excited. With Colleen's approval, I staked her out on the bed. At first, I rubbed Colleen while kissing Jan. Then I started having sex with Colleen.

"I can't handle it," Jan cried as she jumped up and ran toward the front door. I headed her off and calmed her down. Colleen was taken back to the basement, disappointed the sex had ended so soon.

As a solution to our problem, we told Colleen we were going to buy her out of slavery from The Company. She would be free to go anywhere except the police. If she went to the police, The Company would punish her. Before being released, I wanted her to stay with us for three months and help us settle into the mobile home. We were moving because the landlady was giving us trouble.

Colleen helped dismantle her workshop and box which was later used to construct the box under the waterbed. At first, she slept in the box, but later she slept in the back bathroom. Colleen was not restrained because she didn't try to escape. She was a good slave.

Colleen helped fill in ditches for the plumbing and electrical wiring to the trailer. Between April and June, 1978, Colleen also helped me cut fence post in the forest, 35 miles east of Red Bluff. Once, I tied her up to a tree and we spent time talking and kissing. I told Colleen the only restriction, after her release, was not to tell anyone about The Company. If she told anyone about The Company, she would become someone else's slave. I never threatened her family.

In September, 1978, Amber was born. By this time, Colleen slept in the box only if people came over to spend the night or if the bathroom was too cold. She was eating three meals a day and helped Jan clean the kitchen. However, Jan continued to treat Colleen like a slave which depressed her.

One Sunday morning, Colleen came into the kitchen after I had told her I would drive her back to Riverside in two weeks.

"If I stay here, will I have the same amount of freedom I have now?" Colleen asked.

"Yes," I replied.

"I don't want to go back to illegal drugs and my family. I want to stay here."

"Welcome to the family," I said, as we embraced.

You have to understand, Colleen came from a family where her mother kicked her out, her husband kicked her out, and illegal drugs made her life miserable. She wanted the stability of a loving family.

Jan told Colleen, one week after she asked to stay, the truth about her knees and that she had never been a slave. I told her my father and brother was not members of The Company. I never told her the truth about The Company, because I didn't want to lose her. She looked up to people in authority.

A collar, worn since she signed the contract, was removed once she became a family member. A second stainless steel collar and a ring in her labia were like a wedding band. Incidentally, I believe she took the collar home with her in 1984.

I promised Colleen, she could have a child and remain a slave. I also told her what I expected from her, to which Colleen agreed. Colleen wanted a guarantee I wouldn't run her off, to which I agreed. However, Jan didn't like any of these agreements. She wanted Colleen to leave. Jan knew that Colleen and I were falling in love.

From then on, Jan treated Colleen rough and wanted her punished for things she did wrong. For example, when Colleen did a macramé project incorrectly, Jan demanded punishment. I hung Colleen in the frame, but Jan wanted more straps to secure her legs and arms. I went to the shed looking for more straps. When I returned, Jan was shocking Colleen with electricity. I pulled the electrical plug from the wall which angered Jan. She stormed out of the trailer and didn't come back for two hours. I took Colleen down from the frame and gave her a bath. When Jan returned she was really mad.

"Don't interfere again," she shouted. We slept apart for a couple of cold nights.

Colleen and I started having light bondage and sex once a month. I would tie her hands, kiss, and rub her body before sex. Once every four months, we would have heavy bondage with her being hung up. I only punished Colleen twice in 1978 and 1979, once for breaking a dish and I can't remember the reason for the other time. Jan demanded more punishment. Once while Colleen was in a bondage situation in the shed, she accidentally kicked Jan in the stomach. Jan wanted her whipped, but there wasn't enough room in the shed. So Jan went to the trailer and returned with a box of matches. She lit a match and held it under Colleen's breast. Surprisingly, the fire didn't burn or blister her breast.

When Jan started work at Foster Freeze, Colleen cleaned house and took care of the children. I never forced Colleen to have sex. However, she chose to have sex with me on a regular basis. She slept in the back bathroom and started meeting family, friends, and neighbors. I told everyone she's a friend, housekeeper, and babysitter. She talked about wanting to get married and have my baby. Charity and Amber loved Colleen as good, if not better, than Jan, their own mother. When Jan dated other men, it didn't bother me since I was in love with Colleen.

Bondage continued between Colleen and I once a month. We used the frame to take the strain off the trailer ceiling. Since her feet touched the bottom of the frame, the weight on the ceiling was reduced. The whips were used as toys in bondage, never to hurt anyone. I did use a cat-of-nine-tails and a leather strap on Jan, but never on Colleen. When I put Colleen on the stretcher, she didn't cry. Colleen could take more pain than I could dish out. She was one tough woman. After the eye hook on the stretcher broke, I became afraid and we never used the stretcher again.

The Bible was a gift Colleen asked for before Christmas. I'm a poor reader and never read the Bible, but Colleen did read portions to me. Colleen went jogging and learned to water and snow ski with the family on trips to the lake and mountains. She had running shoes, two swimsuits, and heavy clothes for the winter. Colleen met my brother once or twice a week and had dinner with both our families. She wrote letters and made phone calls home which I never monitored.

Colleen would meet me at the door when I came home from work. She had on makeup and would give me a big hug. She would ask for sex and would lie on the floor with her hands on her knees as she looked up. Colleen knew what that position did to me. Sex always followed. Colleen was grateful for: (1) being off illegal drugs, (2) having a home that would be there for her the next day, (3) having a Bible, and (4) the thought of having a child.

When Jan spoke harshly to Colleen she would cry. She also cried when the kids cried, and when I said something wrong to her. Colleen never cried during bondage.

I started the hole under the shed because Charity was getting too old for us to perform bondage in the trailer. The hole would be a mini-dungeon for bondage play. It took all three of us and two years to complete. The niches in the wall were to store whips and other stuff. It was Colleen's idea to tell Jan I wanted more slaves. Colleen hoped the idea of more slave would make Jan treat her better.

As time went on, Jan and Colleen began to argue about everything. How were they going to take care of the kids? Who was going to do the house work? Jan complained about Colleen and Colleen complained about Jan's complaining. I was going crazy.

Colleen wanted to go gambling, so I took her to Reno around Easter. It was her idea to panhandle for money to use for gambling. We slept in the car and gambled about three hours. She also panhandled in Red Bluff and Redding. Colleen panhandled for more money, because she wanted to go home and visit with her parents.

One day, Jan heard Charity call Colleen "Mommy". Jan was very upset and quit her job, quit dating, and wanted Colleen out of her house. I suggested to Colleen she stay with her parents in Riverside after the visit.

Before Riverside, we tried some bondage in my father's barn because it was a nice backdrop for photos. My parents were away on a trip. On the way to Riverside, we stopped off at an adult bookstore to pickup something I had ordered. The original plan was for Colleen and me to spend the night in a motel and visit her father the next morning. However, when she telephoned her dad, she became excited and wanted to see him that night. I took her to his house and stayed 20 to 30 minutes. I introduced myself as "Mike" to her family, because I didn't want another mother-in-law or bothersome relatives.

Jan was fearful Colleen and I would take the kids and stay in Riverside. I was afraid Jan would take the kids and stay with her parents. We were in a crisis situation. Colleen agreed to return to Red Bluff with me because she loved me.

"I will come home only if Colleen stays with us," Jan said, fearing we would elope with the children. When we returned from Riverside, Colleen was placed in her box to keep the family together. Even Colleen agreed she had to go back in the box to save our marriage. For the next three years there was no sex or bondage with Colleen. The kids kept asking over the years about Kay. We told them Kay had returned to her home in Riverside.

When Jan was in the hospital with knee surgery, Colleen and I rekindled our love for each other. I put her on the X frame and had sex with her. The next morning we had a big fight. I had promised her a child and now it looked like our baby would be far in the future. One day when the blower went out, Colleen got mad and kicked the exit panel out of the box. The panel was made to be kicked out in an emergency.

In 1982, Jan and I had a long talk about my sexual activity with Colleen and her dating other men. She told me about the pregnancy lie prior to our marriage. After our talk, the friendship between Jan and Colleen started to grow.

By 1984, Jan decided it was okay for Colleen to come out of her box and see the kids again. Colleen wanted to go to work which was fine. We needed the money and most of her paycheck as a maid went directly into the family bank account. Colleen received $20 spending money from each paycheck, which was the same amount Jan and I got from my paycheck.

During this time, I had bondage with Colleen once or twice a month. I tied her up in the bathroom and on the bed, but I never hung her by the wrists. With Jan, I had bondage two to three times a month and hung her up once a month. Colleen and Jan started to have sex together about this time. Colleen staked Jan out on the bed and Jan hung and whipped Colleen. In 1984, I was present when they had lesbian sex, but didn't force them to have sex together. I would describe the relationship between the two women as "good".

Jan read the New Testament to Colleen, after which they discussed the meaning of various passages. I overheard them talking about Abraham, Sarah, and Hagar one day. Hagar, Sarah's slave, was given to Abraham to have his baby. Soon Colleen was Hagar, Jan was Sarah, and I was Abraham as we role played the story from the Bible.

In August, 1984, Colleen telephoned me and said she knew The Company was not real. She said she was returning to Riverside. Colleen didn't want to come between Jan and I because of Charity and Amber. I told Colleen I loved her.

Once at home, Colleen telephoned me around midnight. She was looking at a picture of me as we talked about Jan's pregnancy lie before our marriage. She still loved me. Five days later, Jan came back to me with the children. Later, we took a drive out to Hogsback Road where I performed bondage on Jan. (Note: Hooker was lying. I didn't learn about Jan's false pregnancy until after Hooker's arrest and Jan's statement to the police.)

After Colleen got home, she continued to telephone me often. She also wrote letters, but I never wrote back. My spelling is worse than my reading. Colleen talked about moving back up north to be near us, but didn't want to come between Jan and I. Jan said if Colleen returned, it would end our marriage. Colleen asked me to destroy the diary she had written. I stalled. Colleen called Jan and she burned the diary. The two women started talking on the telephone and rekindled their love for each other.

A love triangle developed where each of us loved the other two in the triangle. Colleen loved both Jan and I. Jan and Colleen were in love, but Jan was married to me. I loved Colleen, but was married to Jan.

In the end, I was the odd man out in this triangle. Colleen and Jan got together and had me arrested. They could now get back together and not worry about me showing up and taking the children. Their plan was to live together happily ever after with me out of the picture.

In summation, Colleen was kidnapped by Jan and I on an impulse. Not knowing how to release Colleen, without her going to the police, we created a slave contract and The Company. The combination would instill fear in Colleen and keep her away from the authorities.

We still wanted to get rid of her, so Colleen was told we had purchased her slave contract from The Company. Now she was free to go, but she must not tell anyone, especially the police, about The Company. However, when the day came for her to leave, she didn't want to go. She wanted to stay with our loving family, something she never had before in her life. Over time, Colleen and I fell in love and Jan was overcome with jealousy. By 1981, even Colleen agreed she had to go back in the box to save our marriage.

After I told Jan I was having sex with Colleen, Jan turned away from me and towards Colleen. The two women talked, went on long walks, and made love together. Up until August, 1984, Colleen still believed The Company was real, but when Jan told her the truth, Colleen went home which was what Jan wanted. Colleen didn't want to destroy our marriage. However, Jan didn't count on Colleen and I continuing our love over the telephone. She knew someday Colleen and I would get back together again and take the kids away from her.

Colleen and Jan talked over the telephone and renewed their friendship and love for each other. They concluded I had to go so that Colleen and Jan could get back together and live with the children in peace. Both Colleen and Jan are lying to remove me from the triangle and their lives.

Colleen and Jan willingly participated in bondage. Colleen wanted to be my slave because she loved me and wanted to stay with our family. She didn't wear underwear, because when we kidnapped her, she didn't have any underclothes. I never put wax in her ears or a shot gun in her mouth. I dunked Colleen only once and never again. I never raped or held her against her will.

Look at the love letters, the telephone calls, the photographs of us smiling together, and the lack of any physical damage from "years" in the box. These are not the characteristics of a person held against their will. Listen to the testimony of how Colleen jogged, cared for our children, visited her parents, got a job using her real name, and went out on dates with other men. These are the actions of a normal, healthy woman. The only thing I'm guilty of today is being the odd man out in a triangle of love.

"Were you ever hung up by the wrists?" Christine asked Hooker.

"Yes, once I was hung up for 15 minutes, but I never did that again. It hurt," Hooker testified.

"She really tried hard to be a good slave?" Christine asked, near the end of Hooker's testimony.

"Yes. She was a good slave," Hooker answered. "I was impressed with [the woman's] ability to withstand pain. [She] never cried. She would take almost anything I put her through. She could handle it."

With that Hooker ended his testimony and was dismissed by Judge Knight. The trial would continue the next day with the final witnesses for the defense.

Chapter 17 - The Verdict

The next defense witness was Lorena Hooker, Hooker's mother. Lorena testified she knew me as Kay Stan and saw no indications of servitude. "Kay seemed happy and I saw no scars or bruises on her body." When asked if it was unusual for her son and his wife to be able to afford a live-in babysitter, Lorena answered she never thought about it. Lorena did remember Jan saying the night after Hooker's arrest, "I know for a fact Kay wasn't raped."

Donna Marie Merritt, whose sister was married to Dexter, once telephoned the Hooker mobile home for Jan. When a woman answered, Donna assumed it was Jan. Surprisingly, the woman quickly introduced herself as Kay. Donna never met Kay, but once when in the trailer she commented that the couch was made up like a bed. "Is that Cameron's bed?" she asked.

"No," Jan said, "that's Kay's bed." Jan was mad Kay had not cleaned up since it was late in the afternoon.

(Note: I slept on the floor, but never on the couch. I was told my value was the same as a piece of furniture.)

The next witness was Shirley Ann Merritt, who was the daughter of Donna Merritt. Shirley told the jury she met Kay in Raley's, a Red Bluff supermarket, in 1978. There were no visible scars or bruises and her speech appeared normal. However, Shirley noted, "Kay only spoke when spoken to."

Dexter Hooker, Cameron's brother, was the next defense witness. Dexter, three and a half years younger than Cameron, described Kay as happy, never depressed, and always with a smile on her face. He and his wife once took Kay and the children to the city park when Cameron and Jan were away. Dexter also remembered the children referring to Kay as "Mommy" and Kay being absent between 1981 and 1984. When asked if Kay was a quite person Dexter answered, "No, Kay talked all the time."

Rebecca (Becky) Donyle Hooker, who married Dexter in 1982, recalled meeting Kay in 1984. Kay wore shorts and a tank top and always appeared neat and clean. Kay had an outgoing personality and once was seen giving Jan a goodnight hug and kiss on the cheek.

Hooker's father, Harold, testified Kay was a pleasant kind of girl who didn't appear to be afraid of him. He recounted how Kay, along with Cameron and Jan, were over for dinner six to eight times. After dinner, Kay never cleaned up the dishes. He also remembered Kay as being good with Charity and Amber.

Robert Deavers was a Hooker neighbor, described Kay as a carefree woman with a good attitude. He purchased macramé from her and remembered making the check out to Kay Powers.

"Did you ever see Kay showing any kind of affection toward Cameron?"

"No," Robert Deavers answered.

Hooker's defense now called their expert witness Dr. Donald Lunde, a professor of psychiatry at Stanford University. He had participated in the Patricia (Patty) Hearst trial.

Patty Hearst was the granddaughter of William Randolph Hearst, a famous newspaper publisher. In 1974, at the age of 19, she was kidnapped by a revolutionary group called the Symbionese Liberation Army (SLA) and endured physical and emotional abuse. Later, she participated in an SLA bank robbery and was eventually captured by the FBI. At her trial, she claimed the SLA had brainwashed her and forced her participation in the crime. The prosecution claimed she sympathized with the SLA and had willing participated in the robbery. She was found guilty and given seven years in prison. Patty's sentence was commuted by President Carter after she served two years. President Clinton granted amnesty to Patty in the last days of his administration.

I have always thanked God, Hooker never told me The Company wanted me to rob a bank. If he had, I too would have been in Patty Hearst's shoes. I have always felt Patty was a victim because she never participated in revolutionary activities before her kidnapping or after her release. She was a victim of brainwashing while in the hands of the SLA.

The term brainwashing was avoided during the trial. Lawyers and psychiatrist can't use 50 cent words when they're charging $300 per hour. Brainwashing is a method for systematically changing attitudes or altering beliefs. It can be as simple as a television ad to cause a person to switch toothpaste or, in my case, extreme measures to change my view of the world. Anyone can be brainwashed, with young children being the easiest to influence. Even older people, who have had military or police training, can be brainwashed if given enough time and resources. Brainwashing, like advertising, is not a one time event. It must be reinforced time and time again.

Dr. Lunde was at Hooker's trial to convince the jury that I too, like Patty Hearst in his opinion, had been a willing participant rather than a brainwashed victim. Dr. Lunde focused on the term "coercive persuasion" which he defined as a person being forced to do something they wouldn't normally do. Dr. Lunde told the jury, I was kidnapped and forced to become a slave, but once I obtained a degree of freedom, after the first eight months, coercive persuasion ended and I was a willing participant. I could have taken action to save myself if I had been so inclined. With access to a telephone, open doors, neighbors, and the police, I could have escaped if I had wanted freedom. The average person, he continued, would never have believed the outrageous stories about The Company. Therefore, fear of The Company was not a factor.

Dr. Lunde was a psychiatrist with a medical degree, unlike Dr. Hatcher who was a psychologist. Dr. Lunde pointed out to the court that anyone locked in a box 23 hours a day for three years would have physical and emotion problems. Such a person would have trouble standing up straight, keeping their balance, and walking. They would also have difficulty speaking, vision problems from the darkness, and severe emotional problems like depression. Many witnesses, Dr. Lunde pointed out, described me as being without physical problems and outwardly happy.

Dr. Lunde reviewed my "love" letters, numerous phone calls, smiling photographs, public interactions, unsupervised periods, and my job as a motel maid. None of these events would be expected of a bondage slave who was kept in a dark box for years. They are the actions of a consenting adult in love with her so-called master.

Dr. Lunde went on to say the attention drills and the bathtub dunking were not unlike United States Marine Corps drills and under-water escape training. Later, Judge Knight asked Dr. Lunde if the Marines stripped their recruits naked and forced them to stand with their hands above their heads. Judge Knight also asked if underwater escape training included being hogtied to a wooden pole. Dr. Lunde maintained a certain similarity existed between the two situations and Marine training.

After Dr. Lunde had finished, the defense went on to point out that, according to phone records, a total of 29 calls totaling eight hours, 20 minutes were made by me to Hooker or Jan, between August 9 and November 9. With that final point made, the defense rested its case.

In the last minutes of the trial, the prosecution called a surprise witness. Elaine Corning had known Hooker in 1972 when she was a 16 year old high school student. Cameron told Elaine that he had, or wished he had, a dungeon under his parents place to keep women in bondage.

With the last witness dismissed, the court got down to business. The prosecution asked the judge to drop counts 12 through 16 which dealt with forced imprisonment and living in an illicit relationship. Perhaps the prosecution wanted the jury to focus on the more serious counts. Then the prosecution and defense made their final arguments.

Interestingly, the prosecution outlined the events in the *Story of O* that were similar to my experiences. Starting with O's name, a single letter of the alphabet, and continuing with not being allowed to put legs together, hung and whipped, wrists chained to neck, use of the name Master, blindfolded, use of a dungeon, obedience drills, no underwear, directed self-masturbation, labia piercing, speaking only when spoken to, not making eye contact, and kneeling to ask permission. The only difference was O "wanted" to serve her master while K was "forced" to serve Hooker. O was branded while I was spared that indignity. However, I did endure other things such as stretching, dunking, the box, and electrical burns, which were not found in the *Story of O*.

The defense pointed out inconsistencies in my testimony such as when asked, "Did you ever tell Cameron you wanted to stay?" I answered, "No." At preliminary hearing you answered, "I don't think so." The defense repeated Dr. Lunde's points and once again listed the "freedoms" and opportunities to escape I had while with the Hookers.

Judge Knight reminded the jury that a verdict of guilty or not guilty must be decided only on the evidence and facts presented in court. The views of the attorneys were not evidence. The jury members must decide how much weight, if any, to give to the testimonies of Dr. Hatcher and Dr. Lunde. With that, the jury was sent away to decide.

The jury came back with a verdict in two and a half days on Thursday, October 31, which was Halloween, Hooker's favorite holiday. The jury found the defendant Cameron Hooker guilty on all counts except count VIII, rape by Hooker with Jan present in 1984. On that count, the jury hung with six voting guilty and six voting not guilty. There was a question about me being pressured to have sex with Hooker. At the preliminary hearing, I reportedly told Hooker and Jan, "Okay, I'll try it." If I said such a thing, it must have been while under pressure.

I was at home in Riverside when the verdict was announced. I was a nervous wreak and not sure I could go through another trail if there was a hung jury. Suddenly the phone rang.

"Colleen, this is Christine. Hooker's guilty on all counts except one." I was relieved and thankful to God. Hooker had been found guilty of 10 felony counts including one count of kidnapping, six counts of rape, and three counts of sex related acts.

The next day my phone rang while I was at home in Riverside.

"Hello," I said.

"I wanted to give you a chance to chew me out," a voice on the other end of the telephone said.

"Who is this?" I asked.

"It's me, Cameron."

I immediately hung up the phone and called Christine. She contacted the jail and Hooker was not allowed to make any more unsupervised phone calls. The telephone call would turn out to be my last contact with Hooker.

Sentencing took place on Friday, November 22. Under a new California law, I was allowed to make a victim's impact statement. I asked Marilyn Barrett to help me with the statement and to read it in court.

"The victim said one of the results is she's a harder person, she has no trust or respect, particularly for men," Marilyn told the court.

My statement went on to ask for a long prison sentence so Hooker would never be able to hurt another woman like he hurt me. Hooker sat 10 feet away from me, this time wearing an orange prison jumpsuit. The smirk on his face was gone. He looked like he had been hit by a ton of bricks as he realized what lay ahead.

Judge Knight sentenced Hooker to a total of 104 years. He said of Hooker, "I consider this defendant the most dangerous psychopath I have ever dealt with, in that he is the opposite of what he seems. He will be a danger to women as long as he is alive ..."

Hooker was also ordered to pay $50,000 in restitution of which I have never seen a cent. Cameron Hooker was turned over to the California Department of Corrections on November 26 and issued inmate number D-18324.

I soon learned, however, Hooker's 104 year sentence didn't take into consideration time served, time off for good behavior, any future sentence reductions due to ill health or prison overcrowding, or the possibility of parole. Rather than 104 years, Hooker is currently scheduled to be released 14 years from now in 2022.

Normally, after a trial jurors don't return for the sentencing. Of the 12 jurors in this trial, eight of them attended the sentencing. Two other jurors wanted to attend, but one was sick and the other couldn't get off work. After the proceedings, the eight jurors asked Christine if I would meet with them. In the hallway, I had a chance to thank each one of them personally.

One of the jurors, Debbie King, passed me her business card and asked if she could write me. Debbie was about my age, height, and weight. She had climbed into the box to see if it was possible for a person to use a bedpan in such a restricted area. She also tried on the head box. Throughout the trial, Debbie later told me, she never believed a word of Hooker's testimony. The stone faces on the jury, I had worried so much about, were not an indicator of their feelings. Debbie and I have maintained contact over the years and I consider her a good friend to this day.

After the sentencing Christine approached Marilyn and I to ask if we would like to go out to lunch and celebrate. She asked if her friend Carla Norton could accompany us. We agreed so the four of us headed for a café near the courthouse. While at lunch, Christine introduced Carla as a college friend who was a writer. She went on to say that Carla had sat in on the trial and had taken notes for a book. Then Christine added, "We have a publishing deal".

"We are willing to give you five percent of the book deal," Christine said, after she reached under the table and produced a legal contract from her briefcase for me to sign.

Marilyn and I looked at each other in total disbelief and shock. Christine had told me throughout the trial not to speak to anyone in the media about an interview, movie, or book deal. Hooker's defense attorney would have claimed I was trying to profit financially from the trial. I had followed her instructions to the letter. Now, I realized my personal conversations with Christine had been passed on to Carla for publication. What Christine had done was not right to say the least.

"No, it's my story and I will decide what will be done with it," I told Christine. "Whose story is this anyway? I was the one who was tortured, humiliated, and raped, not you [Christine]!" I was mad as hell and, unlike when I was with Hooker, was now free to vent my anger against someone who hurt me. Marilyn and I quickly departed.

Everyone knows criminals aren't allowed to profit from their crimes by making media deals. Few people know that victims, during a trial, can't stop anyone from using their testimony to write a profitable story. I expected this from news reports or writers, but not from an official of the court. Once again, I felt like a victim.

Christine and Carla titled their book *Perfect Victim,* which implied something in my character predisposed me towards being the victim. I have always thought of myself as just a victim, not the "perfect victim". When the book was published, it was dedicated to me, Colleen Jean Stan. One would have expected an autographed copy of the book to have been presented to me, but that didn't happen. Instead, I had to go to a local bookstore and purchase my own copy.

Later, Marilyn saw Christine and Carla on the 'Larry King Show" promoting their book. The next day Marilyn telephoned the producer of the show and asked why I had not been invited? The producer said I "had" been invited, but according to Christine, I had declined.

Marilyn wrote the California Bar to bring Christine's conduct to their attention. The California Bar replied they would take action if other complaints were received. I consulted a lawyer specializing in civil law to learn if I had grounds for a civil suite. I was told I did have a case, but a quarter million dollar retainer fee would be required up front. I didn't have that amount of money. I was now doing something I could never have done under Hooker, I was fighting back.

In August, 1986, I filed a $10,000,000 civil suit against Hooker. My attorney was Charles D. Cummings of Sullivan, Workman, and Dee in

Los Angeles. Hooker had transferred his assets out of his name, so he could declare himself indigent and unable to afford a lawyer. Therefore, my suit was filed against the Puritan Insurance Company, who had issued the insurance policy on the mobile home. Policy number MHC-04-57-75 included $150,000 of personal liability coverage for anyone injured on the Hooker property.

Puritan filed a request in the United States District Court for a jury trial against Colleen Stan and Cameron Hooker contending the policy didn't cover what occurred between 1978 and 1984. I found it odd that Hooker and I were co-defendants in this civil suit. The request was not granted.

At first Puritan tried to portray me as a person out to get money, but in time they realized their case wouldn't fly in front of a jury. Puritan finally reached a settlement with me and paid the face value of the policy, not ten million dollars. I was glad to win the case, but I would have preferred to have made it safely to Westwood on that day in May, 1977.

Chapter 18 - Life after Slavery

Once back home, I knew I needed to jump-start my life. I had missed out on a lot and wanted to catch up fast. I could see a place of my own, a husband, and a baby in my future. I wanted to lead a normal life like other women.

I had missed so much during my years of captivity. People would mention an event, and I would have no idea what they were talking about. Elvis Presley, John Lennon, Bing Crosby, and John Wayne had died. So too had 909 members of the People's Temple at Jonestown, Guyana, under the misguided leadership of Jim Jones. The Soviet Union had invaded Afghanistan, Argentina had invaded the Falkland Islands, and the United States had invaded Grenada. The Shah of Iran had departed, Ayatollah Khomeini had returned, and the U.S. Embassy had been seized. Mount St. Helens had erupted and Three Mile Island nuclear power plant had almost erupted. Ronald Reagan had been elected president, the space shuttle Columbia had been launched, and Sally Ride had become the first American woman in space. Charles and Diana were married, personal computers were introduced, and a new PG13 movie rating was unveiled. "Star Wars, Superman, Raiders of the Lost Ark, and E.T." were the popular movies I had missed.

When the trial had ended, I was exhausted. I wasn't going to let it haunt me for the rest of my life. I wasn't going to let anyone stop me from doing what I wanted to do. I wanted to get on with my life.

First, I needed a new car. Mohammad, who was within two months of returning to Iran, took me around looking for a new car. At one auto lot, Mohammad started talking to the sales person who had recently converted to Islam. The car salesman was a Peruvian, named Ruben, who had dark features and beautiful olive skin. Mohammad told Ruben that he was returning to Iran in the next two months. As I was checking out the cars, Ruben was checking me out. We didn't buy a car that day, but Ruben did get my name and phone number.

After Mohammad had departed, I received a telephone call from Ruben wanting me to come down and look at a car he had just received. I went down and looked at it, but I didn't buy it. As we talked, Ruben asked me out to dinner. I said, "Okay."

With dinner came more conversation and familiarity. I told Ruben I wanted to move out of my dad's house and get an apartment of my own. Ruben suggested we and another salesperson get an apartment together. We could rent a large, three bedroom apartment. I eventually knew Ruben well enough to accept his offer. The third person, an African-American man who was very nice, joined us as we signed the lease on the nicest apartment I have ever lived in.

The apartment was in the shape of a "U" with an atrium in the center. The atrium had lots of sunshine and privacy. Since I didn't go to work until 2:30 in the afternoon, I had the apartment to myself for most of the day. Ruben and the other man went to work early each morning. With time, Ruben and I slowly fell in love with each other.

Ruben told me up-front he had spent time in prison. He had come to the United States from Peru as a young man and had married an American woman. They had a child together and while on a short trip back to Peru, Ruben tried to make a quick buck by transporting a load of cocaine back into the United States. He admitted it was a dumb thing to do, and he got caught. After four years in prison he was released on parole and rejoined his wife. His wife signed a statement saying that if Ruben was deported back to Peru, his American family would suffer a financial hardship. Ruben's wife became pregnant with their second child and then the marriage fell apart. When I met Ruben, he was recovering from the divorce and still on parole.

I didn't approve of his illegal drug smuggling, but in the late 70's and early 80's a lot of people tried to get rich quick by bringing illegal drugs into the United States. After all, Ruben had served his time and was moving on with his life. Since Ruben told me about his past, I told him about mine. We continued to live together in the fantastic apartment and enjoy the great California weather.

A couple of months later, Ruben told me his parole officer (PO) wanted to talk to me.

"Sure," I said, not seeing any problems.

Ruben told me his PO would come by the following Tuesday, around 1:00 PM.

About 30 minutes before the PO arrived, Ruben took me into the living room. "Colleen, I have something important to tell you," Ruben said, in a serious tone.

"What is it Ruben?"

"When I told you I served four years in prison for cocaine smuggling, well that was not what really happened. I actually served time for raping a woman in the San Francisco area. I followed her into her house, raped her, and was caught."

"Oh," I said, not showing much emotion. On the inside I was screaming, "I'm living with a rapist!"

When the PO arrived, he asked me if I knew why he was there.

"I do now," I said, still in shock.

The PO confirmed what Ruben told me and then left. I knew I had to leave also. I couldn't live with a liar and a rapist. I told Ruben there couldn't be a future for us together. He lied to me, and I didn't trust him any more. I told our roommate and the apartment manager I was moving out. I packed up and moved to a small, though not nearly as nice, apartment by myself. However, I soon learned I would not be by myself for long. I was pregnant with Ruben's baby.

We always had protected sex except for one night when some friends were over for a late night barbecue. There had been some drinking, which I have no tolerance for, followed by unprotected sex. We only did it once, but that's all it took.

I was 29 years old and would be 30 by the time the baby came. I always wanted a baby, but not with Hooker. Now, I decided it was time for me to have my baby. Ruben wanted to do the right thing and marry me, but I said, "No." I wouldn't live with a man I couldn't trust. I would rather be a single mom.

As the due date drew near, I was still living in my small apartment and working at the manufacturing plant. Suddenly, another complication arose during my last trimester of pregnancy. I developed a severe case of toxemia, a blood poisoning resulting from the presences of bacterial toxins in the blood. My blood pressure rose, and my ankles started to swell. The doctor told me to stay off my feet and to keep my legs elevated. I followed his orders, but during my next visit the doctor admitted me into the hospital. The toxemia worsened until it started to affect the unborn baby. A cesarean birth was ordered four weeks before my due date. I was scared and concerned about my baby's health.

Danielle was born on Thursday, April 23, 1987, weighting in at four pounds, 15 ounces. It was truly the happiest day of my life. Even happier than the day I came home to Riverside. I have had a number of regrets in my life, but never once have I regretted having Danielle.

Colleen with Danielle, 1987

I chose Danielle's name while locked in the box. During the endless hours, I sang Elton John's "Daniel" time and time again. I knew someday my baby boy would be named Daniel. For me, Danielle was close enough. I was happy my prayers had been answered, and I was now the mother of a healthy baby girl.

Before going into the hospital, I had moved out of my small apartment and back with my dad. Dad had purchased a new four bedroom house in Moreno Valley one week after Danielle was born. The house was in a fast growing community between Riverside and Palm Springs. It had plenty of room, and he later built a swimming pool in the backyard.

Ruben was still trying to get me to marry him, to which I kept refusing. "Let's do the right thing," he would say.

Finally, I agreed to move back in with him. After an argument, Ruben told me, "If you ever try to leave me, I will take Danielle and you will never see her again." Our reunion lasted one week after which I moved back to my dad's house.

When Danielle was about four months old, Ruben came for a short visit to see Danielle. He asked if he could take Danielle out for a three hour visitation. I said, "Okay." A couple of hours later, Ruben called.

"I'm in Mexico with Danielle and we are heading south [toward Peru]. You will never see Danielle again."

"Bring Danielle back!" I cried. "Why are you doing this to me? Why do you want to hurt me?" I called the police and told them Ruben had kidnapped our child. I got a quick lesson in California custody law. Without a court custody order, Ruben had as much legal right to Danielle as I had. I freaked out! For the next three days and nights, Ruben and I talked on the phone.

"Ruben, do you really think this is going to make me love you?" I asked. "Please bring Danielle home."

My dad told me to offer him money, but Ruben, like Hooker, didn't want money. He just wanted to hurt me. I was not eating, sleeping, or working. Finally, I said to Ruben "What do you want me to do?"

"Get an attorney," he said, coldly.

I spent $1,000 retaining a lawyer. His attorney talked to my attorney and they decided the place for Danielle was with me until a court hearing could be conducted. In the parking lot in front of his lawyer's office, I got Danielle back safe and sound.

The first step in the legal process was to meet with a mediator. Ruben started with a personal attack on me.

"She's an ex-sex slave who spent years locked in a box. She can't possibly be a good mother. She's crazy."

"Well, he's an ex-con convicted of raping a woman. He can't possibly be a good father," I replied.

The mediator got more than he had bargained for. He threw up his hands and said, "This is too much for me. I can't mediate this case."

We were both ordered to take a psychological examination at our own expense. I paid $650 and spent hours being evaluated. Ruben never showed up for his evaluation nor did he pay his attorney. In the end, I won custody of Danielle and Ruben won visitation rights. When visiting, he had to have a friend with him I knew and trusted. Ruben was also ordered to pay child support.

"It was 'you' that wanted the baby," Ruben always said. He never paid any child support nor did he visit on a regular basis. When Danielle was older, her dad would schedule a visit on Friday afternoon. Danielle would get so excited, but her dad would never show up. When he would visit, it would be unannounced and he would stay for only a short period of time. Danielle never received any birthday cards or Christmas gifts from her dad. When she became a teenager she missed the approval and love that only a father can give.

"Danielle, I'm sorry I didn't do a better job choosing your father," I said.

Soon after I got custody of Danielle, who was now seven months old, Dad and I had a short conversation with long term consequences.

"Why don't you get off your ass and get a job," Dad said.

"Well find something for me to do," I replied, which was a big mistake. The next day Dad found an ad in the newspaper for a used water truck.

"But Dad, I don't know anything about water trucks."

"You'll learn," he said.

A day later, I was standing in front of a 6X6, army surplus, duce-and-a-half truck that had been converted into a water carrier. It had six tires on the ground and six-wheel-drive, hence the name 6X6 (six by six). The name duce-and-a-half came from army slang meaning two and a half ton capacity. In the back of the truck was a 2,000 gallon water tank. It cost me $6,500.

I started my new job while my mom watched Danielle. Dad was unable to help with the truck, since he was working at his own job site. However, Dad had an old, retired friend who would teach me everything I needed to know about how to operate a water truck. His old friend showed up and after half a day, became bored, and went home. I was on my own.

My first job was to water down some utility trenches so the workers could compact the earth. Not knowing what to do first, I panicked. I then jumped out of the truck and approached a utility worker.

"This is my first job, so watch out for me, and please help me," I pleaded. The utility worker said, "Okay." The job went well except for one problem. I had no brakes, especially when the truck was full of water, on a hill, and rolling backwards.

Once, when contracted to fill a swimming pool with water, the brakes failed, and I started rolling backwards down a hill. As I was dodging parked cars, I pulled the gravity flow lever to dump the water. The truck careened off the road with the back dual wheels falling into an irrigation ditch. The front of the truck lifted up off the ground. I thought the truck was going to flip over, but the front tires dropped back down and bounced until they came to a rest on the edge of the ditch. The man who owned the swimming pool came running down the hill.

"Are you okay?" he asked.

"Yes," I replied.

"Are you going to be able to complete the job?" he inquired.

"Yes, as soon as I stop shaking."

Later, after I had sold the water truck, I was working with Dad at one of his construction sites. Dad was from the "old school" of teaching.

"Get on the loader and dump that pile of trash into the bin," he ordered.

"Dad, I don't know how to operate the loader."

"Get on the damn loader and dump that pile of trash into the bin," he repeated, in a stronger voice.

I got on the loader, cranked the engine, and start pulling and pushing levers and knobs until I got the hang of it. Soon the pile of trash was in the bin.

In time, I was assigned to operate Big Ruth, a bulldozer with a ripper blade in the rear. The ripper blade was used to brake up the soil so a scraper could scoop up the earth and move it to another location. Driving Big Ruth had its own challenges. With my right hand stretched to the rear, I would control the ripper which had to be constantly regulated. With my left hand stretched to the front, I controlled Big Ruth. My feet were stretched out to reach the petals. There I was stretched from end to end trying to keep Big Ruth under control. I was watching the ripper while at the same time watching where Big Ruth was heading.

I still wanted to be independent of my dad. With some of the money from the civil suite against Hooker's insurance company, I purchased a fixer-upper house in Moreno Valley. Randy, my sister Jenise's husband, said when he first saw the house, "You've bought the money pit." He was referring to the movie "The Money Pit" staring Tom Hanks. The movie was about a house where everything was wrong and nothing was right. My house was much the same way. It cost me $65,000 of which I put 10 percent down and spent $10,000 on repairs. When I had finished the house had a new roof, floors, carpet, doors, windows, kitchen, bathroom fixtures, and paint.

Shortly before I sold my water truck, I was filling it up at a fire hydrant when a good looking man came over to talk to me.

"Want to go out for some breakfast?"

"I'm sorry, but I've got to work," I said.

Each time I filled the water tank, the same man, whose name I learned was Ray, would come over and talk with me. I finally accepted an invitation for dinner.

Ray was a big guy of Italian heritage. He was at least six feet, four inches tall, and had dark hair and green eyes. Working outdoors as a carpenter had given him a beautiful, dark tan. After I got to know Ray, I told him about my years of captivity.

"I would have kicked Hooker's ass. I would have killed him," Ray said, in a macho way.

When I hear such comments, my eyes roll to the top of my head. Sure you would Ray, I thought, as Hooker towered 10 inches in height over you. For Ray, Hooker would have been seven feet, two inches tall, proportionally. Men don't deal well with my personal history. They can't understand why I didn't spit in Hooker's eye.

Ray was a nice guy and, unlike Ruben, had no criminal record. He liked Danielle and wanted to have children of his own, but we later learned he couldn't. When he asked me to marry him, I gladly accepted.

We were married in April, 1989, at the Chapel of the Roses in Riverside. It was a fairly large wedding with many people attending from both families. My cousin Amy was my maid of honor while Jenise,

Bonnie, and Cindy, a family friend, were my bride's maids. Two year old Danielle was too young to be a flower girl, but Ray's eight year old niece was just right for the job. I was happy and knew Ray would be a good step-father to Danielle.

As Dad walked me up the church aisle, I noticed Ray was wearing a Jewish yarmulke, the small skullcap worn by Jewish men. It didn't bother me, but it did surprise me because he had never mentioned it before the wedding. After the ceremony we got in a limousine to ride to the reception.

"Well Ray, when were you going to tell me about the yarmulke?" I asked.

"My mom told me not to tell you, because she said it might upset you." Ray replied. It was at that point, I first realized, I had the mother-in-law from hell.

"You may be married to my son, but I'm still number one," my new mother-in-law told me. "And don't you forget it."

A week after Ray and I were married, his mother wanted me to take out a second mortgage on my house so she could buy the house she was renting. I told her I didn't want another mortgage. From that day forward, I was a bitch in her eyes. My marriage with Ray, thanks to my mother-in-law, had started off on the wrong foot. Ray and I went to counseling where he was told, "You need to put your marriage first, and your mother second." Of course, Ray wouldn't do that, because he allowed his mother to rule his life.

Our marriage finally came to an end after four years. Danielle was broken hearted and didn't understand why we were divorcing. I had shielded her from our adult problems. To her, Ray was the father she never had. For years Danielle kept begging me to get back with Ray.

"Danielle, when you are older you will understand," I told her. Today, Danielle is older and recently told me she now understands. The last I heard, Ray had a girlfriend, but still lived with his mother.

Shortly before we divorced, I did take out a second mortgage on my house to pay a tax bill. With Ray gone, I couldn't keep up the payments on the mortgages. I tried to sell the house for over a year, but with a depressed market and new houses just down the street, I had no offers. I reluctantly returned the house keys to the bank and declared bankruptcy in 1993.

While I was in captivity, Dad had purchased 40 acres of land north of Red Bluff. His plan was to move to Northern California after retirement, which he did in 1991. After divorcing Ray and losing my house, I planned to join Dad up north.

Despite my painful experiences in Red Bluff, I still loved Northern California. It was a man, not the region, which held me in captivity. Northern California is beautiful with pine-covered mountains to the east and west and the Sacramento River meandering down the middle. Mount Shasta, to the north, overlooks the entire region. The summers are hot and the winters are wet, but the air is still cleaner than the smog-shrouded Los Angeles basin. The high population growth, stalled traffic jams, and rising crime in the Inland Empire, as the area around Riverside was called, were additional reasons for me to move north.

Before I departed for Northern California, I had a job at Boreal Resources, an Australian owned sand and gravel pit operation. I ran the scales and weighted trucks as they entered and exited the quarry.

"That guy really likes you," my boss told me one day. He was referring to Doug, who weighed his truck each day on my scale and took time to talk to me every chance he got. We started dating and in time Doug became my third husband in 1994.

We were married in my house just before I surrender the keys to the bank. My mom and Doug's mom, along with my dad, were present when a minister conducted the marriage ceremony. After Tim, Ruben, and Ray, I was hoping and praying that Doug would bring me the happiness I had never known and Danielle the father figure she had never experienced.

Once again, my expectations were too high. Doug had a serious alcohol problem compounded with some illegal drug usage. Alcohol was the self-medication Doug used to fight off his depression. I began to think of him as "Doug the slug" when depression kept him in bed for six months. Keeping a job was out of the question for Doug, and soon he was not only abusing alcohol, but Danielle and I as well. When I tried to call the police, he ripped the phone out of the wall.

"I don't want to talk to you Colleen," the psychiatrist at counseling told me. "You're too angry."

"Your damn right I'm angry," I replied.

I do want to talk to you Doug because I can see you're very depressed," the psychiatrist said.

Doug was prescribed the drug Paxil, which is an anti-depressant form of Prozac. The only problem with Paxil, in Doug's mind, was it made him ill when he drank alcohol. One day, I came home from work and found Doug drunk. "How could he be on Paxil, drinking, and not sick?" I wondered.

"I don't need Paxil anymore, so I flushed the pills down the toilet," was Doug's answer. I filed for divorce to end our four year marriage in 1998. Even after the divorce, it took a restraining order and law enforcement officers to evict Doug from my house.

"Mom, isn't it nice with no men in the house," 11 year old Danielle told me. "It's so quite."

Five years later in 2003, I received a telephone message from a man named Doug. "Doug, Doug who?" I thought. "I don't know a Doug." After I returned the call, I realized it was my former husband. He just wanted to talk and didn't say much. It was then that I realized, after five years, I had placed Doug so far out of my mind. I hung up the phone knowing he was gone from my life forever.

I had gone through three husbands, four if you count Ruben, and found none of them to be keepers. It was clear I didn't have much luck with men. Only my dad remained close to my heart. Dad never lied to me, abused me, or hurt me.

Why had I gone through so many men searching and praying for love? I could say the men were cheaters, liars, rapist, mama's boys, alcoholics, and illegal drug users. In truth, it was my fault because I chose each of them. I saw warning signs while we were dating, but refused to acknowledge them. I overlooked their problems, and soon their problems became my problems. I haven't given up on men, but now I listen to what they say and watch what they do. Small clues send up hurricane warning flags which drive me to safe harbors.

Life after slavery has been filled with peaks and valleys. I acquired an AA (Associate of Arts) Degree in accounting which I'm using in my current position with a highway construction company. My mom died in 1998 causing me to cry like a baby at her funeral. There were still many issues between us that had not been resolved with words. I loved my mom, but vowed my daughter, Danielle, would always come first in my life.

Colleen with Danielle in Hawaii, 2003

In 2003, Grandma Gertrude passed away at the age of 98½. She was the "rock" of our family and the one who took my sisters and I to church as little girls. She was also the one who prayed for me nightly when I was in captivity. I loved her so much and have missed her even more.

The same day Grandma Gertrude passed away, another tragedy was unfolding. Danielle had become involved with a bad group of misguided teenagers and illegal drugs. I didn't approve of her friends or the drugs, but Danielle had the same stubbornness I had when I was her age.

One morning, I received a telephone call from the sheriff asking me if I knew where Danielle's friends were staying. I told them they were at the Deluxe Inn and the Red Lion Inn. It wasn't until they were all arrested that I found out the truth.

When a girl in the group said, "I wish my mom was dead," one of the boys said, "No problem." Danielle was not directly involved, but she knew what was going to happen and told no one. While Danielle was waiting down the road, an innocent woman was murdered. Danielle later took items that were stolen from the woman's house and brought them back to my house. I was crushed when I found out about Danielle's involvement and officers came to retrieve the stolen goods from Danielle's bedroom.

As I was driving to my grandmother's funeral, I received a call from my supervisor at the Women's Refuge where I volunteered.

"Have you seen today's newspaper?" she asked.

"No," I said.

"Danielle's mother is Colleen Stan who was kidnapped in Tehama County in 1977 and held captive for seven years before she escaped. Cameron Hooker of Red Bluff was sentenced to 104 years in prison for the infamous 'Girl in the Box, Sex Slave' case."

I knew immediately the media circus would start. Fortunately, my supervisor called the newspaper and reminded them that I was a victim. The newspaper dropped any references to me in subsequent articles.

At age 16, Danielle was tried as an adult. Using a public defender, she was faced with accepting a plea bargain and receiving 10 years or going to trial and, if found guilty, receiving 20 years. It was a difficult choice for any young woman. Danielle chose to take the plea bargain. The girl who wished her mom dead received 35 years to life, and the boy who pulled the trigger received 50 years to life for murder.

Before Danielle got into trouble, I prayed the Lord would save Danielle from illegal drugs. My prayers were answered, just not as I expected. (Be careful what you pray for). Danielle is now drug free serving her sentence in prison. Danielle believes God placed her in prison to save her life. She is using her time wisely helping others and educating herself. She has donated her hair to Locks of Love, an organization that provides wigs to children with cancer. She has also graduated from high school and is now taking college courses. As for me, I'm thankful Danielle is alive.

In a way, there has been a parallel between Danielle's life and mine. We both made bad decisions and lost many years of our youth. I hope Danielle has the strength and perseverance to survive and recover from her ordeal. I pray she too will be a survivor.

With all the problems I've had in life, one might ask why I just didn't give up? If you have been following my story, you know by now

I'm not a person who gives up. My daughter will be out of prison in a few years, if not sooner, and I have a new friend in my life. I met Ralph, through my daughter, a few years ago. Ralph has been good to me, and I'm happy. Concerning my problems, I've learned in life God never gives you more than you can handle.

I am independent
But I don't always like to be alone.
I am strong
But sometimes I let my guard down and am weak.
I am full of love
But at times my heart feels hate.
I have faith
But some days I feel hopeless.
I am locked up and stuck in a cage
But I am free in my mind.
-Poem by Danielle.

Chapter 19 - Life under the Spotlight

The media has always been interested in my story. When a hostage related news story occurs, my phone rings off the hook. In 2008, when Elisabeth Fritzl was released after 24 years of captivity in Austria, reporters sought me out. Reporters were searching for someone who knows what it's like to be in captivity and could answer their questions. My name and phone number must be on many newsroom Rolodexes.

After the trial, I was offered $50,000 for the rights to my story by a producer in Hollywood. The only catch was once I signed on the dotted line, I would lose all control over how my story was portrayed. Since I wanted to make sure the story was not distorted or trivialized, I refused the offer.

Television:

My first television appearance was on the "Oprah Winfrey Show" in 1987. Christine, Dr. Hatcher, Jan, and I were invited to appear together and discuss the story. My only request, before the show, was not to be seated next to Jan. Throughout the Hooker trial, his defense had contended Jan and I were lovers. Seating us next to each other would reinforce that falsehood. A minute before air time, we were escorted on to the stage and told where to sit. I steamed as Jan was seated next to me. Jan and I both talked during the show, but not to each other.

I regretted there wasn't time to talk with Oprah personally, but I realized she was busy. I admire her warm, generous spirit. She is a woman of great strength and is a survivor herself, who has used her influence to reach out and help others.

After the show Ruben, Danielle's father, and I were driven directly to the airport to fly home. To my horror, the "Oprah Winfrey Show" I had just taped was airing on televisions in the airport terminal. I was still wearing the same dress and makeup I had worn on the show.

"Look, there's the twin," a man seated at the bar said as I walked past. I went directly to my gate and hide out while the show aired.

"Go back to the bar and find out what they're saying about the show," I told Ruben. A few minutes later Ruben returned.

"Look, the two women are sitting side by side," one man at the bar said.

"Yea, they look like friends to me," another man said.

In 1989, two women knocked on my door and asked me if I would interview for the television show "Current Affairs." Normally, I would have refused, but for some reason, I invited them in to discuss the show.

"How did you find me?" was my first question.

"Oh, as reporters we have our ways," was their reply.

Lisa Lou was a beautiful Chinese-American woman while Reba was of English heritage. Reba spoke so fast and with such a heavy English accent, I could hardly follow her. The interviewer was Gordon Elliott, an Australian who was so tall he had to lower his head when entering the room. His intimidating size didn't portray his gentle side when conducting an interview. The show, produced by Peter Brennan, was a big success.

Two years later, Peter Brennan produced another television show about me on "Hard Copy." The show was written by Graeme Whifler who interviewed Hooker in prison. After the show Graeme, received a threatening letter from Hooker because Hooker felt the show failed to cast him in a good light.

I also have appeared on "The Montel Williams Show, A&E's American Justice, and 48 Hours." After "48 Hours" aired, something unusual happened to me. For the first and only time in my life, someone recognized me in public as Colleen Stan.

"Didn't I see you on TV last night?" a saleswoman in a New York department store asked me.

"Yes, I'm Colleen Stan," I answered. We talked about the show for a few minutes before I departed the store.

The appearance that surprised me the most was on the "Geraldo Rivera Show." The producers of the show had been after me for months to appear with Geraldo. I kept refusing, because I didn't think Geraldo would focus on the serious nature of my story. Finally in 1992, I accepted and was flown back to New York.

Before the show, Geraldo Rivera met and talked with me. He wanted to know if my hotel room was comfortable and how I liked New York. During the show, Geraldo spoke to Hooker on the phone.

Hooker started to read some of the "love" letters I had written while in captivity. Geraldo cut him off and started a verbal assault on Hooker. Hooker hung up the phone. After the show, Geraldo continued to talk with me. I was surprised by his kindness and concern. I had misjudged both Geraldo Rivera and his show.

I turned down requests from Jenny Jones, Ricki Lake, and Maury Povich. I was concerned they would tell my story in a circus or tabloid atmosphere. Like Geraldo Rivera, I could have been wrong.

I learned that television appearances do not result in big money. My travel and hotel expenses were paid and a small amount of money was given for family photographs that were used during a show. The rewards of such appearances were intrinsic, not financial.

Retaining a media consultant was unheard of for victims of crime in the 1980's. The thought of having someone to advise me on television appearances and media contacts never entered my mind. Even today, I don't have a media advisor. However, anyone finding themselves a victim of a high profile crime would be well advised to consult someone familiar with the news and entertainment industry. There are many human sharks in the oceans of life.

Many enterprises have been started without my knowledge or input. A television movie "The Colleen Stan Story" staring and produced by Jean Kasem was announced in 1997. Jean Kasem stared as Loretta in the television show "Cheers." Nothing has materialized from this effort as far as I know.

A "Law & Order, Special Victims Unit" episode titled "Slaves" was aired on television in 2000. The show was based on my story I have been told.

A Japanese television show about me was filmed in San Francisco for broadcast in Japan. The actors spoke English, which was later voiced over into Japanese. The show was not broadcast in the United States.

A video movie re-enacting my story was produced in Europe. The movie, I understand, will not run in an American VCR. No one consulted me for input nor have I seen the production.

In 2007, I was interviewed by a French film crew for a documentary which aired on French television.

I was contacted by Vivian McGrath of Gecko Productions to assist in the documentary "The Girl in the Box" which aired on British television in May, 2008.

Another documentary, produced by Benjamin Sessoms, Jr. of m2Pictures, is in production for the Discovery Channel. The documentary should be ready for American television in August, 2008.

Newspapers:

At least a dozen newspaper reporters have also contacted me. I have only granted interviews with the *Riverside Press Enterprise, Redding Record Searchlight*, and a student newspaper at Shasta Junior College. The Riverside article, by John Pomfret, was my first public interview. The interview took place in my dad's house the day after Hooker was convicted. I made a follow-up interview with Skip Morgan four years later where I talked about the book *Perfect Victim*. The Redding interview, written by Betty Lease in 2002, can still be found on the Internet today. The interview at Shasta Junior College was written by a journalism student who was working on a special project.

Internet:

Today when information is sought, people go to the Internet. Numerous Internet stories have appeared about my life. A friend has sent me copies of the Internet stories concerning my story over the years.

"Case of the Seven Year Slave" by Katherine Ramsland appeared in the Internet under Court TV's Crime Library. Katherine's account draws information from court records. Rather than Colleen Stan, she uses the name Carol Smith.

A modernistic painting depicting my story was done by Cameron Hayes, a young Australian artist, in 2001. The Internet picture of the painting is small and I'm sure doesn't do justice to the original.

Choreographer Rachel Arianne Ogle performed a dance about my story at the Perth Institute of Contemporary Arts in Australia in 2002. I have not seen the performance.

The song "Jack in the Box" by the American rock band Elysian Fields was in their first album "Bleed Your Cedar" in 1996. The song describes the experience of the box that Hooker kept me imprisoned in under the bed and alludes to the power Hooker had over me.

I have been told Hooker's signature, while in prison, is for sale on the Internet and a Goggle Map will show you an aerial photo of the Hooker house on Oak Street by using the key search word: Cameron Hooker.

Books:

There are 20 books that touch on my story, mostly from a legal or psychological point of view. I have not provided personal input or read any of the books. A list of the books can be found in the related sources section of this book.

Public Events:

The media engagements were a small fraction of my life. Most of my life, I have been busy working and raising Danielle.

In 1999, I saw an ad in the newspaper for "Take Back the Night," an annual event to stop violent crime. Something inside of me told me to volunteer, but I was hesitant. I waited until the day before the event before I telephoned, hoping they wouldn't need me.

"Yes, we would love for you to speak," a lady said, after I told her my story.

My nervous speech at the event the next night was well received. I was invited back the next year and soon became an advocate or sponsor for other people scheduled to speak at the event. As an advocate, my first survivor was a man who had been sexually abused by his father.

I also became active in a Women's Refuge Center where I volunteered to assist women who were victims of crime. Like other volunteers, I hoped my efforts would perhaps help someone find their way back to a better life.

My time in the media spotlight has had its advantages. I have been given an opportunity to tell my story in a serious forum that might help someone in need. The trips to New York and Chicago were fun, but if given a choice, I would have preferred to have arrived safely in Westwood on that day in May, 1977.

Chapter 20 - Looking Back

If you think something long enough and strong enough, it will happen. For our mind is our strongest defense weapon.

If you think that you can survive something, even the most horrific unimaginable thing, it will happen.

Our minds can be our place of refuge.

- Unknown Author

Time has given me the prospective to look back over my life and draw conclusions. This would have not been possible during my first years back home. I will cover lessons learned from my experiences and observations made as to how the media covers captivity stories. Next, I will close the loop on Hooker, Jan, and other important people in my story. I will then follow with an update on various locations in my story such as the Oak Street basement, the mobile home on Weed Court, and the Interstate 5 overpass in Red Bluff. My physical and mental health will be discussed and, lastly, I will answer the three most common questions I have received from both friends and the news media.

Lessons learned:

1. Don't hitchhike or pick up a hitchhiker. I assumed I was safe since a woman and a baby were in the car, but I was wrong. I paid dearly for my mistake. Most abductors want to take you where they feel safe. They will never take you to a better place. Hooker wanted to get me back in his Oak Street basement. I made it easier for him by getting in his car.

Once while I was married to Ray, we saw a beautiful young woman, about 19 years of age, trying to hitch a ride on the side of the highway. Ray pulled over and the girl got into our pickup truck and sat between Ray and I.

"I think she'll do just fine," Ray said, in a menacing voice as he hit the automatic door lock. He wanted the girl to think we were about to kidnap her. Ray then pulled off the road, stopped the truck, and pointed to me.

"She's going to tell you a story and you had better listen," Ray said. After I had finished telling my story, Ray made the young woman promise she would never again hitchhike. We dropped her off safely at her destination and drove off. I think we scared the girl to death, which might have been a good thing.

2. Listen to your inner-voice and watch for warning signs. In my case, I felt the warnings came from God, but I refused to acknowledge the warnings. "Jump out the window, run, and never look back," was the last warning I received before I got back in the car with the Hookers. If you don't feel something is right, it probably isn't. There's nothing wrong with changing plans, delaying, or asking a friend to help you. Follow your intuition. Your guardian angel may be trying to get your attention. The same is true when looking for a spouse in marriage I learned.

3. Escape from your abductor at the first opportunity, hopefully before they can bind you up and take you to a secluded place. I was physically restrained and constantly watched during my first years of captivity. Once the restraints were replaced with a deep fear of The Company, I was allowed greater freedom. I considered escape, but didn't think I would be successful in getting away from a world-wide, underground criminal organization.

For me, the first opportunity to escape came in August, 1984, when Jan told me her husband was not part of The Company. I knew then only one man stood between me and going home to Riverside. For Natasha Kampusch in Austria, the chance came after eight years when her abductor went into his house to answer the telephone. She was vacuuming out his car and left the vacuum running to cover her escape. For Elizabeth Shoaf escape came after 10 days when she was able to text-message her mother. For Marliz the chance to escape never came. Each situation is different, but one must try to escape as soon as possible. Just make sure your escape is successful, since you might not get a second chance.

4. Your abductor will never tell you the truth. Don't believe what you read, hear, or see while in captivity. Your abductor will try to lower your self-esteem and make you feel helpless. You may be told your parents don't want you anymore or no one is searching for you.

"The Company felt you were too ugly to be a prostitute, so you will remain a slave for life. The Company is everywhere, so don't think about escape. Your family will be in danger if you ask for help." These were among the lies Hooker told me to lower my self-worth and increase his control over me.

5. The next point is very important, especially for the news media. When in captivity one does things and says things they normally wouldn't do or say. Telling Hooker I loved him, smiling for photos, and not telling my parents I had been abducted are not the actions of a free woman. They are the actions of a woman under pressure to survive. The news media is especially bad about asking a recently freed hostage why they did something out of character such as not escaping or expressing support for their captor. Some might call this the Stockholm syndrome, but I prefer to call it the survivor syndrome.

The Stockholm syndrome is when a hostage shows loyalty to the hostage taker. The term came about after a failed 1973 bank robbery in Stockholm, Sweden. The bank was surrounded by the police and several bank employees were held hostage for six days. With their lives in the hands of the robbers, the victims became emotionally attached to their captors. Their survival depended on the safety and welfare of their captors. Even after the hostages were released, the victims still defended their captors. This is referred to as the Stockholm syndrome.

Many people have tried to attach the Stockholm syndrome to my case. At no time did I feel love or loyalty to Hooker. My love for him was forced from me or used to lessen my pain. I wanted Hooker to see me as a person, not as a commodity. I was thankful Hooker didn't kill me or sell me to another member of The Company, but I always knew Hooker was an evil man, not my protector. I could never have loved him. I will let psychologist decide if Jan would be a better candidate for the Stockholm syndrome label.

6. If you survived, you did the right thing. No matter what you did, the goal is survival. Some victims feel they may have been partially responsible for their victim status. They may feel guilt, remorse, embarrassment, anger, shame, and humiliation because of what they did in captivity. If they survived, they did nothing wrong. Some people will always blame the victim. These are the same people who have never experienced what it's like to be kidnapped and not know if they will be alive the next day.

An exception to this lesson may be POW's in time of war and hostages compelled to commit crimes. Neither of these situations applied to me. To Hooker, I was much too valuable to waste robbing a bank. As Marliz discovered, Hooker wasn't in the kidnapping business for money. He wanted a woman for torture and sex which, for him, no amount of money would compensate.

The closest I came to committing a crime was fulfilling Hooker's desire for additional women slaves. I would have been responsible for their discipline and training, something that I prayed daily would never come to pass. Thank God, Hooker never fulfilled his perverted desire.

7. Transitioning from a victim to a survivor is a slow process and will be different for each individual. One has to find what works for them. For some it might require months if not years of professional help. For me personally, my recovery came from Dr. Chris Hatcher, my family who were there for me, and my strong faith in the Lord. I knew I needed to get my life back on track. In time, I moved from being a victim full of fear to being a survivor filled with hope for a positive, healthy future. There is no magic formula. Each person must find their own path and discover what works for them. Hooker had stolen years from my life, but I was determined he would not shadow my remaining years. Also, illegal drugs, alcohol, and other destructive habits will turn a victim of violent crime into a victim of drugs and alcohol abuse. So avoid negative self-pity and seek healthy choices during the recovery process.

I was fortunate my family, especially my dad, was always there for me. What I appreciated most was that my family didn't pressure me when I first came home. They let me tell my story when I was ready. They never tried to second guess my actions or judge my behavior either while in captivity or after I returned home. If one doesn't have the support of family or friends, then they must find a substitute or look within themselves for strength.

People:

As for Cameron Hooker, most people are surprised when they ask me something about his personal tastes, desires, or habits.

"What were Hooker's feelings about politics or sports?" they might ask.

"I don't know," I would answer. The Hooker's, both Cameron and Jan, never had a person-to-person or heart-to-heart talk with me. There was always a slave-master barrier between us. Even after seven years, they were still strangers to me on a personal level. They knew many things about me, but I knew very little about them. This trend started as we drove up the mountain in May, 1977, prior to my kidnapping. They kept asking me questions, and I was too tired at the time to quiz them. I wish I had asked more questions when I had a chance, because later I became a slave who spoke only when spoken to. My human traits were suppressed to avoid personal attachment between slave and master.

Cameron Hooker, I feel he must have come in contact with some deviant person or pornographic pictures that fixed his sexual desires at a young age. He told me at age five or six, he was drawing naked women in bondage which usually requires some type of outside influence. His family claimed Hooker had an average childhood and was not exposed to sexual deviance at a young age, but they also claimed I was not a slave.

Once Hooker reached adulthood, he made the decision to fulfill his fantasies. He chose evil. Even today he has shown no remorse for what he did. He denies or shifts the blame for what happened to Jan and myself. I can't see him ever changing because he believes his life style, his desires, and his fantasies are normal. He lacks all feelings of remorse and guilt.

On March 8, 1988, Hooker's appeal for a new trial was denied. The last I heard he was still serving his time at Corcoran State Prison. Sadism and sex are the same in Hooker's mind. They will always be the driving force in his life. If he ever escapes from prison, is released, or is granted parole he will, I don't doubt, find another woman to abduct and torture. His scheduled release date is the year 2022 which is 14 years from the time of this writing.

Jan or Janice Hooker remains an enigma for many people, including myself. She was both an accomplice and a victim. It was her presence, along with the baby, that lured me into their car. Throughout my captivity, I never felt any human kindness or sympathy from Jan. Instead, she directed her anger, jealousy, and hostility towards me. Many times after I had cleaned the kitchen, Jan would tell Hooker my performance was poor which would bring on a beating. The whipping

I received under the arch doorway at Oak Street due to a missing fork and the electrical torture in the trailer while Jan and Cameron watched television, were the results of Jan's complaints to Hooker about me. She turned her back on my suffering and seemed to enjoy the limitless power she had over me.

On the other hand, she too was a victim at the hands of Hooker. With the exception of the boxes, electrocution, piercing, and burning, she suffered the same tortures Hooker put me through. Even when she was pregnant, the bondage didn't stop. Unlike me, Jan knew Hooker was capable of murder after he allegedly killed Marliz. Whereas I feared The Company, she feared Hooker. She was an abused wife who used denial and compartmentalization to survive.

When she came to the motel on that hot August morning to tell me Hooker was not part of The Company, she did so in her own interest. She knew her life with Hooker couldn't continue with two growing daughters and a slave under the same roof. By sending me home and reforming Hooker, she hoped to save her family and marriage. She got the first part right, I went home, but Hooker never reformed. She knew Hooker was bizarre when she married him. Yet she waited nine years before doing anything to stop him. I will always be thankful to her for starting the sequence of events that lead to my freedom. I just wish she had spoken up sooner and saved herself, Charity, Amber, Marliz, and me from all the pain.

After the trial, Jan divorced Hooker on January 28, 1986, citing "irreconcilable differences." She and the children continued to live in the mobile home on Weed Court. Later, Jan moved out of the trailer and received a college degree in family counseling. Unlike me, her education was paid for by the government since she was an impoverished mother with two small children. Today she's working in Northern California helping troubled teens. I'm still waiting for the explanation or whole story she promised me at the courthouse elevator.

Since Charity and Amber were shielded from what had gone on, it must have been hard on them when their father went to prison. I cringe when I think of all the unjustified remarks and stares they endured while in school. I understand they both went on to acquire college degrees and are living in the Northwestern United States. I would love to meet them again someday, but any meeting must be at their request.

I would not want to invade their privacy. As young women they too are survivors and I pray they have gone on to recover and are enjoying rewarding lives.

My dad, Jack, continues to live in Northern California on the 40 acres of land he purchased while I was in captivity. My mom, Lynn, who I dearly loved, passed away in 1998. Dad and his third wife, Ruth, divorced and she now lives in Southern California with her three girls and two boys from a previous marriage. My sister Jenise lost her husband Randy when he died of an unexpected heart attack at age 46 while they were out jogging. Their son Nicholas is now serving in Iraq as a medic with the Marines. Jenise now lives with her second husband Kevin in Southern California. Bonnie, my other sister, was married and has two children. They too live in Southern California. Linda, my cousin who is five years older than me, is married and lives in Redding. Amy, also a cousin, is married, lives in Southern California, and has twin boys. Her husband, Joe, recently retired as a professional Arena Football player.

Tim Stan, my first husband, had filed for divorce after I had disappeared. Under Ohio law, he was granted a divorce because after a number of years no one knew my whereabouts. Tim later remarried and had two girls. He visited me once in California after Danielle was born. He called my daughter a "little n….. baby" because of her Peruvian father. I told Tim he should return to his wife and daughters. Tim, an anti-government, nonconformist in his youth, now works for the government.

Ruben, Danielle's father, remains in the shadows and mostly out of our lives. He made very few child support payments and never developed a good relationship with Danielle. My daughter felt rejected by Ruben rather than loved by him. Ray, my second husband, still lives with his mother. Doug, my last husband, remains out of my life and lives in Southern California. I understand he continues to self-medicate himself with alcohol. Just before this book went to press, I learned Mohammed, the man who touched my soul, is living in Canada with his wife of 18 years and a son. I'm glad he's doing well.

Dr Hatcher, who helped me so much, passed away in 1999 at the age of 53. Judge Knight, who presided over the Hooker trial, has retired from the bench. Detective Al Shamblin recently retired as Police Chief

Shamblin. Christine McGuire continued her legal career and both she and Carla Norton went on to publish additional crime books. My dear friend, juror Debbie King, continues to live in the San Francisco area and corresponds with me. Another close friend, Marilyn Barrett, who helped me so much when I needed her, continues to work and live in the Los Angles area.

Linda Smith, the birthday girl in Westwood, now lives on the California coast. Bobby, my roommate in Eugene, was killed in an automobile crash in his 20's. Alice, my other roommate in Eugene, returned to Oklahoma with her son Tomac, and now teaches at an alternative high school. Tomac, who reportedly was named after a character in the "Planet of the Apes," inherited his mother's free spirit. He works as a carpenter and goes to college off and on. Sadly, Marie Elizabeth (Marliz) Spannhake remains somewhere in the mountains east of Red Bluff, still waiting for somebody to find her and bring her home. I still pray there will be justice for her someday.

Places:

The house on Oak Street has changed little over the years. It's still being rented out by the Leddy family. Before anyone signs a rental agreement, they are told about Marliz and I. The horror in the basement doesn't bother most renters, and many of the renters are too young to remember the events first hand.

I returned to the house on Oak Street three times. The first time, years after the trial, I was passing through Red Bluff by myself and stopped out of curiosity. I parked my car in front of the house and walked to the chain-link fence surrounding the house. I stood frozen as I stared at the house, too afraid to open the gate. Mr. Leddy, the owner, seeing me in front of the house approached me. I told him my name was Colleen Stan. He offered to let me inside, but I declined. I returned to my car and quickly departed town. Later, Mr. Leddy said I looked scared standing in front of the Oak Street house and he was right.

The second time I visited the house was during the taping of the television show "A&E's American Justice." My cousin Linda and I drove over to Oak Street and entered the house which was vacant at the time. The bedrooms, the bathroom, and the arched doorway, where I was ordered to do attention drills, remained unchanged since 1978. I didn't know there was a garage behind the house until 1984 due to my profound isolation. After working up some courage, I went downstairs with Linda into the basement. The stairs were steep as I remembered and the basement had been painted white. Only the stairs, two small windows, a supporting pillar, the gas pipe, and the wooden beam across the ceiling remained. All other items such as the workshop and the box had been removed years before. In the wooden beam, I could still see where the hooks had been screwed into the wood. I couldn't stay in the basement for long. The experience was too frightening and real for me.

The third time I visited the Oak Street house was in January, 2008. A documentary film crew wanted to interview me in front of the house. Once the camera started rolling, the neighbors came out to see what was happening.

"Let's hurry up and get out of here," I told the film producer.

Weed Court remains the same, but the Hooker's mobile home has been removed and someone has constructed a house behind where the trailer stood. Kings Lodge remains the same, but the name has been changed to Travel Lodge. The overpass atop Interstate 5 is still there, but more fast-food businesses have sprung up in the area. The forest and mountains east of Red Bluff are the same with their pine-scented air and fast running streams. The gas station at Paynes Creek remains, but has gone out of business with its windows boarded up. I have never returned to where I was abducted. I believe the site might be along Cold Creek, a tributary of Battle Creek. I searched for the site once, but winter snow forced me to abandon the search.

In the Riverside area, Dad's house on Coolidge Avenue and Mom's house on Victoria Avenue remain as I remembered them during my short visit in 1981 and my homecoming in 1984.

Physical and Mental Impact:

I still carry physical and mental scars from my experience. After I returned home, I was diagnosed with PTSD (posttraumatic stress disorder). I also have arthritis in my left shoulder where Hooker dislocated my arm while on the stretcher. In June, 2008, I underwent bone surgery on my shoulder to try to reduce the pain. Today, I find it hard to sit up for long periods of time without some type of back support. I still have scars on my wrists from being hung and burns on my skin from the electrical shocks. My eye sight is horrible and I now wear glasses to see. Dr. Lunde was correct when he said in court that my eye sight would be poor from all the years of darkness. I also have hearing loss in my left ear caused by the constant whining of the ventilating fan next to my head while in the box. I can't stand to hear a small electric fan running. Even today, if I burn something on the stove, I will open a window before I will turn on the ventilating fan over the stove. I'm also not a big fan of bulk rice or oatmeal.

When I first returned to Riverside, I sought out professional help. At $100 per visit, a psychoanalyst listened to my story, as he puffed on a cigar, and said nothing. Perhaps the fear, pain, isolation, and despair, over more than seven years, was too much for the doctor as it had been for Jan's parents, Pastor Dabney, and the police. After three sessions, I discovered my money was better spent elsewhere. Later in life, I did find a woman in Northern California who did help me.

"Oh my God, your bald," a nurse once exclaimed during a visit to a doctor's office. I was stunned by her remark.

"Yes, I was abducted at age 20 and held for over seven years. During that time I was raped, beaten, and locked in a box. I suffered from a lack of water, food, sunshine, vitamins, exercise, and human contact. Yes, you're right, I have lost some hair on the top of my head." The nurse made no other comments as she went about her duties.

While in captivity, I experienced nightmares constantly. The number of nightmares slowly diminished after I got home. Today, I still have a nightmare about once a year. Now, I wake up, tell myself I don't need to have nightmares, and go back to sleep.

One nightmare does stand out in my mind. After Danielle was born, I had a dream where Hooker took Danielle while I was turned around getting a diaper. When I turned back around, he was standing in front of me holding Danielle with a smirk on his face.

"Don't you ever touch my baby again," I said, as I grabbed Danielle back.

As I went through the day, the dream haunted me. It wouldn't go away. I couldn't stop thinking about it because it had scared me so much. Finally, I called Dr. Hatcher who had told me to call him if I ever needed him.

"Colleen, that dream was a good dream. You stood up to Hooker and told him to never touch your baby again," Dr. Hatcher said.

"Thank you," I replied, knowing the doctor was correct. I had stood up to Hooker even in my dreams.

I'm not as impulsive now as I was at age 20. I've learned to take my time and size up the situation before acting. With people, especially men, I have learned never to trust them by their appearance. Only after I get to know them do I let down my guard. Only after I really get to know them well do I tell them my story, if it's appropriate.

I have received phone calls and letters from strangers. Not knowing their motives, I usually don't return their calls or letters. I received a letter, via the Women's Refuge Center, from a man who said he had known me in the past. According to the man, we had a common friend who had died years before. He never got around to telling me the name of the common friend. I did not respond to his letter.

Another man tried to contact me through the Women's Refuge Center. He told the Women's Refuge that he would make a big donation if they would put him in touch with me. I did some research and found he had a criminal record that included stalking, false imprisonment, and rape. The Women's Refuge told him I didn't wish to be contacted.

Any publication like mine will be viewed by most people as a guide to recovery and an example of the magnificent human spirit. A few will see my story as a blue print for evil. David Parker Ray used the book *Perfect Victim* to refine his iniquitous ways in 1999. It should be noted that of those who chose evil, none have gone unpunished. Hooker is still in prison, the man who held Natasha was killed after stepping in front of a train, and David Parker Ray died in prison. Society does not condone such crimes. When I asked Hooker what he would do if someone did to his girls what he was doing to me, he said, "I would kill them."

Questions I'm Most Asked:

Over the years, three questions have continuously been asked of me: (1) Why didn't you try to escape? (2) How can you be so normal after what you went through? (3) How could you keep your faith in God under such conditions?

(1) Dr. Lunde was not alone in his conclusions. Many people, even to this day, can't understand why I didn't run away. How could I return to Hooker knowing I would face more torture? Over the years, I had access to telephones, the police, and friendly neighbors. Why didn't I just run away and change my name so The Company would never find me? How could I believe in such a thing as The Company?

For me, the answer has always been fear. Fear of The Company, fear of Hooker, and fear of what might happen to my family was what kept me from running away. Initially, I was physically restrained which made escape impossible. After the contract was signed, the physical fetters were replaced with cold, raw fear of The Company. Having my hands nailed to a wooden beam, or crucified, was not out of the question. I had experienced firsthand Hooker's sadism and knew what kind of pain he was capable of inflicting. There was no place for me to run because The Company knew where my parents lived. Even if I changed my name, The Company would eventually track me down through my Social Security records or telephone contacts with my family. Once I was told that Hooker was not part of The Company, I quickly made arrangements to go home. I feared The Company, not a single individual.

Two things most people don't understand are fear and evil. For most people fear is when a car runs a red light or when they almost fall off a ladder. In such a situation, fear runs like an electrical current through their body and mind in a fraction of a second. Once the danger has passed the fear passes. For me fear was something Hooker reinforced daily. Terrible pain was always at hand and death wasn't too far behind. It was the thing I took to bed each night, and it was the first thing on my mind when I awoke. Fear controlled and dominated my life while I was with Hooker. Anytime the box was opened and flooded with light, fear would shot through my body. I never knew what was to come, but I always knew it wouldn't be good. When told to take a shower, my body would start shaking uncontrollably. Even after I arrived home, I still feared Hooker and was reluctant to go to the police. My fear didn't truly start to dissipate until Hooker was arrested and convicted.

Evil is the other thing people normally don't experience. Everybody knows someone who is unkind, short tempered, cruel, mean, or uncaring. Few people encounter true evil in their lives. With his hand on the electrical switch, Hooker set on the couch watching television as he sent surges of power through my body. From under my blindfold, I noted his lack of emotion or concern. In his eyes, my only purpose was to fulfill his sadistic desires. His denial of my humanity is what made him evil. Silence was enforced and eye contact was denied in order to suppress my individuality as a woman.

(2) The second question was how could I be so normal after all I had been through? The answer to this question is much simpler. I was normal before the abduction so why can't I be normal afterwards? Hooker was the abnormal one, not me. I didn't want him to steal the remaining years of my life. I chose to be normal and enjoy life to the fullest. Dr. Hatcher, my family, and my strong faith in the Lord helped get my life back on track. Bad memories will always be with me and nightmares will visit me late in the night, but I will continue to choose life over depression, happiness over sadness, and good over evil.

(3) How could I keep my faith in God under such conditions? Before I was abducted I believed in God, but didn't have a close relationship with Him. I failed to respond to His warnings at Paynes Creek. After I was kidnapped, my faith was all I had. Hooker took everything else away from me. I desperately sought a better understanding and a closer relationship with God. When I signed the Indentured Contract I refused to give up my soul. I asked for and received a Bible in my third year of captivity which I read diligently. I knew God and His angels were watching over me and protecting me. It was discussions of the Bible between Jan and I that helped free me from the box and it was God that I thanked when I got home to Riverside. Throughout my life I have maintained my faith in God.

I don't blame God for evil. All the evil on earth is caused by people because they choose to do evil. Yes, we have people like Cameron Hooker and events like Hurricane Katrina, but we also have good people like Dorothy, who tried to help me, and beautiful rainbows that follow hurricanes.

To me God is like a parent watching over His children. Like any parent, God wants his children to be safe, happy, and to do well. However, God's children, like all children, have free choice. Each child chooses to be good or evil. God doesn't bring evil to the world. People choose to bring evil into their lives and into the world. Like any parent, God continues to love his children and hopes they will turn away from evil.

Why did God try to warn me? I believe God is not willing for any of us to perish and doesn't want to see us suffer. He wants to save us all, but we must be willing to accept Him. God came to save me that day at Paynes Creek, but I wasn't listening. Why did God want to save me? God tried to save me because He loved me and didn't want to see me perish.

I'm still amazed at how powerful His voice was at Paynes Creek. When God speaks to you, your spirit, your soul, and your body will know it. It's very profound, straight forward, and powerful. I just wish I had been listening.

"Why is this happening to me?" I asked God. I never turned away from God, but I did get angry. "Get over it," I would tell myself. A day never went by that I didn't pray to the Lord. I still pray every day.

Why didn't God rescue me from Hooker sooner? It did take over seven years, but who am I to question God's methods. Maybe He doesn't use the same calendar we use. If God had rescued me immediately, He would also have been expected to prevent the destruction of September 11, 2001 or Hurricane Katrina. What kind of world would this be if all pain and destruction was instantly alleviated by God? He gives us warnings and it's up to us to heed them.

Have I forgiven Hooker and Jan for what they did to me? Yes, I had to forgive them in order to move on with my life. The angel at Paynes Creek said, "Jump out the window, run, and never look back." I intend to never look back.

Finally, what single word would I use to describe my overall life? I would say blessed because God has blessed me in so many ways. He has blessed me with my daughter Danielle, good friends, a good job, and of course a good mind that has allowed me to overcome all that has happened to me.

Some may call my religious faith primitive or elementary, but without my faith in God I would never have survived. I had ample time in the box to think and pray. I know God saved me. I know this because I'm alive today.

Colleen in Hawaii, 2003

The Lord is close to the brokenhearted, and saves those who are crushed in spirit. Psalm 34:18

Time Sequence of Events

Cameron Hooker Born	November 1953
Colleen Stan Born	December 1956
Janice Hooker Born	February 1958
Colleen Moved Out of Mother's House	1970
Cameron and Janice Met	April 1973
Colleen and Tim Married	December 1973
Cameron and Janice Married	January 1975
Marliz Kidnapped	January 1976
Charity Born	September 1976
Colleen Moved to Eugene, Oregon	March 1977
Colleen Kidnapped	May 1977
Slave Contract	January 1978
Moved to Trailer	April 1978
Amber Born	September 1978
Colleen Jogged Alone	1979
Colleen Given Bible	January 1980
Colleen Allowed to Call Home	June 1980
Colleen Alone in Trailer with Children	July 1980
Colleen's Home Visit to Riverside	March 1981
Colleen Put in Box	March 1981
Colleen's Last Night in Box	May 1984
Colleen's Motel Job	May 1984
Freedom	August 1984
Janice Allows Pastor Dabney to Call Police	November 1984
Preliminary Hearing	December 1984
Trial Starts	September 1984
Hooker Convicted	October 1984
Colleen with Ruben	1985-1987
Danielle Born	April 1987
Colleen on "Oprah Winfrey Show"	1987
Colleen Married to Ray	1989-1993
Colleen Married to Doug	1994-1998
Colleen's Mom Died	1998
Colleen's Grandma Gertrude Died at Age 98.	2003
Colleen's Daughter Danielle Enters Prison	2003
Colleen Stan: The Simple Gifts of Life	2008

Related Sources

Newspapers:

The Washington Post, "Police Say Woman was Held 7 Years in Sexual Bondage by the Associated Press, November 22, 1984.

The Press Enterprise (Riverside), "Colleen Jean Stan Home, Talks of Ordeal" by John Pomfret, November 1, 1985.

_____, "The 'Perfect Victim' of the Past Lives for Her Future and Present" by Skip Morgan, August 19, 1989.

Sacramento Bee, San Francisco Examiner, San Francisco Chronicle, Red Bluff Daily News, The Times: San Mateo County's Daily Newspaper, the McClatchy News Service, and The Associated Press printed various articles about the story from November, 1984, until November, 1985.

Redding Record Searchlight, "Living on Faith" by Betty Lease, February 3, 2002.

Books (by date of publication):

Story of O by Pauline Reage, Ballantine Books, 1981. (fiction) Story of a woman who was a slave by choice. (First published in French, 1954).

The Collector by John Fowles, Little, Brown and Company, 1963. (fiction) Story of the kidnapping and confinement of a woman.

Holy Bible: New International Version (NIV), International Bible Society, Colorado Springs, Colorado, 1973, 1978, and 1984.

Perfect Victim by Christine McGuire & Carla Norton, Arbor House William Morrow, New York, 1988. Hooker case written by prosecuting attorney.

The Encyclopedia of Crime by Colin Wilson & Damon Wilson, Overlook Press, Woodstock, New York, 1993. Discusses sex slaves and the Hooker case.

Cannibal Killers: The History of Impossible Murders by Moira Martingale, Carroll & Graf Publishers, New York, 1993. Discusses why people, such as Hooker, turn to evil.

Eccentric & Bizarre Behaviors by Louis R. Franzini & John M. Grossberg, John Wiley & Sons, Inc., New York 1995. Dr. Hatcher's 16 techniques of coercion are discussed.

Deadly Innocence: The True Story of Paul Bernardo, Karla Homolka, and the Schoolgirl Murders by Scott Burnside & Alan Cairns, Warner Books, Inc., New York, 1995. A copy of book *Perfect Victim* was found in house of Bernardo and Homolka.

Female Subjects in Black and White, Race, Psychoanalysis, Feminism, edited by Elizabeth Abel, Barbara Christian, Helene Moglen, University of California Press, Berkeley, California, 1997. Discusses my appearance with Geraldo Rivera along with complicity and resistance in the Hooker case.

The Serial Killer Letters: A Penetrating Look Inside the Minds of Murderers by Jennifer Furio, The Charles Press, Philadelphia, 1998. Discusses Janice Hooker's guilt.

Next Time, She'll Be Dead: Battering and How to Stop It by Ann Jones, Beacon Press, Boston, 2000. Discusses my letters written to Hooker and abuse.

Dark Dreams: Sexual Violence, Homicide, and the Criminal Mind by Roy Hazelwood & Stephen G. Michaud, St. Martin's Press, New York, 2001. This book is also marketed as *Dark Dreams: A legendary FBI Profiler Examines Homicide and the Criminal Mind.* Discusses sexual slavery.

Practical Aspects of Rape Investigation: A Multidisciplinary Approach, edited by Robert R. Hazelwood & Ann Wolbert Burgess, CRC Press, Boca Raton, 2001. Investigates the wives and girlfriends of sadistic men.

In the Firing Line: Violence and Power in Child Protection Work by Janet Stanley & Chris Goddard, John Wiley & Sons Ltd., England, 2002. Discusses hostage behavior.

Die Leibeigene, by Christine McGuire & Carla Norton, Lubbe, 2002. German language version of *Perfect Victim.*

Their Word is Law by Stephen M. Murphy and Steve Martini, A Berkley Publishing Group, New York, 2002. Interview with Christine McGuire concerning the books she has written.

Sex-Related Homicide and Death Investigations by Vernon J. Geberth, CRC Press, Boca Raton, Florida, 2003. Discusses Hooker's sadism.

Karla by Stephen Williams, Cantos International, Canada, 2003. Discussed relationship between the Hooker crime and Karla Homolka.

Slow Death: The Sickest Serial Torture-slayer Ever to Stalk the Southwest by James Fielder, Kensington Publishing Corporation, New York, 2003. Story of David Parker Ray and how he was influenced by the Hooker case.

17 Days: The Katie Beers Story by Authur Herzog, iuniverse, Inc., Bloomington, Indiana, 2003. Briefly relates Katie Beers experiences to that of Colleen Stan.

The Logic of Consent: The Diversity and Deceptiveness of Consent as a Defense to Criminal Conduct by Peter Westen, Ashgate Publishing Limited, England, 2004. Discusses nature of wrongful oppression in the Hooker case.

Monday Mourning: A Tempe Brennan Novel by Kathy Reichs, Scribner, New York, 2004. (fiction) Hooker case is tied into story.

I Choose to Live by Sabine Dardenne, Virago Press, 2006. Twelve year old girl kidnapped and survives in Belgium.

Minds on Trial: Great Cases in Law and Psychology by Charles Patrick Ewing, J.D., PhD. and Joseph T. McCann, PsyD., J.D., Oxford University Press, 2006. Discusses the impact of expert witnesses in the Hooker trial.

Internet:

http://www.kinkindex.com/truetales1.htm
The Seven-Year Hitchhike, by Mark Owen, Felicity Press, Newcastle, Australia, 1991 and 2006.

http://www.crimelibrary.com/criminal_mind/psycology/sex_slave/
  index.html
The Case of the Seven-Year Sex Slave, by Katherine Ramsland.

http://en.wikipedia.org/siki/ColleenStan
Article on Colleen Stan.

http://boards.aetv.com/forum.jspa?forumID+414
A&E discussion board about Hooker case.

http://www.koolpages.com/bedlam/hooker2.html
Article on story from Partners in Perversion, Bedlam Library.

http://findarticles.com/p/articles/mi_qn4161/is_20060903/ai_
  n16710011
I Was Locked in a Box and Used as a Sex Slave for Seven Years, by
  Deborah Sherwood, Sunday Mirror, September 3, 2006.

http://www.gospelassemblyfree.com/facts/perfectvictim.htm
Article on brainwashing in a religious cult.

http://blog.myspace.com/index.cfm?fuseaction+blog.view&friendID=
  9143128&blogID=284231571&Mytoken=41A9CD2262504C84
  B73C5284476D90C736841363
Article on Stockholm syndrome.

http://www.spearheadnews.com/OutoftheBox2.htm
Japanese television show article by Bob Ericson.

http://www.pica.org.au/art02/spaceeaters-strut.html
Dance article by Rachel Arianne Ogle.

http://www.imdb.com/title/tt0629734/
"Law & Order, Special victims Unit," titled "Slaves," directed by Ted
  Kotcheff, aired on television 19 May 2000 (Season 1, Episode 22).

http//www.indepdent.co.uk/arts-entertainment/film-and-tv/tv-radio-reviews/last-night-tv-the-girl-in-the-box-fivebr-my-Israel-bbc4-828176.html
The Independent, UK, "Last Night's TV: The Girl in the Box, Five my Israel, BBC4 by Thomas Sutcliffe, 15 May 2008. Article on television documentary.

http//www.people.co.uk/news/tm_headline=1-was-a-sex-slave-too-kept-in-a-6ft-coffin-for-7-yrs&method=full&objected=20413657&siteid=93463-name_page.html
The People, UK, "I was a Sex Slave too, Kept in a 6ft Coffin for 7 yrs" by Rachael Bletchly and Jon Wise, 11 May 2008. Article relates Colleen Stan's experiences to those of Elisabeth Fritzl.

http//www.co.uk/showbiz/tv/todaystv/2008/05/14/the-girl-in-the-box-89520-20417316/
Daily Mirror, UK, "The Girl in the Box, 14 May 2008. Article on documentary about Colleen Stan with references to Elisabeth Fritzl.

http://maps.google.com/maps?q=http://bbs.keyhole.com/ubb/download.php?Number=695139&t=k&om=1
Map and imagery of Hooker house on Oak Street.

http://www.supernaught.com/crimefiles/forsale1.html
Handwritten prison envelope signed by Cameron Hooker for sale.

Interviews and Documents:

Interviews with Colleen J. Stan by Jim B. Green, November 4, 2006 through March 23, 2007.

Notes of Debbie King, juror #10, People of California vs. Cameron Hooker, September 26, 1985 through October 31, 1985.

Information on file in the Library of Congress and Copyright Office, Washington, D.C.

Various legal documents and transcripts from the Cameron Hooker trial.

Made in the USA
Coppell, TX
24 December 2023

26845378R10155